To the rosebowl from the roses

Contents

Acknowledgements

I would like to thank Paul Vaughan and all those who have shown true love and friendship by supporting my family and myself when it would have been so easy to walk away. You will never know how important you have been in ensuring that truth is made available to everyone.

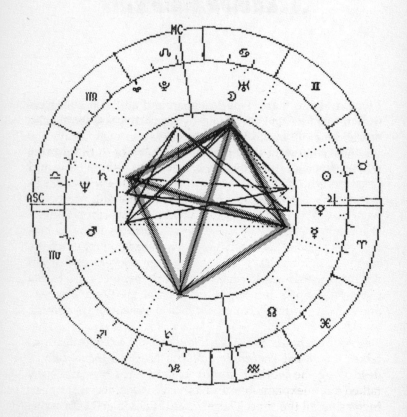

*My birth chart. How the heavens looked at about
1815 GMT on Tuesday, 29 April 1952.*

Introduction

In March 1990 a psychic passed on a series of communications which changed my life forever.

One of them said I would write five books in three years which would bring to people the truth about life and Creation. I thought this was impossible because five books in three years is some going by any standards and my books were going to be on subjects which, at that time, I knew absolutely nothing about. Yet here I am presenting to you the fourth book I have written in two years. So many of the communications I have received through many psychics and directly through myself have either happened or are in the process of happening and it is clear that the basis of what I and so many others around the world are saying is coming to pass.

In my first book, *The Truth Vibrations*, the communications talked of global economic collapse as the system that is destroying the world is removed before it's too late. They talked of unexplainable and extreme weather conditions increasing all the time. These would include great droughts in some areas, fantastic rains and winds in others, and the book also predicted great geological events, gathering in scale all the time through this decade. They said the energies around the planet were changing and how this would lead to more and more people transforming their lives as they

1

rejected the destructive and the materialistic, and encompassed a life of vegetarianism and non-violence which had respect for all things.

The communications also said that those who were not ready to tune in to these changing energies, these quickening vibrations, would find themselves getting out of synchronisation with the planet and this would lead to more violence, terrorism, conflict, crime, social unrest and negative, inexplicable behaviour of all kinds in the period of transformation. We should expect immense and increasing political upheavals, they said, as people demanded control over their own lives in smaller units. The vast empires like the Soviet Union would go, the communications said, to be replaced by independent states which would, in the end, disappear themselves as all borders and boundaries ceased to be in the new world of love, peace and harmony that awaits us beyond these years of turmoil and change. So many things outlined in the earlier books have either happened or are happening.

There are many ancient legends of peoples like the American Indians and others which predict these events at this time. There are the quatrains of Nostradamus, the books of America's most famous psychic, Edgar Cayce (1877–1945), and countless other books and channelled information by people all over the world today to back up all the basics of what my books are saying. Every day more people are accepting this, and even those who have allowed the system of self-destruction to programme their thinking and build walls around their minds will be unable to deny for very much longer that a time of enormous change is upon us.

The reason I came out publicly and attracted such massive ridicule was because I believed, and never more so than now, that people should have this information so they could begin to understand why everything they have come to depend upon is falling apart at every level of their lives. There will be fear and confusion in these transitional years, but how much more fear and confusion would there be if it happened with no-one able to offer a credible explanation for what was going on?

In my previous books I set out the basis of what will happen and why it must happen if the planet is to survive and we are all to realise our true potential as beings of wisdom and love. In this book, I expand on this theme and I have used the story of my own rather extraordinary life to explain how all our lives are constantly influenced in ways we are not ourselves aware of. I know it will help so many to have a clearer understanding of why they do certain things with certain people in certain situations. It offers an insight into human behaviour which I hope will encourage all of us to stop judging each other and see that we are on a journey of experience. On this journey we face many tough and unpleasant times which leave us sad, demoralised, perplexed and confused, but, if we react in the right way, these experiences can also leave us wiser and stronger, speeding our evolution to ever more wonderful levels of life.

The real us never dies as we continually incarnate into different physical bodies and situations on our never-ending journey to greater wisdom, knowledge and enlightenment. No experience is wasted. They all add to the bank of knowledge and understanding that we carry with us for-ever. It may not seem like that sometimes. It can often appear, as it did to me, as a nightmare that will never end, but end it always does. And if we react with courage and compassion both for ourselves and others we can use the experiences to become more loving and understanding people. You will see from my story the parallels with your own life and it will help you to appreciate the forces, negative and positive, that guide and affect us every day. The reasons for our behaviour are many and various and nothing is what it seems when viewed from the wider perspective of life and Creation.

The experiences of my life, many of them very extreme and often played out in the public arena, have left me so much more complete as a person because I understand so much more about myself and the nature of life on this planet. More than anything I understand how wonderful Creation really is and what a future can be ours when this period of incredible transformation is over.

The Background

To appreciate the astrological readings I include in the book and much else in the story of my life, we need to look at the basic principles of Creation before we start.

The main point to remember is that everything in Creation is the same energy. Your house, your mind, your body, the rain, the earth, everything, are all made from the same energy. The difference between them is the speed at which that energy is vibrating – its 'frequency' – and its level of consciousness: evolution. One simple example of this principle is water, clouds and ice. They look very different, feel very different and react very differently, but they are all the same water. The ice and the clouds are merely water in another state of being. It's the same with the energy that is everything. All that exists is the same energy in different forms. I would define energy as movement or motion.

This energy is also what we call consciousness. All thought and all energy is one mind, one consciousness in different states of being. It is this consciousness constantly experiencing through all life forms in Creation that I call the Infinite Mind. So 'God' is consciousness, 'God' is life. We are like droplets of water in an ocean, apparently individual, but in truth a part of the Infinite Mind that is the creator of all that is. Thought creates energy fields and everything that exists is made from energy fields. So the Infinite Mind created everything through thought. All consciousness, the ability to think, is the Infinite Mind, and Creation is the result of its thoughts, its imagination.

But this Infinite Mind does not work in isolation from us; it works through us. It *is* us. When you use your consciousness to think, it is the Infinite Mind – 'God' – that is thinking because your consciousness is part of the Infinite Consciousness. For reasons that will emerge through this book, humanity's connection to the whole is not as powerful as it is meant to be but the principle remains the same.

You might think of us as cells in some gigantic brain. The Infinite Consciousness works through everything, every person, plant, planet, animal, mineral, and universe. How we use this consciousness and what thoughts we create with it is our choice. Each 'cell' is given free will to make its own decisions and learn from them. It is in this way that the Infinite Mind expresses itself in so many different forms and takes on what appear to be individual personalities. In fact those 'individual' expressions of the Infinite Mind are aspects of the same whole. Whatever we experience is absorbed by the Infinite Mind and evolution continues into infinity. Therefore if you want to use symbolic language, we are *all* God, all part of that Infinite Mind, but obviously there are quite amazing differences in understanding wisdom between the highest and lowest levels of consciousness within this whole.

The pioneers of true physics, people like Ronald Pearson in his book *Origin of Mind*, explain how they believe all this evolved. Creation as we know it began when consciousness emerged. This happened, in the language of Pearson's physics, as a result of 'the mathematics of chaos and of positive and negative cosmon collisions. It did not need another creator behind itself.' Cosmons are simply a term Pearson uses to describe certain negative and positive particles of energy which, he believes, are the basis of everything that exists. His findings, achieved through mathematics and experiment, correspond with many of the themes of my own psychic sources of information which I outline in this book.

Once this original consciousness emerged, it began to create and grow, both in size and understanding. It is from this original consciousness that Creation has come, including us. When these cosmons collide and interact in a particular way, the energy and consciousness of Creation 'breeds' and recreates itself. Creation, therefore, goes on endlessly expanding into the void of 'space' and hence I use the term Infinite Mind. It is truly infinite. It is at the highest levels of understanding within Creation that you will find that original consciousness, the super-mind if you like, from which everything began. By now it has absorbed all the knowledge and experiences of all it has created and all its creations have created. It has reached a level of wisdom, understanding and knowledge that is beyond our comprehension. If you feel the need to use the term 'Creator' then it should be directed at this original consciousness. But while it represents the highest level of knowledge and wisdom within the whole, it is a creator and observer, not a dictator. And we are all creators, part of the creative force, at different stages of potential.

Many people dismiss any idea of eternal life or other life forms elsewhere in Creation because they can't see evidence of them. The church asks us to have faith that there is life after death while mainstream science is sceptical, even dismissive, of any claim that life is eternal. Yet the answers to the 'Great Mysteries' are quite simple. These other levels of life, where we go when we 'die', exist on different wavelengths or frequencies.

Around you are all the frequencies of the radio and television stations broadcasting to your area. They are all sharing the same space that you are in now, but you can't see them and they can't see each other because they are on different frequencies and wavelengths. If you tune your radio to one of those frequencies around you, to the radio at that time that will be the only wavelength in Creation. But move the dial to some other frequency and that will appear to be the only one. The different levels of life operate on the same principle. Only a fraction of Creation exists on what we call the dense physical (atomic) level. The rest exists on the non-physical (sub-atomic) levels, most of which our physical senses cannot see or even sense because their energies are vibrating too quickly. Each higher frequency encompasses the ones below it, so the higher frequencies know all about us even if we know little about them.

When people see 'ghosts' they often appear as transparent, misty spirits who pass through walls. This is because the 'ghost' is on another wavelength and just as the radio waves can pass through walls to reach your receiver, so can the 'ghost' which is merely a mind not in a physical body. On the non-physical frequencies, the mind is capable of far more than it is here and can manifest itself in whatever form it wishes. Just as we are limited in what we can do when we are in a space suit on the Moon, so the mind has limitations while working through a physical body. The reason some people see ghosts and UFOs and others don't is because some people are sensitive and can knowingly or unknowingly change their vibration to get closer to that of the ghost or UFO while others cannot. This is why one person will see a ghost and the person next to them will not. It is all about the mind tuning in to different frequencies.

When people have near-death experiences, when they 'die' in Earth terms and are brought back to life, they all tell similar stories of looking down on their physical body watching others trying to resuscitate them. They have the same emotions and personality, but for that period of physical death they are no longer part of the physical body. This is because the real them, the mind, has left the body. When that happens at the end of our physical life we merely move on to another frequency. Life is forever. Those who have had near-death experiences also speak of seeing loved ones who have 'died' and they lose the fear of death after feeling the incredible love that surrounds them on a non-physical frequency free from the misunderstandings and limitations of the dense physical body.

I know that some scientists working outside the rigid scientific establishment have come to this conclusion themselves, although their work is often ignored or suppressed to protect self-interest. There is no such thing as the 'supernatural'. Everything is governed by the natural laws of Creation. 'Supernatural' or 'paranormal' are just other ways of saying human science hasn't discovered it, doesn't understand it, or hasn't even bothered to look.

Mainstream science has always believed that light travels at the fastest speed in Creation, but this is not the case. The speed of light is the maximum speed of this particular frequency, that's all. It is pedestrian compared with speeds on other frequencies. Once energy is vibrating beyond the speed of light, we cease to be aware of it because it has progressed out of the frequency to which we are currently tuned. This is how it is possible to make things appear and disappear. When you increase the speed at which the energy of an object is vibrating to beyond the speed of light, it 'disappears' to our senses. It hasn't really disappeared, it has merely reached a speed of vibration beyond the limitations of our physical senses. It has moved through the barrier of this frequency (the speed of light) to another one. This is how what we call UFOs can suddenly 'disappear' before our eyes. Highly evolved beings can also reverse this process by raising their consciousness to tune in to a higher frequency, create something there through thought power, and then lower its vibration to, at, or below the speed of light. At that point whatever they have created on the higher, non-physical, level through thought appears 'miraculously' as a physical object or situation.

Once you appreciate these principles you begin to understand how people can perform what are called 'miracles'. They are not miracles at all, they are the skilled use of the natural laws of Creation. You can see that when we understand our true potential we will have no need to ravage the Earth. We will just create what we need ourselves and there will be no hunger. Moving from one side of the planet to another in seconds will become quite straightforward for those beyond a certain level of evolution, once those gifts have been activated. You use your thought power to raise your vibration to beyond the speed of light. This causes you to 'disappear' on this frequency and move to another one. Now once you leave a frequency you also leave its version of 'time'. What we see and measure as time is very different from other frequencies. What can take months or years here can take a fraction of a second elsewhere. So having left this frequency you move to where you wish to be and then lower your vibration and 'appear' on the physical level again. In this way you can disappear in England and re-appear in Australia a split second later. It is also possible to be in two places at the same time by creating a sort of duplicate you! All this will be possible once the transformation is complete or at least well advanced.

This raising and lowering of vibrations relates to something called a vortex. Think of it as a whirlpool or whirlwind shape. Some people believe that every form and object from a sub-atomic particle to a person and planet is created by a wave of movement or a vortex or combination of vortices which hold energy together in a concentrated way. (For more on this, see *Science of the Gods* by David Ash & Peter Hewitt; Gateway Books.) The speed at which the vortex or 'whirlwind' is spinning determines the speed at which the energy vibrates – its frequency. Even those things which look 'solid' are really energy vibrating within a vortex or combination of vortices. Light is created by waves of movement at a certain speed.

All that I have just described, the appearing and disappearing, involves increasing or decreasing, through thought, the speed at which the appropriate vortices are spinning. Once this ability is mastered you can go up and down the frequencies at will and create whatever you wish. By 'you', I mean your mind, your consciousness, the eternal part of us. Many call this the 'soul', but I prefer the mind. It is important to remember, however, that your mind, the real eternal us, is an aspect of the Infinite Mind. Our minds are like spiritual transistor radios tuned to a particular frequency at any one time depending on our stage of evolution. The mind and the brain are not the same thing. The brain and the physical body are vehicles through which the mind can experience this physical world. If you go to the Moon, for instance, you need a space suit to surround the body or you cannot exist there. In a similar way the mind, which is a nonphysical energy field, needs a physical body, a genetic space suit as I call it, to operate on the physical level. This nonphysical energy field called the mind can tune itself to the different frequencies of Creation just like that radio dial. At this time our minds, or at least part of them, are tuned to this frequency and therefore this is our reality. But around us sharing the same space are all the other frequencies.

Sensitive people like psychics, mediums or channellers raise the frequency of their minds, their consciousness, and the communicators lower theirs enough for them both to get into synchronisation. This is why some channellers tend to go into a sort of trance. They have retuned their consciousness so completely to another frequency that they lose consciousness, at least to some extent, on this one. Every time we think we create an energy field and at this point with the channeller and the communicator in sync, information in the form of thought energy is passed from one frequency to another through the channeller who decodes the energy and turns it into spoken or written words. The channeller will obviously choose their own words to interpret the thought energy and this is why some will talk of a God, others a Godhead, and still others the Infinite Mind. I have only used the term Godhead in my other books because that was the term used by the channellers I was working with at the time.

We are all capable of channelling to some level and we are all receiving telepathic thought communications to guide us through our lives without being aware of it, although some people are more gifted in this area than others. It depends what we have come to do and whether we choose to develop these gifts. The number of channellers is increasing rapidly because there is so much information that needs to be passed to us in these decades of transformation. I have heard religious dogmatism condemn channelling as working with the forces of 'evil' and yet they are quite happy to stand up on a Sunday and read extracts from the Bible which talk of an angel of the Lord speaking to so and so or God speaking to this or that person. How do they think these communications, symbolised in the biblical text, were actually passed on? By a loud voice from the sky? By telephone? It was done, of course, through channelling, the very process the church now frowns upon. What's more, they only have to look around them to see what not communicating with higher intelligences, and not understanding who we really are, has done to the physical body of the Earth and all who live upon it.

It is vital to appreciate that the real us is not our physical body. Once that leap in understanding is accepted a whole new world begins to open up before you. The physical body is a shell we take on to allow us to go through certain experiences in any one of a succession of physical lives. These lives are designed by us to speed our evolution through greater understanding, wisdom and balance. The eternal us is a series of non-physical energy fields working together as one. Our emotions are an energy field, our mental level is another, and so on. Linking these energy fields together are a series of energy points or vortices known as chakras. These are linked to the physical body during an incarnation through the endocrine system. In relation to the physical body the chakras are at the base of the spine (base chakra), the navel area (sacral chakra), the solar plexus (solar plexus chakra), the centre of the chest (heart chakra), the throat (throat chakra), the forehead (third eye chakra) and on top of the head (crown chakra). There are others, but these are the main ones. Some sensitive people see the fields as spinning wheels of brilliant colour; others say they appear like gas jets. (See the illustration at the end of the picture section.)

The chakras are constantly passing energies between the various levels and so an imbalance on one level can be passed on to another. This is why when we get emotionally upset and out of balance the first thing that happens is we stop thinking straight. The imbalance on the emotional level has been passed on to the mental level. I call the nearest level to the physical the 'etheric'. This is the organiser of the physical body and the template for its shape and characteristics. Part of its job is to organise the constant replacement of cells. When the etheric energy field is imbalanced in some way this cell replacement process can get out of control. We know this situation as cancer. The cure for cancer and Aids lies in understanding the etheric level.

If something is amiss in the etheric energy field, perhaps caused by mental or emotional imbalances, it will eventually manifest as a physical disease, or 'dis-ease' as it should really be pronounced. This is how emotional upset and stress leads to physical dis-ease. During spiritual or 'hands on' healing, energies are passed through the healer to the patient to balance out their energy levels, their dis-ease. I have seen this described as 'faith healing', but it is nothing to do with faith. It is about using the natural energy forces of Creation to heal and this, along with other forms of healing that use these non-physical energies, will replace the drug-obsessed, surgery-obsessed medicine we have today. This is how the genuine 'miracle' healers worked and work. They remove the imbalance on the etheric and other levels and so remove the cause of the physical problem.

It is also the case that the mind has the power to heal, indeed the power to make the body do its will. The phrase 'mind over matter' describes one of Creation's great truths. The body is the vehicle for the mind and so the body will react as the mind reacts. If the mind thinks negatively, the body will act negatively, but if the mind is positive, the body will react accordingly. You can think yourself to illness and think yourself to health by affecting the etheric organisation of the body. Yet because this knowledge of who we really are has been lost or suppressed, millions are mutilated by unnecessary surgery, devastated by unnecessary drugs, and massive amounts of money go to drug companies that need not do so when gentle, non-violent healing alternatives are available. Those who work in traditional medicine are mostly highly dedicated people trying their very best to do the right thing and they do some wonderful work, but until medical science opens its eyes far wider it will go on missing the vital point – the mind, the real us, is not the same as the physical body and any form of healing has to reflect this fact if it is to be truly effective.

Everything has an etheric energy field and this can be measured through technology and something called Kirlian photography. This has shown that even if you take away part of a leaf or any living thing, the etheric energy field around it will stay in the shape of the original leaf. The same is true of human amputations, although this may later change as the energy field responds to the new situation. It is possible that the etheric level sends messages to the DNA molecules in the cells (DNA is the body's genetic code and inheritance material) to guide the workings of the physical body and make genetic improvements through the generations.

The amalgamation of the chakras and energy fields working as one, the mind as I call it, is the sum total of all we have learned since we were first created. The mind is both male and female, and we only enter male or female bodies because they offer different learning opportunities. One of humanity's imbalances is that of male energy swamping the female and this reveals itself in a world controlled by male values. This is in the process of changing because there should be a male-female balance, not one dominating the other, and that applies both within ourselves and to the planet as a whole.

The process of reincarnation and the different experiences

we choose comes under the heading of karma. This word karma is another way of saying 'a balance of experiences'. To know what lukewarm feels like – in other words balance – we need to have experienced hot and cold and that, in the simplest of terms, is what karma is all about. We are constantly experiencing both sides of the balance point so that we learn where the balance point actually is. How far from the balance point we stray in our behaviour is up to us and we are making that decision all the time in how we think and act. It is true that what we do to others we will need to have done to us in this physical life or a future one. We will need to experience what we make others experience so that we can eventually find that balance point of understanding known as wisdom. Our own behaviour is reflected back at us through others so we understand the consequences of that behaviour. I feel that the karmic 'debt' is created not so much by the action, but by the motivation behind it.

What a nonsense this makes of so much human behaviour; the bigotry and prejudice like racism and sexism. The physical body is a vehicle to allow the mind to experience this physical level and so what people who consider themselves racially and sexually superior are actually saying is: 'I've got a genetic space suit that was made in a different country and it is a different colour or design from yours, so therefore I am superior!' Because of this basic misunderstanding of life, we go to war, we have concentration camps, ethnic cleansing, and endless other horrors. The rest of Creation must shake their heads in disbelief. Those who today put women or black people or homosexuals through pain and anguish will themselves go through that experience in a future life. If they don't choose to do this, and they can always refuse because there is no compulsion, they won't be able to evolve to ever more glorious frequencies of life. Here on Earth at this time we live on a very low and unenlightened frequency, but this is about to change, in fact is changing, hence the transformation I constantly speak of.

I should emphasise that karma has nothing to do with punishment. It is about seeking wisdom and balance through experiences that *we* choose to have because we know it is the only way to enlightenment and progress up the frequencies. To progress from one frequency to another we need the perfect interaction of negative and positive energies within us. Once this is achieved through negative and positive experiences we reach the vibration of the next frequency. These alternative forces of negative and positive can be found in many cultures. The Chinese call them Yin and Yang.

Maintaining the correct balance between negative and positive energies is important not only for a mind, but also for a whole frequency. A significant lack of balance between the two has serious consequences, as we shall see.

There is no such thing as empty space. What appears to be space is really energy vibrating at speeds beyond the ability of most people to see. But while we can't all see this energy, we can all feel it. When we go into a house and we say, 'Hey, I don't like it here – it feels eerie', we are sensing non-physical energies dominated in this case by negative energy. It's the same when we meet someone and say, 'I got bad vibes from them.' Again we are feeling the negative energies being generated by the thoughts of that person. On other occasions we will immediately feel at home at a place or feel joyful and elated whenever we go there. That is the result of sensing positive non-physical energies.

To follow parts of my story and to understand why the Earth is in such trouble, it is necessary to appreciate that all life forms are creating energy fields, positive or negative, with every thought and action. We are constantly sending out energy into the sea of non-physical energy all around us and affecting its positive–negative balance. If the life forms of this planet generate far more negative energy than positive, then the sea of energy will become increasingly dominated by negative energy and so encourage us to think and act more negatively. This is what has happened to planet

Earth and unless the energy sea is 'cleansed' and restored to balance this planet will be no more. You could think of this sea of energy as an ocean. If you pollute the ocean you affect all life within that ocean and it is the same with the energies that surround us and flow through us, the energy sea.

Karma is designed to lead us through experience to balance and so, as a result, generate balanced energies into the environment. Not all of our experiences, however, are due to past life behaviour and the need to balance out karma. It is also the case that some minds choose to go through certain experiences for the good of humanity and the planet in general and many of these are attacked, ridiculed and condemned because they challenge established and misguided thought. Others choose to go through experiences not only because of past behaviour, but because they feel they will help them along the road to greater understanding. There are as many different life plans as there are people on this planet and this is one of so many reasons why we should stop judging each other. What we may see as unacceptable behaviour might be exactly what that person, that mind, needs to experience for its eternal journey to wisdom and balance.

When the mind enters the physical body at some time between conception and birth it would be of little use if we knew exactly what we had come to experience, who with, and how we hoped to react. We would go through the motions and learn nothing. So when we enter the physical body we 'forget' what we have come to do so we experience everything 'cold' as it were. We only need to know enough for us to stay on the life plan. The link with this life plan is guidance from the higher levels of our mind – the so-called subconscious, super-conscious, or 'higher self'. These levels of the mind do not enter the physical form and are not subject to its limitations. I feel there is an even higher level, too, which I call the 'true self'. We are guided, through the process of thought transfer and astrological influences, into situations we have come to experience with those people

who have come to experience them with us. This guidance
shows itself as intuition, a 'gut feeling', a feeling of being
drawn to certain places and people. It also shows itself when
we say, 'Oh, fancy meeting you here', 'What a small world',
and the classic, 'What a coincidence'.

Although we choose these experiences before we incarnate, we can use our free will once we are in a physical shell
to ignore this guidance and go another way. Learning comes
from making free will decisions in the situations we face and
experiencing the consequences of them. But this use of free
will can get out of hand if we ignore this guidance too often.
Countless numbers of minds on Earth over the centuries
have done precisely this and continue to do so today, which
is one reason why the planet is in such a state. When we use
our free will in this way, we are not guided into the
experiences we need and we will have to return in another
life to try again. This is why the population of the world is
so high today. It is the result of billions of minds returning
to try to work through the karma of many lifetimes before
the transformation. If we do follow our guidance, in most
cases unknowingly, we will find ourselves in karmic situations with the opportunity to balance out past behaviour
and this is not always pleasant. But what we might seek to
avoid on this level might be exactly what we need in
evolutionary terms. A channelled communication I received
for *The Truth Vibrations* said:

> True love does not always give the receiver what it would
> like to receive, but it will always give that which is best
> for it. So welcome everything you receive whether you
> like it or not. Ponder on anything you do not like and see
> if you can see why it was necessary. Acceptance will then
> be very much easier.

Sometimes people need negative experiences to change their
thinking and the negative aspects of the transformation now
underway will have this effect. If you live in a big house in

the country and earn £500,000 a year, this will colour your view of those who are homeless, unemployed, and poor. You might see them as lazy scroungers who don't want to work. But if you no longer have a big house, big car, and big bank balance, if you yourself become homeless and unemployed, you will see such people in a very different light and your thinking and perspective will be radically changed. I know an advertising executive whose life and thinking were transformed for the better when he had a heart attack in his thirties and he took a whole new look at his life and priorities. Our perspective is the result of our experiences, and karma is designed to give us a balance of experiences and, so, a balanced perspective.

Another enormous influence on our lives and life plans is astrology. There is a great deal of nonsense peddled under the heading of astrology and we see some of this in many tabloid newspapers. But true astrology is the key to understanding so much about why we react in certain ways at certain times. Conventional science does not accept this, but then 'science' is now so confused in its desperate desire to hold on to outdated ideas. On one hand, it accepts without question that one planet, the Moon, affects whole oceans, yet laughs at the very suggestion that planets affect people! We each have a unique overall energy pattern which is formed from all the experiences we have had since we were first created, but we also have impregnated within us another energy pattern for each new physical lifetime. This is the reason why the timing of our birth is so painstakingly worked out. It is no accident.

Every life form in Creation is generating energy and the planets are no different. Each planet is generating a certain type of energy and as they move through the heavens the energy mixture around us is changing second by second. An incoming mind will have worked out, some better than others, what is the best time to be born and so be impregnated with the energy pattern, the energy mixture, most suited to its particular life plan. In effect, from the moment we are born the energy pattern within us reflects the universe as it was at that precise second. The pattern is called the birth chart. Throughout our lives the energies of the universe now within us are continually interacting with the changing energy mix generated by the physical universe as the planets move in their orbits. This means that the planetary movements will not affect everyone in the same way. They will affect us according to the energy pattern within us at that moment we came into the world. If you then add to this the fact that our experiences in past lives will also ensure that we will react to the situation in a different way from someone else, you can see that the idea that planetary movements will affect everyone the same is simply not credible.

The inner universe, the birth chart pattern, is static while the physical universe is always moving. But from that moment of birth there is a third element to add to the mixture. There is another energy pattern picked up at birth which is, at that precise second, a reflection, like the birth chart, of the physical universe at that time. Then, however, this pattern begins to move like a ticking clock around the static pattern and this 'clock' is called the 'progressed chart'.

Now we have three 'universes' reacting and affecting each other: the physical universe; the static birth chart within us; and the moving 'progressing' birth chart within us. It is like one static wheel interacting with two others moving at different speeds. They are designed to affect each other in ways that will create the form of electro-magnetism necessary to attract to us the people, places and experiences needed for our life span to be successful. That is what karma actually is, a kind of electro-magnetism which draws to us other energy patterns – people, places and experiences. Everything from the tiniest thought to a planet and universe is an energy field and everything that happens is caused by the interplay of these fields.

The birth chart patterns within us will also pre-programme certain responses which will lead us into pre-arranged situations. We will react in ways that will start a chain of events that will take us into the situations we have come to experience. The programming can often suspend the conscious thought processes if they are preventing a life plan experience from being set up. This is why we often look back at things we have done and say, 'What on earth was I thinking of, why did I make such a stupid decision?' It is often because we were meant to. It was the interaction of pre-programmed energies which ensured that we did and, as a consequence, had a life plan experience to face. If this programming was left to itself we would all complete our life plans perfectly every time. There are, however, other forces that can pull us off course.

First of all there is free will to react to those situations in different ways and so affect the next stage of the life plan. This free will is fuelled, obviously, by all the information we receive through the senses from the media and the misguided world around us. It can, and does, encourage us to make decisions that can take us way off the life plan. There is also the free will of others which can change our lives in ways that make the life plan more difficult to complete. These forces can be very powerful, but all the time the birth chart programming will be trying to pull us back on course and for this reason so many people find themselves constantly facing the same situations. This is the programming offering us the same choices over and over again in the hope that the choice appropriate to the life plan will eventually be made.

The 'battle' between the life plan programming and the other forces pulling against that programming can cause such inner conflict, as people are pulled in two directions, that it can manifest in scrambled emotions, mental problems and serious physical illness. But let us not get the idea that everyone who is acting in self-serving and destructive ways has lost touch with the life plan programming. Many will need that experience to make them and others think. The time of birth, and therefore the programming, is decided by us and for reasons that will become clear later in the book,

many minds in this part of Creation have so lost touch with
understanding that they design life plans which will lead
them to serve themselves rather than the whole or even to
work for the destruction of the planet.

I have used two astrological readings of my own life to
help to illustrate how the birth chart programming works
and affects us. I will use information or small extracts from
both of them at the relevant points. The two readings were
done in slightly different ways. One, by Judy Hall, is called
Karmic Astrology and she uses basically the interaction of
the physical planets with the static birth chart energy
pattern I received at birth. She also adds to that an analysis
of past life experiences that would create a unique response
to the various situations I have faced. The other reading was
by an astrologer called Tumi which looks more at the
interaction of the static birth chart pattern with the moving
birth chart pattern, the ticking clock, as well as the physical
planets.

These are the main astrological terms you will see. The
signs of the zodiac – Aries, Taurus, Gemini, Cancer, Leo,
Virgo, Libra, Scorpio, Sagittarius, Capricorn, Aquarius, and
Pisces – are areas into which the heavens are astrologically
divided. As Judy and Tumi explained, they display specific
characteristics which are common to each sign and can
indicate karmic issues to work on. The signs also indicate
how a planetary energy or energies are likely to affect us.
'Houses' are divisions in the chart, each one representing a
different sphere of our life, and they indicate which area of
our lives will be most affected by the changing energy mix
around us and within us. The planets – the Sun, Moon,
Mercury, Venus, Mars, Jupiter, Saturn, Chiron, Uranus,
Neptune, Pluto and others as yet undiscovered – affect
those patterns within us and can trigger great changes in our
outlook and behaviour. When we are children the mind is
getting used to life in a physical body again and does not
need all the energies and knowledge it will require later.
Over the years, certain planetary sequences release these

latent energies as we need them to fulfil the life plan we have chosen. This can bring enormous transformations in the way we think and act and there are particular times in our lives when many of these energies are released within us. Puberty and the so-called 'mid-life crisis' when we tend to reassess our lives completely, are but two of these.

You will notice that I have included a planet called Chiron which most people will not have heard of. Chiron was discovered by the astronomer Charles Kowal on 1 November 1977. It had actually been seen as far back as 1895, but not recognised as anything of importance. It is a small body positioned between Saturn and Uranus, although its orbit is so erratic that it actually passes between Saturn and Jupiter at times and will reach its closest point to the sun in 1996. It is something of a puzzle to scientists and it has in the past been designated an asteroid or 'planetoid'. Astrologers have linked the Chiron energies to wounds and the healing of wounds, both personal and collective. Anyone with Chiron as a major planet in their birth chart is either here to heal themselves, the Earth, or both. Some believe that when Chiron is in the area of the heavens known as Capricorn at the time of birth, as in my chart, it indicates someone who has agreed to undergo a lot of pain and suffering. Chiron is one of the planets in my chart that form what astrologers call a Grand Cross or Cardinal Grand Cross, which is literally a cross created by drawing lines between the planets. The Tumi reading said:

Of the ten main planets in your chart, only one, Pluto, doesn't seem to be involved in the Grand Cross and even Pluto is aspecting [affecting strongly] a good half dozen of those planets, so you could say your chart *is* the Grand Cross. I think most astrologers would take a step back if they saw your chart. It is a very powerful chart, very tense and taut. What a Grand Cross tends to do is create lines of tension in your energies, your consciousness, which almost force you into certain situations. I hesitate to use the word force because we have free will, but in your chart force is the only word I can think of. I'm sure you have noticed in your life that there is some kind of invisible hand guiding you and leading you, not always consciously, and if you look back at the major events in your life you will see, if this is the right word, that they have been 'Divinely' orchestrated, or at least orchestrated from another realm.

The Grand Cross is very often related with quite heavy karma, but I say immediately that I feel in your case this is not karma that is personal to you. My understanding and very strong feeling is that there are today a number of people on Earth whose reason for being here is purely service. There are not that many, but these people tend to carry Grand Crosses in their birth chart. They have come to take on some of the collective karma of humanity and the Earth, and the Grand Cross is there to make sure that they are not diverted from this path. In other words I feel the Grand Cross is there to guide you almost like a puppet and I feel the major experiences you have had in your life have actually been there to open the doors to your higher vision and understanding that would allow you to do the job you have come to do.

Judy Hall's reading of the birth chart said:

Your chart indicates to me someone who has the potential to become a 'parent' to the planet and humanity and someone who has a great love for humanity ... You have the potential for developing totally unconditional love, really loving the other person warts and all, for accepting them the way they are, allowing them to learn their own lessons in life, to be their own person, and still loving them even if they do not fit our idealised picture ... The position of Saturn and Neptune in the karmic twelfth house of the chart indicates that you have come to clear some of the collective karma humanity has developed.

Both of these planets reveal the potential to be a 'positive scapegoat' working for the evolution of the whole. The chart also indicates that you are here to move away from the exercise of personal power and into using collective power to bring to humanity the realisation that the Earth needs to be healed. The north Node of your Moon, which reveals your karmic purpose, is in Aquarius and Aquarius marches to a different drum. It can see that little bit further than other signs, so it is often the rebel or the visionary and it frequently encounters opposition from the established order ... The Grand Cross also has tremendous potential for understanding and channelling information and energies.

The readings are remarkably similar and the only real difference between them is that Judy would say that more free will and personal karma is involved than would Tumi. My own feeling after all that I have experienced is that free will is constantly there for minute-by-minute, day-by-day decisions, but that when something major has had to be done to keep to the life plan, the Grand Cross has imposed itself so powerfully in my consciousness that it was virtually impossible to resist its insistence on a certain course and direction. I think you will see several examples of this as we go along, but I can only say what I feel is the truth; others have every right to see it another way.

You will see the term 'collective karma' a few times during the book and all it means is the sea of energy, the sum total of the energies generated by humanity and all life forms on this planet. Those energies have increasingly become dominated by negative energy and there is a massive 'karmic' imbalance in the energy sea. Personal karma is the imbalances we retain in our own energy fields – minds – and collective karma is the imbalanced energy we generate into the environment around us. Just as individuals need a balance of experiences, so does humanity and this frequency as a whole. This is clearly not the case today and has not been the case for thousands of years. Somehow this very severe collective energy imbalance has to be removed and many minds have incarnated at this time to try to take out negative energies encircling the planet and replace them with positive. This is what is meant by working out collective karma. So many minds on the Earth today are swamped by the experiences needed to balance their own personal imbalances from past lives that they could not possibly take on the burden of removing collective imbalances too. Instead others have agreed to do this.

So there you have the basic background to life on Earth and the nature of astrology. All you need to appreciate is that the movement of the planets is constantly changing the mixture of the energies around us and activating energies within us, and this affects our behaviour. But you will see that there are also many other forces influencing us on our journey through this tapestry of experience we call a physical life.

1

The Nervous Child

I was born at a time of great change with the world in transition after the war. By 1952 many changes were already underway and so many more were to follow.

The Attlee Labour Government had laid the foundations of the welfare system in Britain in the immediate post-war years, but they had lost the 1951 general election to Winston Churchill's Conservative Party. President Truman was in power in the United States. There was, understandably, a mood among people to sweep away the old and start afresh after half a century of war, oppression and injustice. The old terraced streets gave way to vast municipal housing estates all over Britain and as the 1950s progressed the young would express themselves as never before through a new kind of music called rock and roll. These were the days of the teddy boy, espresso coffee bars, and the cheap and cheerful holiday camps at Britain's seaside resorts.

It was a time of hope and optimism, a moment in history when the world had a comparatively blank sheet of paper on which to design a new tomorrow. Unfortunately the new design had the same fundamental flaws as the one it was trying to replace. There is no doubt that many of the decisions made at this time were motivated by the best of intentions, but they were to lead the world down a dark and destructive road. The obsession with 'science' and economic expansion would take the planet to the brink of non-existence and leave us with the human and environmental catastrophe we survey today.

With the demise of Adolf Hitler, new 'bogey men' emerged in Joseph Stalin and his successors in the Soviet Union. The Iron Curtain came down across the borders of Poland, Hungary, the new East Germany and elsewhere. The Atomic Age which had dawned with the horrors of Hiroshima and Nagasaki gathered pace with every year, and in February 1952, two months before I was born, Britain exploded her first atomic bomb in the Australian desert. The Cold War and the fear of nuclear armageddon had begun.

As I've explained, we all come into a physical incarnation with a life plan, a series of experiences we wish to have, and the minds who will share those experiences with us are agreed before we and they incarnate. This is normally because there are karmic links from past lives between those involved which need to be balanced out and removed. We choose our parents and our brothers and sisters and they choose us. The further we get away from birth the more chance there is that our free will and that of others will lead us away from our chosen path, but at birth we are in control when we incarnate and so we are definitely born into the situations we ourselves have chosen, hard as that may be to accept when you look at the circumstances in which some children enter this physical world. But everything looks very different when we are free of the limitations of the physical body and what we would seek to avoid from our perspective on Earth may be exactly what we need to evolve in eternal terms. It can also be, especially today, that minds incarnate into highly negative situations to bring in positive energy for the good of the planet or to highlight wrongs that needed to be addressed.

I was born in the City General Hospital in Leicester, England, to my mother Barbara and father Beric. They already had a seven-year-old son, Trevor, and seven years after me came Paul. We have all shared many previous lives together in many different situations. For the first three years of my life we lived in a tiny rented terraced house in Lead Street, just off Wharf Street, in the run-down centre of the city. To say we were skint is like saying it is a little chilly at the North Pole.

My father was the product of the toughest of lives and as I grew up he was the biggest influence on how I developed. He was born in Leicester before the First World War to a father of great intellect, but an even greater capacity to consume large quantities of booze. His father was an expert on horses and local dealers would pay him to advise them on which ones to buy. He could have made a good living, but the local publicans prospered instead. Eventually he left his family. My father, who was still a youngster, had to go to work to help them survive. This meant he could not follow his ambition to be a doctor, or at least work in some way in medicine, and these times left scars on his character that stayed with him to the day he died.

He told me often through my childhood about his experiences and they did so much to shape my own attitude to life. In the Depression in the 1930s he spent the only money he had to buy a train ticket to London to search for work. He could find nothing, but he was told he would be certain to find a job in Blackpool, Britain's biggest seaside resort, during the holiday season. With no money for the train, he walked all the way there from London, a distance of some two hundred miles. I remember him saying that his long, long journey took him past Leicester, but he could not bring himself to go back home until he had money in his pocket.

When he arrived in Blackpool there was no work. Still unbroken, he heard of a job in the shoe trade in Preston and he walked another eighteen miles to the factory to find there was still a vacancy and it was his. This is just one example of the man's incredible determination which only left him in his final years. Unsurprisingly he had an enormous impact on my early life. His many stories and our own financial straits instilled in me from the start a sense of right and wrong, justice and injustice, which has been behind so many of the things I have said and done since. The Conservative Party in our house was about as welcome as a rotweiller in a cats' home as my father would hold court on how they had made so many suffer over the years. He never forgave them for the policies that gave him and others such a difficult life and denied him his ambitions.

My life-long rebellion against control and authority also emerged under the influence of my father. In the end I was far more rebellious than even he was. During the Second World War he was in the Medical Corps and so good at his job that he was given virtually a free hand. There were not many, particularly those in charge, who would do what he would do in the face of the horrific injuries and mutilations that arrived at the medical centres. He became indispensable and, as a result, when he went absent without leave down to the local bar they would look the other way. Many a time, he told me, the military police would find him, put him in the jeep, and take him back to sleep it off with no questions asked. The next morning he would be up and back at work doing all the jobs most of the others did not have the stomach for. He would also put his life at risk to help others in a most extraordinary way. He won the British Empire Medal for going into blazing aircraft to rescue people after crash landings. Once he had a medal of that distinction he was able to go his own way with even more freedom from authority. He was never one for rules, and among his endless sayings which I have always remembered is: 'Rules and regulations are for the guidance of the intelligent and the blind obedience of the idiot.' That attitude rubbed off on me in a big way.

As I grew up and listened to him I hated the thought of war and conflict and this has always stayed with me. Anyone would have felt the same after an hour with my father explaining what it really involves behind all the pomp, the glorification, and the triumphalism. War stinks, the glorification of war stinks, and I am so grateful to my father for letting me see that almost from the moment we could communicate. This also triggered the deep loathing of war and conflict that was already within me as a consequence of experiences in so many previous lives. In fact when I say I learned this or learned that, it is more that such experiences bring to the surface, the conscious level, the knowledge carried within the higher self which has been amassed over all my lifetimes. It is a 'triggering' process as much as a learning one and the more channelled information I receive from people, the more I feel that the experiences I have been through were designed to bring that part of my mind within the physical body, the 'lower self', to the point of understanding it needed to reach before my main work was due to begin in the 1990s.

My father was such a complex man and the product not only of his own past lives, but also of the experiences of the present. He had so many rows with other members of the family that, even today, I am still learning of relatives I didn't know existed. He had an unfortunate way of having an argument with someone and then just cutting them out of his life. At the same time he was kind, compassionate, and full of love in his own macho kind of way, but he was also capable of considerable verbal, though not physical, violence. When he wasn't pleased you would be sat down and blared at for what seemed an age before he calmed down. He would say many things that he regretted, but some of them stuck.

I feel he always struggled with a large chip on his shoulder which resulted from the way the life he really wanted – that of a doctor – was snatched away from him by poverty, circumstance and war. But when he left the physical body he would have realised that he had chosen to experience that frustration and cope with it.

My mother Barbara also had a significant influence on me in another way because she was so different from my father. This, let me tell you, is some woman. There can be few women who would have taken what she took from my father at times and still stayed there to take some more. Throughout her married life she was dominated by him, just as I was as a child. It was always 'do this, do that', and the way he spoke to her when he lost his considerable temper was quite astonishing. Again there was never any physical violence, only verbal, and despite these occasions he and my mother were extremely close. Behind all the front and the words, he depended on her as much as she did on him, more so in fact.

It is often those who put us through difficult experiences who love us most on a higher level. They are not consciously aware of this in a physical body, but they love us so much they are putting us through what we have decided we need to balance out past behaviour or prepare us for a role later in this life. In my mother's case I think my father was either providing an experience to teach patience, acceptance and unconditional love, or perhaps to encourage her to break out of a rut of subservience to others and refuse to bow to another's will.

There are so many reasons why we choose to experience such situations. That is not to say that everyone who behaves badly towards us is doing so out of love. They could be using their free will to be unpleasant and it may have nothing to do with our own life plan or theirs. But we don't know and we should not judge because the way we are treated by others can look very different when viewed from the wider perspective of our eternal evolution. What I would say is that as the mind has total control over where it incarnates, the overall way our father and mother treat us is almost certainly the way we chose to be treated, unless they go way off their own life plans once we have incarnated which is always possible.

As I grew up we lived from week to week. Every Thursday I would go with my mother around the back of the Gents Clock Factory in Leicester so my father could nip out with his pay packet and give us some money for that night's tea. He worked in the drawing office and earned very little.

By now we had moved from the 'Coronation Street' environment of Leicester city centre to one of the massive 1950s council house estates in the suburbs, a place known as the Goodwood, and our new home was across the road from the General Hospital where I was born. That house holds so many memories for me.

The Tumi astrological reading picked out a sequence when I was between two and three which suggested a massive shift at a higher level of my mind. The sequence involved the interplay between the static birth chart within me and the progressing or moving one, the ticking clock: 'Something quite enormous must have happened at some level, a really huge shift in understanding, although it could have manifested on the physical level as simply moving house or something.' That was, in fact, about the time we moved to the Goodwood. When shifts take place within us at higher, unconscious levels the reflection of this on the physical level can be quite mundane, almost symbolic.

On occasions like Christmas my father would make toys for us and I recall one year he made me a large wooden bus. He would also make toys to sell at Christmas to pay for little extras and one story sums up my mother. He was making banjos out of round pie tins and wood, and he had sold some to shops in Leicester. They were laid out all over the living-room floor as the paint was left to dry and then my mother had to deliver them. My father had indicated that he was a toy producer of some standing and he said he would deliver the banjos in a van. Van? We didn't even have a bike. Instead my mother would put the banjos on my pram, with me in it, and deliver them to shops all over Leicester on foot. 'I'm sorry,' she told each shopkeeper. 'The van has broken down and rather than make you wait I have brought them on the pram.' There was nothing my mother would not do for her family. Over the years she had many jobs in shoe factories, the school meals service and as a hospital cleaner.

When we eventually could afford a car, they would be held together on a wing and a prayer. One was so short on power that my mother would have to get out and walk if the hill was too steep. There was one old banger after another. So, the first twelve years of my life were ones of financial struggle and make do, but looking back on what I learned or what was triggered in those years I would not have had it any other way. To those people in dire circumstances today I would say sit down and think what you are meant to learn from such a situation. That doesn't mean that we shouldn't try to improve our lives, far from it, but it would help to ask what, at any moment in time, we are meant to learn from the circumstances we find ourselves in. Once we have learned what we need to learn or activate we will find that our lives change as we move on to the next experience. It is the same when we ask: 'Why am I so unlucky?' 'Why do these things always happen to me?' If we look at such questions in terms of our eternal development and growth it is much easier to find answers. 'What am I supposed to learn from this?' is a question we need to ask ourselves when we are trying to make sense of apparently inexplicable events that affect our lives. From my point of view that early childhood with its financial struggles helped me to see that there is far more to life than money and, along with my father, it brought out a sense of justice and a desire to see fair play for all.

One incident as a youngster was to set a pattern that would continue throughout my life – that of being falsely accused. This has happened to me so often since that there are too many instances to mention and they appear to be getting progressively more severe. This one was the first I can remember and it affected me to a far greater extent than the incident would normally justify, something that always indicates a link with past life experiences. I was playing football with a friend when the baker's van stopped nearby. The baker went off to deliver to the houses and my friend went to look in the back of the van. He was looking at the array of cakes when I joined him.

'I'd buy that cake if I had the money,' he said, pointing at one of them. 'Which one would you have?'

'I'd have that one,' I said as I leaned in to point at another.

At that precise moment, the baker appeared and went mad, accusing me of stealing cakes. I could not speak such was the horror I felt. 'But ... but ... I wasn't stealing anything,' I thought. 'Why is this man shouting at me?' He said he was coming around to see my father, and although he never did the baker always had me down as a thief from then on. This pattern of false accusation apparently shows up clearly in my birth chart and was at least in part a preparation for what was, and is, to come later in life.

My father's influence helped me to overcome a lack of self worth. I needed to work this through and let it go before the main purpose of this incarnation began to emerge thirty-nine years later. From the start I was a bit of a loner. I played with the kids in the street, but basically I liked to play alone with little push-along trains. I did this for hours every day. I loved steam trains and I dreamed of being an engine driver. I particularly fell in love with the railways of the Isle of Wight when we scrambled enough money together to have a holiday there. In fact I quickly fell in love with the whole Island. It felt like home because, in past lives, it had been and my electro-magnetic programming was designed to be attracted and drawn by the energy field of the Island. Part of my wish to be alone so much was the lack of confidence in myself. I always thought others were better than me and looking down on me. Although later my father's personality helped to bring out my own strength and determination, it worked the other way during this period. He sapped my confidence and I was intimidated by him.

The Tumi reading of my birth chart, without any prior knowledge of my childhood, picked out this lack of self-worth. It involved Saturn, or rather the energies of Saturn impregnated within me at the moment of birth. They were interacting with that progressing birth chart in my energy field and the physical planets themselves:

Saturn energies are like the school teacher of the chart and not a very kind school teacher. It is like those who rip into a young child dashing their self confidence, and they end up really struggling for any kind of self worth, self value. I feel that between the ages of two and three to about seven or eight, all this would have been very strong for you. It would have made you, if not shy, then certainly withdrawn in some way and lacking confidence. But again I feel this was all part of the build-up to your own realisation which, in turn, has led you to the work you are doing now.

That is absolutely spot on. My mother still tells people how I used to cross the road just to avoid meeting someone. I spent most of my time at Whitehall Infant School with nerves in my stomach. I did not like school one bit. My confidence reached its lowest ebb when I was in a school play. It was Sleeping Beauty and as usual I got the biggest part. I played a tree! I was dressed in a green jumper and long brown trousers, with a paper hat on my head which was supposed to be the leaves. The idea was that the prince would come along with a make-believe axe and the trees would all fall down. The problem was that he didn't come near enough to me to credibly cut me down and I stood there alone amid this sea of prone bodies while the audience fell about at the sight of this silly sod still standing there with his arms in the air. I was gutted and what little confidence I had in myself drained away. This was made worse, if that was possible, when the headmistress, Miss Wilkinson, pulled me to one side the following day and laid into me about spoiling the play and letting down the school. Such incidents in childhood when we are so vulnerable emotionally are quite common for those with a certain type of life plan, particularly those who end up in the public eye.

Like everything that happens to us, it is done for many reasons. In my case, given what was to happen later, it helped me to see that you can overcome the experience of being laughed at and ridiculed. It may not be pleasant, but you survive. Bringing you to your knees emotionally can also break down the 'ego', those imbalanced character traits picked up in this or previous incarnations which need to be let go if the higher mind or higher self is to be able to manifest its wisdom and knowledge through the physical form. The 'ego' can take over the lower self, that part of the mind in incarnation, and ignore guidance and information coming from the higher self. It is often part of a life plan to put the ego in its place at some point. Some of the experiences that people go through to bring about this disintegration of the ego can be very, very tough. I know people who have been into the depths of drugs, alcoholism and mental breakdown before emerging from those experiences as 'new' people with their higher selves able to manifest through the physical form with no ego in the way. In my case, this process of removing all potential blocks to the higher mind began very early. In this incarnation nothing was going to be left to chance and nothing would be allowed to get in the way.

I was frightened of everything as a youngster and not least the dentist. Whenever I had toothache I would go out into the garden with a big lump in my stomach and play alone. I knew a visit to the dentist was imminent. Whenever I was frightened I wanted to get outside and stay there. Walls made me feel anxious and claustrophobic. Usually when the school dentist came I would throw away the form they gave me listing the treatment I needed so that my parents would never know the dentist had even been to the school. But on one occasion at infant school one form slipped through and I went with my mother to the school dental clinic.

It was half an hour's walk from where we lived. My mother would tell me on these occasions that I was only going for a check-up, but I knew that if I was not allowed something to eat before we left home then it was the gas and a tooth out for me. This was one such day. I walked to the dentist like a prisoner on his way to the gallows. By the time I was sitting in the dentist's chair the pressure was too much.

As the gas mask was placed over my face I panicked, whacked the dentist in the chest, and made a run for it. I was across that surgery like a rifle shot, side-stepping the nurse on the way, and I hared down the corridor and across the waiting room into the street. I was still going at full speed a hundred yards down the road with my mother running after me shouting in the distance. Eventually I realised I had no choice and nowhere to go and I walked solemnly back to face it all again. One of my school mates was in the waiting room as I sped through followed by my mother and sundry people in white coats, and my self esteem fell even further.

This continued when I moved on to the Whitehall Junior School. I was always the one who felt ill in the morning assembly and had to go out before I fainted. This happened on my first morning at the new school which I faced with the usual nerves and fear. I walked out of the assembly and ran home. My mother took me immediately to the doctor who gave her a letter to take me to a child psychologist. My father arrived home that evening and went potty. 'No son of mine is going to a child psychologist,' he said. 'You are going to get a grip of yourself.'

From that moment I did, slowly at first, and then more so. I would not have dared to do anything else! But the biggest boost to my self respect and confidence, my salvation in so many ways during this period, was about to make its first appearance in my life. It was the game of football.

2

The Schoolboy Star

I was walking home one afternoon from the junior school when a friend ran up to me. He said the teacher in charge of the third-year football team had seen me playing in the playground and wanted me to have a trial after school the next day.

I would never have had the confidence to go without an invitation because the idea that I was good enough to play for the school would not have entered my head. Such things happened to other people, not David Icke. I ran home so excited to tell my parents. The main problem was a rather basic one. I had no football boots. There had been no need because I only played in kickabouts in the park or at playtime and, anyway, there were more important things for my father to spend money on than football boots for me.

But to play in the trial and the team I needed boots and my father took me out just before the shops closed that night to find the cheapest pair of boots available. They cost seven and sixpence, about thirty-five pence in today's money. This was in the early 1960s just as football footwear was evolving towards the sort of design we see now. My boots would have been modern in around 1920! It was like wearing diver's boots and whenever I kicked the ball my foot felt nothing, such was the thickness of the massive toecap. My mates found them extremely funny, but somehow I squeezed into the team, the last player to be selected. The teacher had wanted me to be the goalkeeper, but someone else turned up for the trial who he considered was better in that position. I then tried playing out on the field and got in the team that way. I scored in my first match, but then almost everyone did because we won fifteen–nil. Soon after that the goalkeeper was selected for the fourth-year team and I took over in goal. This was the start of a journey that was to take me into professional football.

I took to goalkeeping immediately and the more I played the more confident I became in myself as others recognised that I was pretty good for my age. I found a new determination. There was one occasion I remember which showed how my attitude to myself was changing. The fourth-year children at the school were the only ones who had a games lesson, but as my performances for the third-year team were being noticed I was invited to take part in this games period every week. To do this I had to get permission from my teacher to miss his lesson and play outside with the fourth-year footballers. One afternoon I thought I had permission, but he felt otherwise and while I was playing on the school field a boy came over to say my teacher wanted me to return to the class immediately. I had to get changed quickly and walk back into the classroom to face the teacher in front of my classmates. He had not given permission, he said, and how dare I slope off to play football without asking him. There was a time not so long before when I would have dissolved with embarrassment in such an unpleasant situation. Now, though, from somewhere deep within, I reacted differently.

The teacher said I would do better to think about my class work than football and the spelling test he had planned for that afternoon was much more important for me than kicking a ball about. It was true that I was not academically successful because I was bored stiff most of the time and so constantly nervous that fear affected everything I did. That afternoon, however, although my spelling was normally terrible, I somehow managed to get every single one right, more than anyone else in the class. Even at that age I could feel the teacher's embarrassment when he read out the results. 'Yes,' I thought. 'That's shown you.' At the end of that year's exams I came top of the class, something I had never done before and would never even nearly do again.

My improvement during that year to finish top was so inexplicable when viewed against what had gone before and was linked so much to the afternoon of the spelling test, that it can only have been my higher self stepping in to lend a hand. We all have times when we achieve something and think, 'How on earth did I do that?' These are occasions when 'fate' takes a hand and the higher self comes forward to ensure that something within the life plan is achieved if possible. Certainly that academic success added to my growing confidence in myself. The incident also illustrates the effect that people like teachers can have on children in both negative and positive ways and because of this teaching is a profession, like politics and journalism, where much karma can be amassed or removed. But again it is important to remember that a teacher or anyone else who behaves badly towards a child could be doing so either because they are misguided or out of a deep love on a higher level. We don't know which it is until we leave the physical body, but one way of getting some idea of whether something is meant to be is to look at how often you find yourself facing the same situation. If you face the same circumstances again and again the chances are that karma and your life plan programming are trying to tell you something about yourself.

My growing self confidence was not just due to the influence of football. The astrological situation was geared through this period to let go of the lack of self worth and move into a phase of self belief. I came under the influence of Mars' energies which not only led me into sport, but also activated feelings of determination and ambition. I decided what I wanted and set my sights firmly on getting there. I walked into the fourth-year football team the following year and we won everything in sight. There was no doubt in my mind; I wanted to be a professional footballer and what's more I *would* be a professional, no question. At no time did I even consider any other future. I was going to do it and that was that. My father would tell me often when I was out playing football and ignoring my school work: 'You'll never make a living from that.' But I knew differently, I just knew it would happen, and many others will recognise this feeling or sense of destiny from experiences in their own lives. This is the knowledge of the life plan held by the higher self filtering through to the conscious level, and it shows itself as a sort of 'knowing' although you can't say why you know.

There was an afternoon in that fourth year at junior school which I have never forgotten. It's funny how little incidents can have the most profound impact on us. We were in the classroom talking about fossils. The teacher handed a fossil to a boy at the front and the idea was that it was passed along the rows to everyone. When it came to me I looked at it and used my fingers to see how strong it was. To my utter horror it snapped. 'Oh my God, what do I do now?' I thought. I decided in my panic to ignore it and pass it on to the person behind me. They knew no different because they didn't know if it was in one piece or two.

The next fifteen minutes were agonising. I could see the two pieces of fossil being handed from child to child and all the time they were getting closer and closer to being returned to the teacher. I prayed that the bell would go for playtime before he realised it was broken, but it was not to be.

'Who's broken this fossil?' I heard him say angrily. There was silence. I could not bring myself to own up. I thought I had got away with it until I heard the words I dreaded:

'Was it broken when you passed it on, Michael?' he said to the boy at the front.

'No, sir.'

'Was it broken when it got to you, Jane?' he asked the girl on the row behind.

'No, sir.'

Eventually he came to me. I knew the game was up. The only way to get out of it was to pin the blame on the one in front of me and even in my distress I was not prepared to do that.

'Was it broken when it got to you, David?'

'No, sir.'

'Was it broken when it got to you?' he asked the boy behind me.

'Yes, sir.'

Every eye in the class glared at me. Had the teacher lost his temper I don't think it would have been so bad, but he didn't. We had a good relationship and I knew he had respect for me as I did for him.

'Well, David,' he said. 'I am so disappointed that you could not own up to this. I would not have thought it of you.'

I cannot tell you the sense of shame that poured over me and I vowed that afternoon that never again would I avoid saying something I knew to be true unless it was to save somebody else's feelings and never again would I try to evade my responsibility. This all happened in one short space of time in one afternoon, but the experience shaped my character as much as any other single incident in my life, or, perhaps more to the point, activated that part of my eternal self involved with truth so that it manifested more powerfully on the conscious physical level. This would be extremely important in the future as we shall see. I hope you can begin to appreciate that a life plan is designed to arrange a series of choices and it is from the consequences of those choices that we learn and evolve. This is why we learn so much from mistakes and the bigger the mistake often the quicker we learn because the consequences of our choices are so extreme. In fact to me there is no such thing as a mistake, only learning from experience.

One thing that I never overcame during this period, despite my increasing confidence, was the fear of water. It plagued my childhood. I feel this came from past life experience, but it was triggered when I fell over while paddling in the sea on holiday. I can remember panicking and thrashing about and then everything went still and calm. I lay there under the water looking up at the sky and I had given up trying to survive. Then I saw the figure of my brother Trevor appear and he grabbed my arm and pulled me out. I was gasping for breath and thought I was going to die, but I recovered. Trevor was laughing because it seemed to him like his little brother had fallen over in the water and nothing more. He will never know how close I was to going home before he pulled me out of the water.

From then on I was terrified of water. I would never go swimming to the local pool and when I had to go with the school I would either ask my father to write a note for the teacher to get me out of it or hide my swimming gear and say I had lost it. I was well into my thirties before I had overcome this enough to learn to swim. This is by no means unusual and often relates to past life experiences of drowning, being ducked as a 'witch' and other unpleasant events related to water. For many, a fear of water goes back to the end of the Atlantis civilisation around twelve thousand years ago when tidal waves swept across the planet. Most phobias of all kinds result from past life experiences.

In the 1960s when you reached the end of your time at junior school you took an exam called the eleven plus which most people in Britain will remember. If you passed you went on to the academically superior grammar school and if you failed you went to the so-called secondary modern. I failed and so did most of the junior school football team. We should have gone by rights to the nearest secondary modern called Spencefield, but they only played rugby not football, and our parents all wrote to the education authority asking for special permission to move to a football-playing school. They agreed and we went to Crown Hills Secondary Modern.

I remember the names of the players so well, Howard Petty, Paul Burdett, David Bell and others. We all became good friends and at different times I became particularly close to Paul and David and later to a group of players we met at the new school, including Tom Murtha and Malcolm Fahey. David Bell had been the star sportsman at the previous school, the best footballer, runner and cricketer, and I had always felt a little inferior to him. But this ended as my own progress in football and as a person continued to move on. David looked like being an outstanding footballer at junior school, but he fell away dramatically in the years that followed. I feel it was in his life plan – his own choice remember – to experience that disappointment and learn from it. From this perspective we can see that what we call 'failure' in Earth terms can be success in eternal terms.

I have always said that Crown Hills was so rough when I first arrived that if you didn't have a broken nose and a cauliflower ear they called you sissy. Just a little over the top, but my goodness there were some hard kids there. I spent the summer holidays after leaving Whitehall worrying about what I would find at Crown Hills. Its reputation was well known in the area and we were told how the older children would beat up the first-year children and push their heads down the playground toilets. That did indeed happen, but I was 'lucky'. When they came for me one playtime a teacher was there just at the right moment to stop them and they never tried again. Three years later I was held against my will by a group of boys from the Roman Catholic school next door and the same teacher once again came along at precisely the right time to get me out of trouble. It is in these apparently small ways that karma is constantly being repaid for what has happened in past lives. Maybe I got that teacher out of trouble in the past or maybe he got me into trouble. Either way it's now all balanced out.

This was a period of great change at Crown Hills. The year we started the teaching staff was transformed. A new headmaster started when we did, along with a large number of teachers who were to become friends. They turned the school into a wonderful place to be and I couldn't wait to get there every day once the first year was over. It was one of the happiest times of my life and it was to take many years to get over the disappointment of leaving.

I couldn't win a place in the first-year football team as a goalkeeper and I played outfield until the third year. I was all right as an outfield player, but not that good. I would certainly not have become a professional and that ambition was now looking less likely to be fulfilled. The turning point came when the school sent me and several others for a trial with the Leicester Boys Under-Fourteen Team. By now I was playing as a goalkeeper once again, but there was a highly rated goalkeeper called David Vallance playing for another Leicester school who looked certain to get in the team. With this in mind the sports teacher, a really great bloke called Norman Stone, told me that I would be wasting my time going to the trial as a goalkeeper and I should go as an outfield player instead. This I did.

There were a large number of boys at the trial that crisp winter morning. I played hopelessly and after a short time I was told politely that they had seen enough. While the trial game continued I was told to kick a ball around on another pitch with a few of the other discarded trialists. Suddenly I heard a shout from where the trial game was going on.

'Hey, can any of you lads play in goal?' said the manager.

'Yes,' I shouted and I ran towards him as quickly as I could before anyone else could lay claim to the offer.

One of the two goalkeepers in the trial match had been injured and I took over, played OK, and was asked along to the next trial. I was still not building my hopes up because the manager made it clear what he had in mind for me. 'We are looking for a good reserve goalkeeper to Dave Vallance,' he said. This lad was already playing for the Leicester Boys Under-Fifteen team and it was taken as read by everyone that he would also play for his own, younger age group as well. It would have been very strange for a player to be good enough to play for the Under-Fifteen team and not the Under-Fourteen.

I turned up for the next trial with no pressure. I accepted I would be the reserve, but at least I was making progress to be in a Leicester Boys' Squad even if I was not in the team. I was going to enjoy myself and I did. Of all the games I played in my career as a schoolboy and as a professional I never played better than I did that day. I stopped everything and to his credit the manager said he had to pick the goalkeeper that played best in the trial, and that, he said, was me.

If we close off our links with the higher self, refuse to follow its guidance through our intuition and inner feelings, or resist the astrological programming, we can go wildly off our life plan. It is the same if some of those who have come to work with us lose contact with their guidance. If, however, you stay open, amazing things can happen just when you need them. That combination of the injury to the goalkeeper which gave me the chance, my display at the second trial, and the manager's decision to pick me ahead of the highly rated goalkeeper, were no accident. It was a combination of higher selves at work and the planetary energies triggering, or at least, encouraging, certain responses within everyone at the right time. I know it's hard to take in that such situations could be pre-arranged, but so much is possible in Creation that we could not begin to comprehend within the confines of the dense physical form.

My ambition to be a professional footballer was suddenly back on course. It is very important that you get into your town or city schoolboys' side because these are the matches the scouts from the professional clubs go to watch. My father was now getting very keen and beginning to believe that maybe my talk of a football career was not as fantastic as it once sounded. A scout from Arsenal Football Club was showing interest and I was starting to get very confident about my ability and myself, maybe even a little too confident at times. This was a glorious period of my life.

The following season I was up against Dave Vallance again for the Leicester Under-Fifteen goalkeeper's spot and

I just knew it would be mine. I was playing with such
assurance and the scouts began to take notice in larger
numbers. I was going along to Leicester City for training just
after Peter Shilton, one of the finest goalkeepers of all time,
had joined the club following his performances for Leicester
Boys. A string of other clubs were watching me and asking
me for trials. My father always wanted me to play for
Coventry City, then managed by Jimmy Hill who was later
a colleague at the BBC. They were a successful Second
Division Club who were about to be promoted to the First
Division. My father wrote to them asking if they would give
me a trial and I played a game with other trialists one
Sunday morning. I played pretty well and after spending a
week training with the club they asked me to sign as an
apprentice professional when I left school. My ambition to
make a living from football had been realised, at least for the
next two years. The choice of Coventry was all part of the life
plan as you will see from the people I came into contact with
there, one in particular. My father was clearly guided to
guide me to that club because I would have happily signed
for anyone in what was then called the First Division.

My progress in the game had been very rapid since the
day that goalkeeper was injured at the schoolboys' trial and
I was asked to take over. Football had given me self respect
and pulled me out of the nervous jelly stage of my earlier
childhood. It has also presented many opportunities to
harden me up emotionally and help me overcome setbacks
and adversity. I remember two incidents as a schoolboy
when I played at Filbert Street, the home of Leicester City,
the team I supported. It had always been my ambition to
play there on the ground where I watched Gordon Banks,
the then England goalkeeper. But on the two occasions I had
that opportunity I made mistakes and went through agonising disappointment, especially the second time when an
Arsenal scout had come especially to see me. In those
situations, as with the verbal attacks from my father, you
either picked yourself up and carried on with even greater

determination or you went under and fell apart. Sport is a microcosm of life and such a wonderful vehicle for learning or 'triggering' because it is so full of highs and lows physically, mentally and emotionally.

My relationship with my father had changed through this period too. In those early years I was intimidated, but now I was coming back at him. There would be tremendous rows between us as he tried to control my life completely. On and on he would go with his criticism for doing this or not doing that. You could take his advice ninety-nine per cent of the time, but on the odd occasion you didn't, off he would go. 'You never listen to anything I say ...' These marathon lectures would often happen several times a week when things were particularly fraught between us and always when I let in a bad goal or had a bad game. Again he was venting his own frustrations on me. Something had gone wrong which he didn't like and so someone had to be to blame. When you think about it, this is how so many people and, indeed, humanity as a whole, so often respond to events. Humanity always demands a scapegoat in every situation. Blaming someone else means we don't have to look at ourselves. I have come to see that the way we behave towards the world around us is really the outward manifestation of what we think of ourselves. My father also had a problem letting his children go and allowing them to make their own mistakes in their own way. He always wanted to control, to be at the centre pulling the strings. When anyone rebelled against that, which I did increasingly, then he erupted.

My own inner determination was coming to the surface and clashing with his. During the first few years after we are born we are generally getting used to life in a physical body again, but as the years pass we learn new lessons and have our inner knowledge awakened and brought more and more to the conscious level. This was happening to me in this period and I wanted to do my own thinking and make my own decisions while still listening to the views and advice of others, especially my father. Like him, though, I could be very stubborn and the more people told me to do things in a domineering way the more determined I became not to do them under any circumstances.

The relationship with my father was one of enormous contrasts because, between the verbal onslaughts, we would be very close and I was learning so much from him. He said to me once that you are never finished until you sit down and tell yourself you are finished. Until that point, he used to say, it doesn't matter what anyone says about you, there is nothing you cannot achieve no matter how bad things might be. That is a piece of wisdom I have always remembered and lived by and it has got me through some very difficult times.

He helped me once when I faced a personal crisis at school. I became for a short time the focus of hostility from a gang of boys who had once been friends. For some weeks they ignored me and I was subjected to much mental and emotional torment. It built up to the point when the one among the group who thought he was the hard man said he would be waiting for me after school the next day to beat me up. I was so distressed after weeks of this that I persuaded my mother I was ill and could not go to school for the last few days before a half-term break. My father could see I was not myself and asked me what was wrong. I told him and I thought he would say he would go to the school and sort it out. 'No,' he said. 'You tell the biggest one you will take him on – that is the only way to stop this.'

At the end of the first day back at school the biggest one said he was going to fight me. 'OK,' I said. 'I'm ready – I'll wait for you.' He was a little taken aback by this because he expected me to run for it. We met in a fight in the boys' toilets and all my anger and frustration of the previous weeks came to the surface. Funnily enough I didn't actually touch him, but there were so many punches flying around his face as he tried to defend himself that he fled and within days they were all speaking to me again. I don't recommend meeting violence with violence because that is usually the fastest way to even more violence, but I learned from this whole episode another instalment in the lesson my father had been drumming into me: When you have got a problem or you face adversity, stand up tall and face it. Running away only prolongs the agony and postpones the moment when everything can be sorted out. I should say that the way I was treated by the boys was instant karma for me because I had played a part in ignoring another lad for a long time a few months earlier. In fact so often whatever I have done of a negative nature in this life has been returned to me within a short time and this has been an excellent way to develop very quickly.

The theme of false accusation showed itself again from time to time. Once, I recall the teacher, Miss Gaskell, left the classroom and everyone started messing about. The class overlooked the playing field and I spent the time looking out of the window at the football match going on in a games lesson. I vaguely remember seeing a paper dart flying around the room, but I was much more interested in the game. Miss Gaskell returned to see the paper dart in mid-flight.

'Who threw that paper dart?' she demanded to know.

Silence.

'Right, everyone will write an essay on the importance of telling the truth and I will know from those essays who is responsible.'

The following lesson she announced to the class that she had read the essays on truth and she now knew from reading them who had thrown the dart and got everyone else into trouble by not having the courage to own up. I was only taking half an interest in this because I couldn't see how she could tell from reading an essay and, anyway, it had nothing to do with me. But then turning her head to look directly at me, she said: 'I know who threw that dart – don't I, Icke?'

'What? My God, she's accusing me,' I thought. 'How can she do this?' What I remember most was that those in the desks immediately around me, who knew I had nothing to do with the dart because it was happening on the other side of the class, looked at me with equal contempt to all the rest.

When I first arrived at the school I was seen as a bit of a troublemaker, a disruptive influence on others, which was again a travesty of the truth. A disruptive influence on myself, maybe, but not others. I remember David Bell was advised by one teacher to keep away from me because I was having a bad effect on him. What she didn't know is that, if anything, *David* was getting *me* in trouble. He had this ability to whisper something funny to me during a lesson and keep a perfectly straight face while I was laughing helplessly next to him. I spent many a lesson standing outside the classroom after being thrown out. I was often bored and I found learning French particularly tedious. So much so that I spent as much time during those lessons in the corridor outside as I did in the classroom. The headmaster used to take the class next door and time and again he would come out to find me standing there. Every week he would give me the double-take when he saw me. 'My goodness, not you again!' his face would say.

But gradually the perception of me changed and in my last year they made me a prefect, someone with certain duties and privileges within the school. I was simply amazed when I was told I had been selected because only those considered by the teaching staff to be the most sensible and trustworthy were picked. It was another boost to my confidence to think that I was being seen in that way after what had gone before. I wasn't the greatest prefect, however, because I was constantly turning a blind eye to misdemeanours I should have been sorting out or reporting to the teachers. I didn't feel comfortable in this position of authority over others and I never have.

Another aspect of this whole period of the mid-1960s was the emergence of Flower Power. I just loved the music and the idealism, and so many of the songs were so prophetic of what is happening now. Among them were Bob Dylan's

'The Times They Are A'Changin" and Thunderclap New-
man's 'Something In The Air'. I will always remember
seeing pictures of young people walking along a line of
soldiers guarding an air base and putting flowers down the
barrels of their rifles. The soldiers did not know what to do,
but then aggression is always uncomfortable when faced
with peace and love.

I also discovered girls at Crown Hills or mainly one girl,
actually. I was quite the shyest person you could ever meet
when it came to girls. All the confidence of the football pitch
was nowhere to be seen. I fell for a girl called Janice in a big
way, or at least as big as a fourteen-year-old knew how. By
the time I plucked up the nerve to say how I felt I was
leaving school for Coventry and we had to keep in touch
through letters. She eventually ended this long-distance
relationship the following Christmas and it took a long time
to get over it.

This was not only because I liked her as a person, although
she was very nice. It was more that she was a continuing link
with a period of my life that I never wanted to end. Those
last two years at Crown Hills were paradise for me. I was
doing well in football and I could dream of all the things I
would do when I became a famous professional footballer. I
was respected at school, got on marvellously with the
teachers, and was besotted with Janice, although she didn't
know. In the years that followed, I used to sit and ponder
many times on those days at Crown Hills when life seemed
so easy and full of promise. I ached for them to return and I
still look back on them with enormous affection.

When I walked out of the school on that final afternoon I
knew that the days of dreaming were coming to an end. The
time to turn dreams into reality had arrived and awaiting
was the big, bad world my father had told me so much
about.

3

The Footballer

I could never say that, overall, I enjoyed my time as a professional footballer. There were many great moments, but in general I didn't like the pressure of expectation from myself, my father, and those who played with me or managed the clubs. The fear of letting others down was at the bottom of it, I think.

I had moved on so much in my self-belief, but I started to go back again almost from the moment I arrived in Coventry to start my career as an apprentice professional footballer. It was a repeat of those early childhood years almost, but on a more advanced level. It is a little like walking around a mountain. You keep returning to face the same view, but from a higher perspective.

I was nervous on the first day I trained with the club in the summer of 1967 and I was still nervous when I played my last professional game. Don't get me wrong, there were periods when I was playing well that I loved the life, but far too often I let nerves get the better of me. I was determined in that I worked as hard as possible to improve and I practised more than anyone, something that continued throughout my career, but in matches I too often thought negatively and expected the worst. I was a perfectionist for a start. I saw every goal that went past me, no matter how unstoppable, as a personal reflection on my ability and I was so concerned about letting people down, especially my father, by not making the grade as a footballer. I saw the disappointment on his face when I played badly and I felt so responsible. I also often thought of my old friends at school. I know this may sound daft, but I didn't want to let them down either. I remembered how they had said when I left school: 'Good luck, Ickey – see you on the telly.'

I always found it difficult to cope with other people's disappointments and sadness. I could cope with it in myself, but not in others. All the time when I look back I was saying to people in different ways: 'Don't you worry or be sad, pass it on to me, let me do the worrying, you just be happy and then I'll be happy.' I have always been extremely sensitive to the emotions of others, particularly pain, sadness and disappointment and I still am. I now understand that those emotions may be necessary for the growth of the people involved, and balancing both compassion and caring on one side and seeing people's experiences in a wider, eternal context, is something we all need to do, especially through the period of turmoil now underway. For as long as I can remember I have felt emotions that I could not understand because there was no apparent explanation in my own life for why I was feeling the way I was. The Tumi reading saw this in my birth chart:

The Moon was conjunct [in strong relationship with] Uranus in the area of the heavens called Cancer. Traditionally this would mean that you were someone who needs emotional independence and freedom, and there would be sudden shifts in your emotions. But with you I feel you are tuning into, and carrying, the emotions of others, particularly the Earth. Sometimes you can be really hurt or an event could come into your life that would cut you to shreds. The Moon–Uranus combination would make you a very, very sensitive person. It cuts through all the veils and leaves you kind of wide open so you can pick up on what people and the planets are feeling. Sometimes you will have feelings and emotions which really aren't your own. You will be feeling very good or very bad and not always understand why.

I became a loner once again in these first two years at Coventry and my self esteem began to diminish. My fear of failure turned me into an inconsistent player. It was ridiculous. If I made a good save early on in a game my self confidence would grow and I would play well. If I made a little mistake, even if it didn't cost a goal, I would take this as a sign that this wasn't my day and I would play below my best.

The biggest competition for young footballers in England is the FA Youth Cup, the under-eighteen version of the FA Cup. I was the Coventry Youth Team goalkeeper at the age of fifteen and most of the players around me were older. I was intimidated by some of them and this affected my confidence and the way I played. We progressed through the early rounds of the FA Youth Cup and I kept my place, just, despite having a real stinker in another important youth competition. By now every match was an ordeal to be got through. We reached the semi-finals and played Crystal Palace over two games. In the first match I played fairly well, although I got away with one mistake. But when the team was announced for the second match my name was not there. I was dropped and the coach said to me 'It's a tough game, son', which I was later to use as the title of a book about professional football. The team went on to reach the Youth Cup final and it was a time of tremendous disappointment for myself and my father, but the biggest blow was still to come.

I was training just after I was dropped when I jumped for a ball with another player. As we clashed his knee collided with my thigh. It is what is known in football as a dead leg. The next day the thigh had stiffened and I went to see the physiotherapist, Norman Pilgrim. He diagnosed a haematoma, a sort of hard lump at the point of impact. These are quite common injuries in football and we called them week-at-homers because Norman always strapped up the thigh and sent us home to rest for a week before beginning the treatment. It was almost a blessed relief to know that I would not play for a few weeks. The pressure had been building up to such a pitch that I was frightened at the very thought of playing football. My whole world was falling apart.

When the bandage was removed from the left thigh we noticed that my knee was swollen on the same leg. There was no apparent reason for this because I had not hurt the knee and there was no pain. Norman said he could only think that blood and fluid disturbed by the blow on the thigh had gathered around the knee.

The treatment went on and the thigh recovered in the usual way, but the knee remained swollen and this could no longer be explained by Norman's first thoughts. He sent me to the local hospital for an X-ray and fluid was drained from the knee and tested. All the tests were negative and everyone was baffled. What on earth was the reason for the swelling? I didn't play again that season and my knee was strapped for several weeks during the summer. But once the tight bandage was removed the knee just ballooned again. After more hospital consultations they said they had no idea what the problem was, but if the knee felt strong, perhaps it would be better just to start playing again and see what happened. Maybe it would just go away in time.

The knee did feel strong despite the swelling and I started to play again. By now I was sixteen. I could not get a place in the main youth team because Coventry had signed another young goalkeeper who was a year older than me, but I played regularly for the club through that season without any ill effects from the knee. I had one wonderful bit of 'luck', too. Coventry were drawn in the Youth Cup away at Leicester City and I was desperately disappointed that I would not be playing at Filbert Street in front of my old school mates. That match was called off six times because of the pitch conditions and when at last it was played, the new youth goalkeeper was not available and I took his place. We won one–nil and it was the highlight of my season. The next year I was the club's first-choice youth goalkeeper and I began to play consistently well. I had signed as a full professional and played again in the FA Youth Cup. With no other goalkeeper to challenge me and my form so sound, I was enjoying the game more than at any other time since I left school. We got to the final of the Youth Cup before losing to Tottenham after two replays. We won the youth league we played in every week, and I had several good games for the reserve side. This was more like it; we had a First Division goalkeeper in the making at last. I was also getting more confident away from football and became quite a jack-the-lad around the discos during the summer break.

The following season I was too old at nineteen to play for the youth team and rather than play me in the reserves on alternate weeks with another goalkeeper, the Coventry manager, Noel Cantwell (Jimmy Hill's successor), decided to send me 'on loan' to another club, Oxford United. This meant that I continued to be a Coventry player, but I would play for Oxford for an agreed length of time to the mutual benefit of both clubs. Coventry would ensure that I was getting a regular game in a good class of football while Oxford had a second goalkeeper which they urgently needed at the time.

I didn't enjoy my three months at Oxford because I never felt at home there and I faced a series of setbacks. I played badly in my first match for their reserve side and soon afterwards I broke a thumb in training. I was in goal with players taking shots at me alternately from both sides of the penalty area. Eventually the manager shouted 'stop' to give a player a telling off for taking a lazy shot. I stopped and looked over to see what was going on. Unfortunately, the assistant manager, Mick Brown, didn't realise the situation and blasted a shot in my direction when I was looking the other way. The ball landed slap bang on the end of my thumb, breaking it in three places.

I was out for several weeks and Oxford were forced to use a local goalkeeper who had been with them before, but didn't make the grade. This time he did. He played brilliantly and he was signed full-time. This was important to my life plan because had I not broken my thumb and had the stand-in goalkeeper not played so well, I would probably have ended up signing for Oxford and that was not what was required. As it was they had no further use for me when I was fit again and I returned to Coventry. I was quite relieved because I felt at home at Coventry City and I still get a good feeling when I go back to the club even today. I never got on, really, with the Oxford manager and I remember he accused me once of leading the apprentices astray. Again this was totally and utterly untrue and indeed I had never been out with any of the young players at the club, never mind taken them to the local bars or whatever I was supposed to have done.

The most significant development at Oxford was the discomfort I was getting from my right ankle. Like the knee it swelled up for no apparent reason, but unlike the knee it was painful. I went to see Norman Pilgrim, the Coventry physiotherapist. I had become quite friendly with Norman because we spent a lot of time together when I was an apprentice. Apprentice players had to clean the dressing rooms, wash the baths and suchlike after training. My job had been to help Norman with his work and keep the treatment room clean and tidy. He diagnosed a problem with the tendons in the ankle and treated me for that. It took some time to settle down and there was one farcical situation I recall when Coventry played in Germany against Bayern Munich in a European competition. The first team goalkeeper was injured and the reserve came into the team. This left me to sit on the substitutes' bench to be brought on if necessary during the match. The truth was that I could hardly walk, let alone play against one of the best sides in Europe. Coventry lost six—one but goodness knows what the score would have been if I had been forced to play for any reason. This was another bleak period in my career because I knew there was more to this injury than first appeared.

The ankle settled down enough for me to continue to play, although it was definitely weaker than the other one. Coventry sent me on loan to Northampton Town and soon after I arrived there the left knee that had been swollen since that original blow became very weak. I was told I needed a cartilage removed and as the Northampton Town medical set-up was far less sophisticated than Coventry's, I went back again to Norman Pilgrim. I met up with him after a first team match at the Coventry ground and he gave me a brief examination. I could tell he was concerned. By now I had a swollen left knee, a swollen right ankle, and, most recently, a swollen left elbow. Soon afterwards the right knee also became swollen and painful. I could not pinpoint a cause for any of the swellings, they just appeared. Norman and the specialist at the hospital agreed it would be wise to remove the cartilage, but they did not believe that was anything like the whole answer. During the operation the surgeon took samples of tissue for testing. This and other tests, while far from conclusive, led them to the diagnosis that I had rheumatoid arthritis. My career, they said, was over. I was numb. I drove back to Leicester and the clock factory where my father still worked in the drawing office. He came out to see me on the pavement outside the main entrance and I told him the news. I think that was the hardest part of this sad affair, telling him it was over after all those years since that first match in those great big boots. It was a big emotional blow for a nineteen-year-old to take.

But through all this something told me I wasn't finished yet and I was certainly not prepared to let go without a fight. That would seem to be madness when you think that both knees were swollen along with the ankle and the elbow. It is now that a man I will always be grateful to made the first of two timely interventions. He was John Camkin, a former Fleet Street sports writer and television football commentator, who ran his own string of travel agencies in the

Midlands. I had met him briefly on a few occasions when he was a director of Coventry City and I liked him immediately. 'JC', as he is known to everyone, asked me what I was going to do. I said I wanted to see if I could continue in part-time football where I would not have to train every day and the joints would be subject to less strain and wear. They had begun to settle and I wanted to make sure I really did have no chance of playing on before I finally accepted defeat.

JC was magnificent. He gave me a job in his travel agency and promised to look around for a club that would give me a chance. That club turned out to be Hereford United, the best part-time club in the country, and then managed by John Charles, one of the finest players Britain has produced. I went on trial for a month and they signed me. Ironically I was earning more money playing part-time in Hereford's first team than I had been playing full-time in the reserves and third team at my previous clubs.

The most important moment in my entire life before or since also happened in this limbo period between Coventry and Hereford in the summer of 1971. It was 8 May when I went to a dance and disco at the Chesford Grange Hotel between Kenilworth and Leamington Spa in Warwickshire. I was with my best mate in football, Bob Stockley, with whom I shared my short jack-the-lad period. I looked up and into the room walked Linda. Our eyes met and something just went 'wham' in both of us. Within a day I had decided this was the girl for me. We were engaged on 26 June and married on 30 September. It was the best decision I would ever make. She is one of the most caring, loving, supportive human beings it has been my privilege to meet. She was, is, and will always be, the most wonderful friend anyone could ask for.

When we have an instant reaction to someone, be it love, warmth or dislike, it is because on the mind level we recognise each other from past lives and experiences, pleasant or unpleasant. When you look at the background to Linda and myself over so many past lives, it is no mystery why we met and married so quickly. The astrological reading talks of the enormous bond between us. Judy Hall, like most people, uses the term 'soul' for that eternal part of us which I call the mind. You just need to remember that soul and mind are interchangeable terms and mean the same. Her reading said:

We could probably write a book just on your relationships with Linda over the centuries! I see these relationships extending over many lives and countries with all kinds of relationships and interactions. This is typical of the pattern we have with 'soulmates', although it is not always such an idyllic relationship as yours is with Linda. Sometimes our soulmates are the ones who put us through unpleasant experiences out of love to help us learn. And, remember, we have more than one soulmate. Naturally this can cause confusion if we happen to get entangled at a sexual level with more than one in any lifetime, but again this may well be planned and necessary for our development. In Linda's case she is here to support you through thick and thin. There is a deep spiritual link between you and Linda revealed in your birth charts and you can almost read each other's minds. The timing of your meeting was also significant in that you were aged nineteen. When we have sexual contact we generate energy which, if moved up from the purely physical level, can help us grow. What is called the Nodal Return at eighteen and a half is a time when the energy centres of the body (the chakras) are stimulated and the creative energy begins to move upwards from the lower to the higher chakras. So making love with someone with whom we have a soul bond and energy compatibility, helps us to transmute this energy to a higher vibration. For you this was a preparation for the second Nodal Return at thirty-seven when the time came to use these energies for healing.

Linda had a similar background to me. Her parents, Ron and Rose Atherton, were always short of money and she was living in a Leamington council house when we met. She did not, however, have the clashes with her father that had been such a part of my life. My relationship with my father deteriorated rapidly after the news of the arthritis. I now know that he was once again venting his own disappointments and frustrations at the situation on me and I hold no grudges for what happened. But this was a particularly difficult time while I still lived at home in Leicester. One day soon after I met Linda I had the most enormous row with my father and the next morning I packed my bags and left in my little battered car. The last words my father said to me were: 'Don't come to my funeral – I don't want you there.'

I arrived at Linda's workplace, a Leamington garage where she was a van driver. I had everything I owned in that little car and a few pounds in my pocket. I had no idea where I was going to sleep that night. With Linda's help I managed to find some digs for a week and then I was extremely 'lucky' to find a bedsit in Leamington. It was one small room with a shared kitchen. I couldn't cook to save my life and I had some spectacularly awful meals when Linda wasn't there to help. I bought an all-in-one tray meal one day, with different things in separate compartments. I thought that couldn't fail because you only have to put them in the oven and warm them up, but somehow I ended up with red-hot peas and stone-cold potatoes.

I lived there until I married Linda. I worked at a local travel agency during the day and twice a week I drove all the way to Hereford and back to play or train in the evenings. I won a place in the first team and I was playing well with league clubs watching me.

Things began to go wrong two days before the wedding. I was playing at Worcester when I injured a hip and had to be carried off. I couldn't play for two weeks and when I was fit again the reserve goalkeeper who had taken over from me stayed in the team. They went on to have a marvellous

season which included a famous FA Cup run when they beat
First Division Newcastle United and very nearly West Ham,
then captained by the former England captain, Bobby
Moore. I watched all this from the sidelines thinking of what
might have been, but for that injury.

In fact, I left Worcester that unfortunate evening unable to
walk and I was only fit for the wedding thanks to acupuncture. Linda had told me of an acupuncture clinic in
nearby Kenilworth soon after we met and I went there for
treatment for the arthritis. It was my first experience of
alternative medicine and the pursuit of a cure, or at least
some relief, would lead me to many more unconventional
treatments. This, too, was all part of my life plan. I had been
offered only painkilling drugs by the hospital doctors and I
refused to take them. If I had taken them over the long
period since then my body would have been devastated by
now just as so many other people have been by the drugs
handed out by reflex action by the medical profession.
Conventional medical science has such a limited view of
who we really are that it treats us like a machine that exists
only as a physical form so it's no surprise their drugs can do
such damage. Acupuncture is based on the belief, true as it
turns out, that the body has lines of energy known as
meridians which carry the lifeforce energies around the
body. I talk about this in some detail in *The Truth Vibrations*
and *Love Changes Everything*. The treatment was certainly
effective for the arthritis and miraculous for that hip injury.
I hobbled into the clinic and walked out an hour later.

The wedding was very simple and quiet. We had some
money to start our married life only because Linda fell on
her head at the age of nine! She was riding her bike with her
father and as they passed a parked lorry the driver on the
pavement side threw a rope across his cargo and it came
down on the other side, wrapped around Linda's handle-
bars, and sent her careering, head first, onto the road. A
tribunal awarded her £150 to be paid on her twenty-first
birthday and that was just after we met. This was the money

that allowed us to set up home together.

My father was not going to come to the wedding at all, but my mother persuaded him to be there and we slowly began to patch up the rift. But there would be many others. We had our honeymoon at the Claverton Holiday Flats on the seafront at Ryde on the Isle of Wight and our transport was quite the most ramshackle vehicle I have ever owned and that, I can tell you, is quite a statement. It was a Riley sold to me by John Charles, the Hereford manager. What harm I had done to him to deserve that I could not imagine. He sold me a pile of rust with four wheels attached! While we were on honeymoon we heard a loud banging sound under the bonnet. When we looked we could see that the front of the car which supports the engine was banging against the main body because the joint between them had broken. It was absolutely lethal when I look back, but as we all know from experience if we are honest, we ignore such things if we are in dire straits. We went into Woolworths and bought a square of green sponge material and some black tape. We taped the sponge between the clanging pieces of metal and the noise stopped! Bits were always dropping off that car and every time we went out in it or any of the stream of old bangers it was an adventure, a journey into the unknown.

We lived in a two-room flatlet and had very little money to spare, but we so loved being married to each other that such struggles didn't seem to matter. Fortunately the money I earned with Hereford was enough to get us by with Linda working as well. I say fortunately because it was clear that I was not cut out to be a travel agent. Sitting behind a desk writing out tickets was a real struggle for me. My days were numbered after I made a mistake with the train tickets for an executive from the town's major company, Lockheed. He was going from Leamington to London and then from London to Dover to catch a ferry. I got the times mixed up and our important executive, important to the travel agency anyway, arrived in London at roughly the time his ferry was leaving Dover! It was all sorted out and the travel agency kept the Lockheed contract, but after a decent interval I was out of work.

At the end of my first season with Hereford they were voted into the Fourth Division of the Football League and they became a full-time professional club. Linda and I left Leamington and settled in Hereford at the start of the most successful and painful season of my career. It was also to be my last. These were great times in that quiet city near the Welsh borders. Up to now it had been best known for its cathedral and cattle market, but the exploits of Hereford United in the FA Cup the season before had made it famous for its football club.

John Charles had been replaced as manager by Colin Addison and his assistant, John Barnwell, a man who helped me more than anyone to become a better player in the short time he was at the club. I was in the reserves to start with, but as the first team struggled to compete against the higher quality professional opposition I was given my chance. I was never to lose my place again. I established myself as the unquestioned first choice and was playing better than at any time in my life. I was only twenty and here I was after all the struggles and disappointments, a Football League goal-keeper with bigger clubs taking an interest in me. It is only now that I realise just what an achievement that was after all that had happened, and until recently I have only appreciated my achievements later, never at the time.

Hereford's poor start to the season turned into a long unbeaten run of matches which took us to second place in the division. We stayed there until the end of the season and completed the outstanding feat of winning promotion in our first season as a league club. We were playing to crowds of ten and twelve thousand at home, which is incredible in the Fourth Division. We were carried along on a wave of enthusiasm and that season only one other goalkeeper in the entire four divisions conceded fewer goals.

The only really bad moment came in an FA Cup match at Torquay when I let in the silliest of goals. It went through my legs and the ball was travelling so slowly it didn't even have the pace to reach the back of the net. I noticed that when such incidents happened, it almost appeared to happen in slow motion. To the spectators it took a split second, but to me it happened much more slowly. It was almost as if I had entered a different world or dimension for the period it took to make the mistake and create the experience of coping with the consequences. Everything seems to stop, somehow. It's hard to explain, but other goalkeepers have noticed this when they have made their biggest and most crucial blunders. I'm sure it's because we are 'switched off' for the time it takes for the mistake to be made and the karmic situation set up. This same process happens in all walks of life all the time to present us with experiences we would like to avoid.

Certainly that was a terrible weekend for me to get through as only another goalkeeper would fully understand and I knew I had to avoid any mistakes in the next match or my place would be in danger. It was against Aldershot at home and I went down too slowly for a shot along the ground. It went underneath me, but enough of my body touched the ball to slow it down. As I lay on the floor with the ball rolling towards the line, I somehow managed to reach back and stop it a few inches short of becoming a goal. Had that gone in, my place in the side would have been in question, but as it was the ball stayed out and I went on to have a tremendous season. By such fractions are success and failure measured, at least in Earth terms, for all of us.

Behind the success of that season was a secret that only Linda and I knew about. The arthritis was getting worse again and I spent most of my season in pain. Through the winter as we trained in the cold and damp I would be in agony. We would go through a warm-up routine of running and exercises before each session and I could have screamed some mornings. Once the joints were warmed up they felt less painful, but during that routine every morning I came close to tears sometimes. I developed a reputation for always having something wrong with me as I gave my team mates different excuses for why I was limping. 'Oh, the calf muscle is a bit stiff,' I would say, or, 'These boots are rubbing and I think I've got a blister.' All the time of course, it was the same problem – arthritis.

The excitement and the adrenalin would make sure I would get through the matches without noticing the pain and somehow, quite unbelievably, the club never found out the truth of what I was going through. I continued to play well and so, I suppose, there was no need for them to suspect. Towards the end of that season the pain suddenly disappeared and I thought the miracle had happened. Even in training I felt good and I wondered if I would be free from pain forever. We won promotion to Division Three on a wonderful day in front of a capacity crowd and went off to Spain for a celebration with the club. I did not feel well for most of the time in Spain and I had this sense of foreboding without knowing why. A few days after returning home and still not feeling too clever, I glanced down at my knees as I climbed into bed one night. What struck me was that the swelling had gone. Even the left knee which had been swollen since I was fifteen looked normal. This gave me even more confidence that I had beaten the arthritis after all these years. What a shock was awaiting me.

I will never forget the next morning. I was in that sort of half sleep when you first start to wake up. I realised that I couldn't breathe. It wasn't that I was short of breath, I literally could not take a breath at all. I panicked for what seemed an age, although it was only a few seconds, before I managed to gasp a breath. The awful truth dawned. I could not move. It was as if my whole body was encased in concrete and every time I tried to move any joint it was excruciating. Linda had to do everything for me over the next few days, even carry me to the toilet while I screamed with pain. It was the summer of 1973 and there were many weeks to get well for the next football season. Deep down, though, I knew it was over. There would be no way back from this. I went to see my doctor, who was also the football club doctor. He sent me for tests at the local hospital, all the ones I'd had before. It had become a familiar process. The tests had never been conclusive about the type of arthritis and neither were these, but the symptoms fitted perfectly with rheumatoid. I decided to spend the next few weeks having acupuncture before making a decision on what to do. The treatment eased the pain and I was able at least to limp along in some form.

When the time drew near to start training with Hereford for the new season I had another examination with the club doctor and the local orthopaedic specialist. They said they would discuss the situation and I made an appointment to see them a few days later to hear the verdict. It was, ironically, on the first day of training after the summer break and I tried to take part. The pain was unbelievable and there was no way of hiding it any more. The manager, Colin Addison, came up to me afterwards and asked me to see him in his office that afternoon. He said I hadn't been trying hard enough in the training session and wanted to know why. Before that I went off to see the doctor and he told me the news I was expecting. There was absolutely no way I could continue to play football and if I tried I would cripple myself. After the morning I had just been through I had nothing left to fight back. It was almost a relief that the battle was over. I could not have taken any more. I was mentally, physically and emotionally wiped clean.

The meeting with Colin Addison was well timed because I could tell him he needed a new goalkeeper. It was a bizarre conversation. Colin was a nice man and a fine manager, but in my experience he had the habit of speaking to you and then, while you replied, he was miles away thinking of what he was going to say next. It was almost funny when I look back. He was giving me a telling off for not trying hard enough in the training session and I was telling him I was never going to play again. Two totally different conversations were going on at the same time and, for a few minutes, they remained out of sync. Eventually he heard what I was saying and my football career was officially terminated. After all those years of struggle against the arthritis I had conceded defeat at last.

People were amazed that someone so young could be struck down by arthritis. 'How unlucky,' they said. But illness is not random. There is almost always some past life, present life, or life plan reason for it to affect some people and not others. It is worth asking at these times what we are supposed to learn from it or why it is necessary in eternal terms.

Imbalances on our other non-physical levels, in the emotions for instance, can filter down to manifest as a health problem. Cancer and heart disease are classic examples of this. If those imbalances are not removed they can recur when you return for a later physical life. When these imbalances show themselves on the physical level then they have to be dealt with or faced and this is often part of our pre-programming. Facing pain or the possibility of death can make us start to think in another way, see through our misunderstandings and illusions, and help others around us do the same. Some people also take on illness as part of their life plan to absorb negative energies from the energy sea to transmute them through their bodies. Again this can manifest as cancer and countless other forms of dis-ease.

There are so many reasons for illness. The Tumi reading has an astrological explanation for my arthritis and what makes it more impressive is that he was under the false impression that I did not become physically aware of the arthritis until I was twenty or twenty-one. He couldn't understand this because he was sure from the birth chart that it would have started about the age of fifteen, which of course it did. This was the time when the Moon energies in the progressing chart within me, the so-called 'progressed Moon', crossed and activated the energies of Chiron in the static chart. This would have set off all the combined power of the Grand Cross to create something very significant in my life. The Chiron energies which were triggered are about wounds and healing them:

People who have come here for service often take on a wound for the planet and I feel this is what you did. You took on a wound for the Earth so she would not have to deal with it herself in her present state of turmoil and pain. Chiron in your birth chart is in Capricorn which is ruled by Saturn energies. Saturn, in turn, rules the bone structure. Saturn is very strongly placed in your chart. Within your energy field the progressed Moon would have gone over your static Chiron when you were about fourteen or fifteen. I feel that is when Saturn's influence on your joints would have begun. In the period between then and your twenty-first birthday your progressed Moon passed through Pisces, the twelfth house, and this often indicates the end of a phase in our lives, the point when we change direction. Suddenly what was sparked off when you were ten by those Mars energies would have dissolved as the strong influence of Neptune in your chart came into play.

It is also interesting that Chiron is symbolically represented by the wounded king. The wounded king was King Arthur and he was wounded in the thigh. It was a thigh injury that set off your arthritis and it was almost as if you were playing out the legend of King Arthur wounded on behalf of the Earth. Ancient myths and legends are symbolic of actual happenings and I believe that the one who became known as King Arthur in the stories carried the Christ energy as did Jesus and others through history. The Christ is an energy of immense purity and power from the highest levels of Creation and I see that you carry that energy. I don't think that it's personal to one person anymore, I think it's carried by a group of minds, but I do recognise that you carry it very strongly.

With my career ended by arthritis when I was so young, my retirement from football attracted quite a lot of publicity and during this period I was told my contract would be honoured and the club would arrange a testimonial game to give me some money to start a new life. At least, I thought, I am going to have time to think what I want to do next. But a fortnight after the doctor's decision and after the publicity had blown over I was asked to see the club secretary. 'As you can no longer play for us,' he told me, 'you are in breach of the terms of the contract and it is being terminated immediately.'

On top of all that had just happened I was now without an income and the testimonial game never materialised either. I couldn't pay the mortgage and the house had to be sold urgently to keep us afloat. At the lowest point we had £36 in the bank, no income and a mortgage of £66 a month. Once again it was Linda and me against what looked a very tough and unwelcoming world.

4

The Journalist

Of all the bad times I have had in my life this was, until 1991, the worst, but I was determined not to wallow in self-pity. That was, is, and always will be, a disaster whatever the circumstances.

I was shattered, of course, but like anyone in such situations I had two choices: to fall apart or stand up, brush myself down, and get on with it. If I were to choose the first alternative who would be the biggest loser? I would. It would have been so much easier had my contract not been cancelled so quickly or if the testimonial game had happened, but my life was not meant to be made easier. It was my life plan to experience these pressures, and it was I who agreed to it. I needed another ambition, another goal to aim for at this time to help me to think positively and shut out my disappointment and concern for the future. I decided I would become a professional cricketer. This was simply daft because I wasn't even very good, but in the few weeks I had that in mind at least it helped me to focus on something positive.

Then on the day when my enforced retirement was confirmed and announced in the papers, I had a phone call from Chris Moore, the football reporter on the local Hereford paper. He was a nice guy, very genuine, and I had known him since the day I first signed for the club. 'Gary Newbon has just called me,' he said. 'He wants to know if you will go on his programme tonight for a live interview about what's happened.'

Gary Newbon was the main sports presenter for ATV, the independent television company which has since become Central Television. I jumped at the chance to appear in a television studio for the first time. I set off with Linda for the studios in Birmingham and what a turning point this was for me. I just loved the atmosphere of the studios and while we waited for the interview to start I thought: 'Ickey, my old son, this is for you.' I was interviewed with another sportsman, the cricketer Mike Hendrick, who had just been selected to play for England. The interview was billed as one man who was starting his international career and another, me, who was being forced to retire from professional sport altogether. It went pretty well and I left those studios determined that I was going to be a television presenter. As usual with me, there were no half measures. I set my sights on presenting sport for BBC Television and my ultimate ambition was to present 'Grandstand', the most prestigious sports programme in the country at that time.

When I announced my plans to some of my friends they didn't believe it was possible. Why should they? Here I was, a twenty-one-year-old has-been footballer with a serious illness, no money, no job, no educational qualifications and no prospects. But I did have advantages that far outweighed the problems. I had in Linda a wife who would support me to the death, a fierce, unquenchable determination to achieve whatever I set out to achieve, and someone up there, as they say, who was looking out for me whenever I needed a break at the right time.

Just after the television interview a letter arrived from John Camkin. He was sorry to hear what had happened and would I like to meet him and see if he could help me in any way? What a guy and what timing! JC had been a top Fleet Street sports writer on the now defunct *News Chronicle* and the *Daily Mail* and I knew from my inquiries that the best way to get into television sports presentation was through journalism. I told him what I wanted to do and he said he would help if I could show him I had the ability. He asked me to compile an article on an aspect of football and write a report on a football match. I had always had an interest in writing which was encouraged and stimulated by my father who was always reading books. I became interested in sports reporting as a youngster through reading the *Leicester Sports* paper and in particular the reports on the Leicester City matches written by a man called Lawrie Simpkin. JC liked my work enough to introduce me to Bill Hicks, his former sports editor on the *Mail*, who had become head of journalism at Harlow College. Bill was such a nice man and I liked him from the start. He gave me the standard entrance exam to see if I could justify a recommendation to editors he knew. To my relief I passed.

Bill said he was holding a conference the following week of all the editors of the papers which sent young journalists to the college, and he would recommend me to them. It would not be easy because they were looking for people with A Level exam passes or university graduates and I had never passed an exam in my life. There was also the stigma of being an ex-professional footballer and the common belief that all footballers were a bit thick with their brains in their feet. Only two papers were interested, the *Kent Messenger*, and another in, of all places, my home town of Leicester. It was called the *Leicester Advertiser* and they gave me a job as a news reporter.

I went to stay with my parents in Leicester while the house was sold in Hereford and I only saw Linda at the weekends. When the house sale was completed she had to move in with her parents in Leamington Spa because we could not find anywhere to live in Leicester. There was no way we could afford to buy a house and rented accommodation was extremely scarce. It was terrible not being able to live in the same town, never mind the same house, as your wife, but this went on for many weeks as I followed up every advertisement for a place to stay. The arguments continued periodically with my father, but he also tried so hard to help us find a home. One evening when Linda had come over to Leicester to see me, we were just driving away from my parents' house when another car stopped outside. A middle-aged couple got out and asked to talk to us. They owned one of the flats my father had applied for on our behalf and they wanted to know if we still wanted it. What a moment!

It was above an electrical shop on the Narborough Road, one of the main roads out of Leicester. It wasn't the Ritz and the place used to shake when a bus or lorry went past, which was every few minutes. But a caravan in a field would have been a mansion to us. My home life settled again.

My work on the *Leicester Advertiser* was a world away from Coventry City or Hereford United. The *Leicester Advertiser* was no London *Times*. I think it was a bit of a tax write-off for the main paper in the group, the *Leicester Mercury*. It came out every Friday and covered the whole of Leicestershire except for the main areas of population. Most of the area I was responsible for had more cows than people. We would report anything and at some length just to fill the paper every week. When I announced proudly to one local vicar that I was from the *Leicester Advertiser* he replied: 'Oh yes, that's the paper that even reports what size shoes people take!' He wasn't far wrong. If the paper's circulation had been human it would have been on a life support machine. No wonder I got the job – no-one else wanted it.

It was an excellent grounding, however. When you are faced with a few villages, the odd very small town, and endless swathes of farmland, it takes some ingenuity to fill a paper with 'news'. I used to go out on a Monday to all the post offices and village shops picking up the gossip about this fête or that meeting or speaking to the local vicar about whatever the church was doing that week. This was the big time all right. Watch out, Woodward and Bernstein. Actually, I spent so much time in village stores that my level of journalism was not so much Watergate as Cow and Gate! It was all rather a culture shock. Only a matter of weeks earlier I would run out in front of a full house at Hereford with the crowd chanting 'David Icke, David Icke'. Now I was sitting in damp and draughty village halls listening to parish councillors talking about street lamps and cracks in the pavement. One night it was so cold during a power strike that the few councillors who turned up decided to move into the village hall kitchen and we sat around a gas cooker with the oven door open as I scribbled into my little notebook. It seemed such a long way from 'Grandstand'.

I worked hard to develop a style of writing which was simple and economical. I wanted to write in a way that could turn complex information into an understandable form for everyone and this has been such a help in writing the books all these years later. Again this period was all pre-arranged before incarnation to develop the skills I would need today. It has always irritated me when people have used long words or jargon. It means that information is lost to those who are not in the know. I also began to see that those who use such language often do not understand what they are saying. To write simply you have to understand the subject because you can't hide behind the lack of clarity offered by vague wording and jargon. This is often used by government departments so that they can deny the intended meaning of something if that meaning turns out to be unpopular.

I also knew that if I wanted to be a broadcaster I had to lose my Leicester accent and my tendency to drop every 'h'. I love the Leicester accent. It has a life and character all of its own: 'Ooooh, me duck, if you want mi to cum airgently I berra cum straight the way.' My mother 'talks Leicester' and so did I, but it would not have gone down well if I was reading the news. I practised talking a little more 'proper' and I asked Linda to pick me up on every dropped 'h' and 'g'. Slowly I learned to speak without an accent. It became sort of middle of the road, not slang but thankfully not posh either.

After a few months on the *Leicester Advertiser* I met a well-

known local journalist called Roland Orton. He ran the
Leicester News Agency. Every area has a news agency,
particularly the cities. They sell their services and news
stories to whoever will buy them: newspapers, radio
stations, television, whoever. They are invaluable within the
media because if an organisation wants something done in
an area quickly and they don't have time to send their own
journalist, they can ring an agency and get the job done
immediately. Roland's agency also did a lot of football
reporting. I can't remember exactly how we met, but I know
I started to work for him at the weekends. He asked me if I
would report a Leicester City versus Birmingham game for
BRMB Radio, a new independent station. I had never done
any broadcasting in my life before and yet here I was being
asked to ad lib live football reports down a telephone. I
would be crazy to agree to do that, I thought. I agreed.

It went like a dream. Every few minutes I would ring the
radio station from the press box at Leicester and they would
put me on the air to describe what was happening. Birmingham won six–two I think and so there was a lot to talk about,
and I enjoyed every second of it. The name David Icke did
not hit the airwaves, though. I shouldn't really have been
doing it at all while working for the newspaper and I was
given a new name for the afternoon – Nick Gray! Once I had
experienced the excitement of live broadcasting the *Leicester
Advertiser* seemed even more tame and soon after that
Roland offered me a full-time job with the agency. He was
such a character and Leicester journalism will not see the
likes of him again. His office was across the corridor from
BBC Radio Leicester and through his agency I was employed
as their football reporter.

Roland was always trying to save on expenses and one
weekend he organised me a lift all the way from Leicester to
Newcastle to report on a game for Radio Leicester. It was
only when I was picked up very early on the Saturday
morning that I realised my lift would be in a furniture van!
We had a few words about that on the Monday morning as

I recovered from a stiff back, but I soon saw the funny side of it.

Working for the agency also gave me my first experience of the extreme end of the press. It was quite an eye-opener to see them in action, especially those who fearlessly seek out sexual indiscretions – as long as they think it will titillate the readers and make them buy the paper. Not long after I joined Roland, the phone rang in the office: 'Hello, mate, *News of the World* newsdesk here. I'm just ringing round the agencies to see if you've had any good court cases this week.'

'Well, er, yes,' I said naïvely. 'We've got court cases in Leicester all the time.'

'No, I'm looking for our kind of court cases.'

'Sorry?'

'Rapes, mate. Have you had any interesting rape cases? We are a bit short of them for this week's paper.'

I dread to think what we would do without the press to protect the moral fabric of our society.

I think Roland toyed with asking me to become a partner in the business at one stage to allow him to have more time at home. But it would never have happened. He is a journalist from the top of his head to the soles of his feet and he was never going to take a step back, at least not then. Besides, I was looking to move on. The life of an agency reporter is so unpredictable. You are never off duty and often they use agency reporters for the boring jobs the staff journalists don't want to do. I wanted more stability and regular hours for a while and my aim was a job on the Leicester evening paper, the *Mercury*. That didn't happen immediately, but I did move to another weekly paper in the same group, the *Loughborough Monitor*. From my first morning I hated it. The paper's circulation was in the same intensive care unit as the *Leicester Advertiser*, but without the pleasant surroundings of the main *Mercury* offices. The *Monitor* was run from a dingy, depressing little building and I used to dread every morning. Linda and I were still well and truly broke. By now we had moved into our own house in a village near Leicester called Croft which was dominated by a massive road stone quarry. The siren would go off followed by a big bang and often the village would be covered in dust. Linda was expecting our first child, Kerry, and working in an office in Leicester.

Loughborough was some distance away on the other side of Leicestershire and we had to run a car we could not afford. Our cars became legends in the family. We ran a sort of old people's home for motor vehicles. We were in serious transport trouble when our Ford Anglia developed a very expensive fault. We couldn't afford to have it repaired and sold it for as much as we could get – £35. That is all we had to find another vehicle and even in 1974, that was laughable. We saw an advert in the paper for an old Morris Minor for £25 and my father came with us one Sunday to see it. Hard as it may be to imagine today, it wasn't even worth that and we were very depressed. We went to catch the bus home and as it appeared in the distance our eyes turned to the little cards in a newsagent's window alongside the bus stop. In particular we saw one which said: 'Ford Corsair for sale, £25 or nearest offer.' Now a Ford Corsair at that time was still quite an up-to-date motor car and we could not believe the price. The bus was very close now and with so few buses on a Sunday we had to decide quickly if we would follow up the advert or catch the bus. We had no choice, really, because we needed a car desperately.

The Corsair was around the corner and to us it looked great. It was light green and was the most modern car I had ever had the chance of owning. 'So what's the catch?' my father asked the owner, a reasonable question in the circumstances. 'Well,' he said, 'it doesn't have a starter motor and it will cost a lot to put right because the wheel inside the engine which links up with the starter motor is knackered.' That didn't mean anything to me, but my father used this information to knock him down to £20! I became the proud owner of a Ford Corsair – with a difference. Everything was OK as long as I parked it on a hill because this allowed me to start the car on the run using the gears and the clutch. It made parking a little tricky, but at least I had transport. After six months of this I learned of another reason for the price; something the man had kept to himself. I was driving along the motorway when I heard some banging from under the bonnet. I pulled over and looked inside. What a sight. Two great holes had appeared in the bodywork on both sides of the engine where there had clearly been some patching up in the past. End of car and end of transport. I was fortunate that it had lasted so long in that state, but I managed to sell the car for scrap for £15 and it was the best deal I had done in my life. Six months of motoring for a fiver!

With no car I had to get up early every morning, catch a bus to the station in the next village, catch a train to Leicester, then another to Loughborough, before completing the journey with a walk across the town to the *Monitor* offices and, of course, I faced the return trip every evening. I could not afford the cost and when I explained my situation I was given what I always wanted, a job on the *Leicester Mercury*. The man I had to thank for that was Lawrie Simpkin, the football reporter who covered the Leicester matches when I was a youngster. He was now the news editor on the *Mercury*. Lawrie was a compassionate man with a big heart who, for some reason, chose to hide these qualities behind a rather loud and aggressive image which misled those who didn't know him well. I had two wonderful years on the *Mercury* and if it wasn't for something that was driving me ever onwards towards my goal of 'Grandstand', I might still have been there today. I loved the place.

I was also starting to realise that passing exams is not the same as intelligence. Some of the least gifted journalists I worked with had the most impressive academic qualifications. The education system with its obsession with exams and testing can often find no place for those who cannot, or see no point in, amassing in the memory endless amounts of useless information, the vast majority of which is not true anyway. I always struggled to concentrate at school because

I had a sort of sense that much of what I was being asked to believe was a load of baloney. 'What on Earth am I wasting my time learning this for?' I used to ask, and my son Gareth thinks in the same way today. This attitude can get children labelled as a bit dim or lazy when the opposite can be the case. Our natural skills are not created through education, although that can help us to develop them if it is the right kind. Those gifts are pre-programmed into us at birth and they are activated at the correct time in line with the life plan. When people are described as 'born footballers' or 'born musicians' and so on, it is literally true. It was at the moment of birth that those energy patterns – gifts – were programmed into us. Look at me as an example. Just as I was entering journalism, the Sun in that inner progressing birth chart was entering the area we call Gemini in that mini solar system within my own energy field. People with Gemini Suns are natural communicators and many journalists and communicators of all kinds have this combination in their birth charts. If you try to become a journalist or communicator without this pre-programming you might go on courses galore and pass endless exams, but you will never be naturally gifted. It is the same with any skill. Sensible education can awaken and polish skills, but it cannot create them. We do that before we even incarnate.

It was during my time on the *Mercury* that Kerry was born on 7 March 1975. As I have said, our children are not born at random. They are minds who have agreed to incarnate with us and this is because either they have karma with us to work out or they have come to help us, or we them, with a certain task. It is usually both. The incoming mind is also looking for the right combination of energies and genes carried by the parents to create for them the physical body that will best help them in their life plan. It's funny, down here on Earth we get ourselves in such a moral tizzy over unmarried mothers and children outside of marriage while on the other levels of Creation they are concerned only with matching the right combination of energies, genes and circumstances for the good of the incoming mind. This is particularly important today with the time of transformation now upon us. Kerry's birth chart has her Sun in the mystical sign of Pisces and with Mercury in Aquarius at the moment she was born, this indicates under the laws of karmic astrology that she is one of the minds who have come to help with the transformation of the Earth.

I moved in with my parents during the time that Linda was in hospital and the touch paper between my father and me was set alight again. It was incredible how at times we could be so close and yet such hostility could explode so quickly. With Linda now unable to work, our money troubles became even more serious. She had to get a job packing ladies' tights at home and eventually had to leave Kerry with a child minder to work in a hosiery factory. I saw an advertisement for a journalist at BRMB Radio in Birmingham, the station on which I made my broadcasting debut as Nick Gray. I got the job and worked four days a week as a news reader/reporter and two days on sport. It was a good place to be if you wanted to learn how to work under pressure. It was very competitive and if we did not have a story on the air ahead of the opposition there was trouble. BRMB had started during the miners' strike which brought down Ted Heath's Conservative Government. The country was on a three-day week and advertising revenue was scarce. By now, though, the station had overcome its serious financial problems and was operating successfully. It was also full of characters.

One was the main sports presenter, Tony Butler, a Black Country legend and a source of much hilarious material for the comedian, Jasper Carrott. Tony used the enormous rivalry between the fans of the Birmingham City and Aston Villa football clubs to the advantage of the station. He would make rude remarks on air about Villa and on would come their fans to complain. But they would still go on listening to see what else he said about them and he built a cult following among Brummie football fans. His budget was limited and he would use many people on his Saturday afternoon programme who were, shall we say, not born broadcasters. This led to some memorable moments. Before I arrived I was told of an agency reporter who got very confused one afternoon. Agency reporters at a football match have to earn their money by reporting for perhaps two radio stations and some newspapers, too. This one got himself in a right pickle. Tony Butler, so the story went, bellowed in his classic Black Country accent, 'And now we are going over live for a report on the Villa match today from so and so ...' There was a short silence followed by the reporter dictating his report slowly and deliberately to what he thought was a typist in a newspaper office. It went something like this: 'Villa midfield star, Gordon Cowans, that's G for going, O for Orange ...' and before they had got over the shock and cut him off he completed his opening sentence with 'full stop, new paragraph'.

We had so many laughs with Tony and this next story I know to be true. Another Saturday he asked one of his football reporters to bring the West Bromich Albion goal-keeper, John Osborne, to the phone for a live interview after Albion had won promotion to the First Division. Somehow the wires were crossed and Tony was told that John Osborne was waiting on the line to speak to him. The music faded and in came Tony at the top of his considerable voice. 'Right, the Albion are celebrating after winning promotion to the First Division and on the line from the ground is their goalkeeper, John Osborne. John, great news, what was the game like?'

In fact it was the reporter who was on the line and without knowing he was on the air he replied in a broad Brummie accent: 'He's pissed off, Tone.'

No-one worked for BRMB in those days without having scores of tales to tell about Tony and many others at the station. But while there was a lot of fun at BRMB, journalistically there was no messing about and it was in this period that a none-too-confident reporter became a competent broadcaster and journalist. It was an important stage of my career and I will always be grateful to the people I worked with, among them a lovely man called Brian Shepherd who was the news editor.

In the middle of my spell at BRMB I spent two months in Saudi Arabia. John Camkin and Jimmy Hill were involved in a company that was contracted by the Saudis to run their national football team and generally improve the standards of football at all levels. Jimmy rang me at BRMB one afternoon and offered me a contract worth £10,000 a year tax free for two years. Given the Saudi attitude to women, he said, I would have to go alone without Linda and Kerry. I discussed the situation long and hard with Linda, but after all those years of financial struggle going back to childhood, we decided that this was an opportunity to set us up at last. You could count on one hand the number of times I have cried in my life since I was a young child. I wish I could cry sometimes to let emotions out. The one exception was the morning I left Linda and Kerry to fly to Saudi Arabia on New Year's Eve, 1976. I knew by the time the plane was leaving Heathrow that I would not last the course. We were given two trips home a year and I knew the first time I returned it would be to stay.

I loathed every second of my two months in Saudi with Linda and Kerry so far away. But I would not have missed the experience of seeing the country. It was a place of such contrasts. On one side unbelievable wealth from the oil and on the other people living under corrugated iron. I remember the horror of seeing people with hands missing because they had been caught stealing, and the thought of living in a country where they still chopped off people's heads was just sickening. I was also astounded at the way women were treated there. The nearest I came to seeing the face of a Saudi woman were two eyes peering through black veils because the religious law says women must be covered at all times in public. It was hard to believe this actually happened and it was yet another case of religion being used as a weapon of control to prevent sexual and financial justice. It's always made me smile when I see religions so obsessed with covering up the human body. On one hand they say God created our bodies and yet on the other they say we should be so ashamed of what He created that they must be covered up at all times. It's the same when they won't allow you into Roman Catholic churches if you are wearing shorts or your dress is considered too low-cut. Words fail me.

The Saudi system is appalling, but I found the people as individuals to be very pleasant and willing to help. I became quite fond of a place deep in the desert called Buraydah where I met some nice people. It looked like a Wild West town and you expected Wyatt Earp to walk out of the only hotel. It was not a place to be a chicken if you went by the hotel menu. You could get roast chicken or roast chicken or even roast chicken, unless, of course, you preferred roast chicken. Oh yes, and for dessert you could have crême caramel or crême caramel. Every meal was served by a waiter who wiped his nose on his hand before passing you a bread roll. Funny, but whenever I went to Buraydah I had this overwhelming desire to go on a diet.

The agony of being away from Linda and Kerry got worse and John Camkin suggested I go home for a holiday and see how I felt then. We both knew when I left for the airport at Riyadh that I would not return. It was wonderful to be back and we had, for us, some decent money in the bank even after only a couple of months, but if we were to keep that I needed another job quickly. I was also straying away from my ambition to present 'Grandstand' and I wanted to get back on course. As things turned out, I went to see my friends at BRMB and everything fell into place perfectly. My job had gone, but another reporter was leaving and there was a vacancy. It was mine if I wanted it and I returned to the fold. More than that I was back with a little more money to my name. We were able to buy the first healthy car we had ever owned.

In two months, I had broken free of the financial difficulties I had always had. I spent another year at BRMB until

I saw an advertisement for a job in the television newsroom at BBC Pebble Mill in Birmingham working on a programme called 'Midlands Today'. I filled in my application and the next stage in what was turning out to be a most eventful life was about to begin.

5

The Television Presenter

Something strange happened in the two days between BRMB and starting the new job at the BBC. I left the radio station a competent reporter and broadcaster, but I was still the quiet guy who could have done with more confidence.

Over the weekend I had my hair permed, bought some new clothes, and when I arrived at Pebble Mill on the Monday morning I was a new man in more than one sense. I had begun to change my attitude as well as my appearance and within weeks I had developed a more ruthless, calculating streak, and the fiery, 'angry young man' stage was upon me. I had made it this far and I was going to go for it – nothing was going to stop me.

The job description was for a journalist who would write news items for the 'Midlands Today' programme with 'occasional appearances in vision'. I didn't really want to know about writing news items for others to read. I wanted to be a presenter myself and I worked out the best way to achieve this. Every morning the reporters and presenters would be given their work for the day from the diary. These were the events the programme producers knew were going to happen; court cases, feature items and suchlike. Once the reporters had left to cover these stories they were obviously not available if something turned up on the day, like a big fire or bank robbery. On these occasions the report would have to be filmed by one of the news writers like me, the ones the BBC called regional journalists. What's more I noticed that by the time news of an event that happened in the morning had filtered through to the newsroom, it was often around lunchtime. So I used to take sandwiches to work and spent my lunchtime alone in the newsroom outside the programme producer's office. It worked perfectly. The phone would go or someone from the local radio station down the corridor would come in to pass on a story and the producer's head would pop around his door to find little me sitting there with my salad sandwiches.

'David, are you doing anything?'

'No,' I would say, looking surprised.

'Well, get a film crew quick and go to so and so ...'

They must have liked what I produced because they soon began to give me reporting jobs ahead of the main reporters. This caused friction between the reporters and the other regional journalists and myself. It wasn't a pleasant atmosphere at times and I could understand their point with this young newcomer taking their work. But I was in full flow by now and I wanted to get through regional television as quickly as possible and on to 'Grandstand' and the network. Circumstances also helped me enormously. I was always in the right place at the right time and far from having occasional appearances in vision, I was on every night. When you remain in touch with guidance and follow your instincts you always find yourself in the right place just when you need to be, although the free will of others can get in the way. In my case at this stage, however, my life plan was spot on course. I was progressing in television just as I needed to be in preparation for 1991 and I was also having triggered within me by planetary movements a great deal of rage and frustration, again in accordance with the life plan. I would release so much more over the next few years. The Tumi reading could see this anger and the point where I became almost ruthlessly ambitious:

Pluto on your chart is in the tenth house and that gives drive, a ruthless drive, to succeed. People with this placement are invariably successful in career terms. As your progressed Moon passed through Gemini from the age of twenty-four to twenty-seven, something like that, you would have felt this Pluto energy very strongly and ambition to succeed would have been absolutely foremost in your consciousness. I can also see a pent-up anger within your chart which I feel relates to a mother figure, possibly your inner frustration at the treatment of Mother Earth. Shortly after this time your Moon in the progressed birth chart would have completed its first cycle around the static chart. This is the Lunar Return. I feel that those who have come in to serve the planet spend the first Moon cycle getting themselves ready for the second cycle when they begin to consciously wake up and start their real work.

The first examples of the 'luck' that was to speed my progress with the BBC at Pebble Mill arrived in my first week there. Three days after I started I interviewed the American tennis player Roscoe Tanner at a tournament in Birmingham and my face appeared briefly when I asked one of the questions, much to the delight of my mother! Two days later as I was eating my lunch, I was sent out to interview a lady with severe arthritis who was taking the government to court over benefit payments. I arrived back at the studios with the film very close to the start of the programme and I was met by the producer who was in a bit of a flap.

'There's no time to record anything,' he said. 'I want you to introduce your report live in the studio and then round it off in vision at the end.'

My heart began to thump. Apart from that interview with Gary Newbon as a footballer I had never been in a television studio before and within an hour I would be sitting there presenting a live report. Part of me was delighted that the opportunity had come my way so quickly, but there was every chance I would be so bad that I would not be asked again. I sat in the studio only a few minutes before I was on and I even had to ask where to look. In those days we didn't have the technology known as autocue which projects the words you are reading onto the camera lens. We had to memorise the script to ensure we looked down at the paper in front of us as little as possible. My mind was a blank and I think 'Midlands Today' viewers saw quite a lot of the top of my head that night, but the producers seemed to be satisfied and the appearances increased.

There was another bonus that day, too. The story was used by the nine o'clock network news and so by the end of my first five days in what was supposed to be mainly a backroom job, I had produced two reports for 'Midlands Today', one for the network news, and presented live in a studio for the first time.

Once I had my BBC pass, which allowed me access to all their buildings, I went down to Television Centre in London to watch Frank Bough, then the best-known sports front man in Britain, present 'Grandstand'. Soon I was reporting Midlands football matches for the programme occasionally and presenting most of the sport for 'Midlands Today'. The speed at which things were happening was hard to believe, but typical of the way my life has unfolded. I spent hours in front of a closed-circuit camera improving my presentation and studied others to pick up tips. It reminded me of my days in football when I was still out on the field practising when all the others had gone home. Something was constantly driving me on to achieve.

Soon after I joined the BBC I had a call at home one morning from the 'Midlands Today' producer. He said that a young boy had been murdered at a place known as Yew Tree Farm in Staffordshire and would I get there immediately to a police news conference. This was the saddest story I was ever to cover: the murder of the newspaper boy Carl Bridgewater, who was killed with a shotgun at point-blank range when he delivered a paper to the farm. He recognised a burglar who was stealing antiques and he was shot to keep him quiet. It was awful.

I covered the story throughout the week for 'Midlands Today' and the network news, and I did several follow-up reports on the continuing police investigations which led to the arrest of four men. The experience of covering that case from the start and subsequent evidence that has come to light, convinced me that the four men arrested for that crime are innocent. At the time of writing one of them has died in prison and the other three are still inside. I believe that the campaign to free them is fully justified and I hope they will be released because yet another severe miscarriage of justice has taken place.

I was a regional journalist for only a few months before I was offered a job as a full-time reporter. This came after I was approached by a man who has been a great friend ever since. His name is Paul Vaughan, a former researcher with the BBC, and by now a successful agent for many presenters and performers. I was asked to call him by one of his clients who I'd worked with at BRMB. Paul said he had seen me on the television and had recommended me to the rival programme, 'ATV Today'. Would I be interested? I was. They were offering me double the money to become a main presenter of their programme. I met them and agreed verbally to join them.

But there was still something that made me doubtful. I felt I should be loyal to the BBC for giving me my opportunity and I wondered what effect this would have on my ambition to present 'Grandstand'. On the Monday I told the 'Midlands Today' editor, Gordon Randall. He was extremely disappointed. After hurried discussions they came up with the offer of a job as a full-time reporter, although on nothing like the money I would be paid at ATV. But the money didn't matter to me and I stayed with the BBC. But these events did introduce me to Paul and he later became both my agent and a close friend. We have had many lives together and he is also here to play his part in the planetary transformation.

After eighteen months at Pebble Mill I was asked to apply for the job of Midlands Regional Reporter for the network news. It would mean continuing to work for 'Midlands Today', but every time a national news story broke in that region I would cover it for the main BBC bulletins. I was told that if I applied for the job it would be mine. This is the case with many BBC jobs in my experience. Although it was advertised nationally they knew who was going to get it. Even so I almost blew it at the interview. What would I do, I was asked, if someone had been killed or murdered and I knew where to find the relatives? Would I approach them and talk to them? 'No,' I replied. I could see from their faces that it was the wrong answer from their point of view, but I was sickened by seeing distressed people put under even more pressure by the media just to get a story. It didn't seem right unless they made it clear through the police that they wanted to speak to us. I still got the job, but I was told later that I had almost ruined everything with that answer.

In fact it would not have mattered. Within forty-eight hours of the interview I had turned down the job, put in my notice, and agreed to join a then new BBC programme called 'Newsnight'. I had a phone call from the editor, George Carey, whom I had met when he was an editor with the network news. Would I be interested in presenting sport for the programme? Yes, I would. This was the chance of national television and I would be in London where 'Grandstand' and the BBC Sports Department were based.

Leaving 'Midlands Today' was a sad moment. I had so much to thank that programme for. It gave me my opportunity in television and Gordon Randall, the editor, was a valued supporter who did much to help me behind the scenes. The move to 'Newsnight' brought many changes. I was now living in Leamington Spa and the house prices in the London area forced me to commute to the main BBC studios near Shepherd's Bush. I worked three twelve-hour

days a week with 'Newsnight' and I stayed in a cheap dingy
hotel on the nights I couldn't get home.

At the start, 'Newsnight' was fine and the sports news was
given a regular spot of a reasonable length. Gradually this
was cut back and back every night. They tried to pack in too
much and from the moment the programme started they
were dropping items galore. They could not cut back on the
filmed reports when the programme was already on the air
because they were finished and ready to go and so it was the
live element that had to pay the penalty. That meant sport
and it became extremely frustrating to see a whole day's
work being dropped in the bin just as it was about to be
broadcast. The show fell apart at the seams quite often in
those early days and it took a few years before it evolved
into an excellent programme.

What was most important for me in this 'Newsnight'
period in 1981 and 1982 was being seen by those in charge of
the BBC Sports Department, the home of all the major sports
programmes on the BBC. I was now doing regular football
reports for 'Grandstand' on a Saturday and then came the
call I had been waiting for. I was in the 'Newsnight' office
when I was told that Martin Hopkins, the 'Grandstand'
producer, was on the phone.

'Tony Gubba can't do his football round-up in the studio
in a couple of weeks' time,' Martin said. 'Would you be
available to do it?'

'Was I available?' I thought. 'What is the man saying? I
would swim the Channel to do it.'

There was nothing definite yet, he said, he would have to
check with a few people and he would ring me back in half
an hour. It was the longest thirty minutes I could remember.
Tony Gubba had a spot near the end of 'Grandstand' when
he would round up all the relevant football news that day
which had not been covered in other reports from the main
matches. It was the next best thing to presenting the
programme. Martin called back. The job was mine. I said
thank-you as calmly as I could, put the phone down, shouted

something very loudly, and did a jig around the office. Yippeeeeeeeee!

Two weeks later I was shaking when I sat down alongside Frank Bough, the main 'Grandstand' presenter, and began to read from the script. This period when the results are coming in can be quite pressurised and it was my first experience of 'open talk-back'. All television presenters have a sort of hearing aid and it is through this system known as talk-back that the producer and editor can communicate with the presenter even when they are actually on the screen. On most programmes the presenter hears nothing unless those in the operations area, or gallery as it is called, press a button. This would be no good on a live sports programme because so much is happening at once that the editor and producer don't have time to keep pressing buttons when they need to talk to the presenter. Sports programmes have open talk-back and during the whole programme the presenter hears everything that is said in the gallery from the latest football scores to 'Who's getting the tea?'

On that first appearance in the 'Grandstand' studio, it was like having one conversation while listening to several others. There were instructions for me, for cameramen and videotape operators, and for Frank Bough all going into my ear while I looked at the camera and talked about the football news. This soon became second nature, but that day my legs would hardly support me when I stood up at the end. I felt like I'd been fried. I did OK, I suppose, but I was very disappointed with myself really.

The next week that thin margin between success and disaster was clear to see again. I used to write the football news very close to the moment I would deliver it to camera. I would be in vision within minutes of the final whistles at the games and there were usually so many late goals that to write the report earlier would have been a waste of time. As close as possible to my deadline I would rush across to the desk alongside Frank Bough and he would introduce me.

That second week I sat in the chair in front of the camera

and looked down to check my script. To my absolute horror
I found myself looking at a blank sheet of paper. Hell fire,
where had my words gone? A football report was going out
on the programme at that moment and I knew that when it
finished less than a minute later, Frank would be handing
over to me for the football news I did not have. I called over
to John Tidy, the man in charge of the captions on the
programme. 'What's up?' he said.

'I've lost me bloody script,' I replied in utter panic.

I heard the football report coming to an end and the editor
said over the talk-back: 'Frank, out of this, hand to David
Icke.' I don't know about my whole life passing before me,
but my whole career did. Then John Tidy leaned over my
shoulder with a piece of paper. 'Is this what you want?' he
said and there was my script in his hand. That is the nearest
I've come to kissing anyone on camera. I placed the paper in
front of me as Frank said, 'Now with the rest of the football
news, here's David Icke.' I was close to professional catastrophe because I doubt if I would have been asked again in
those circumstances. I was so relieved I was as calm as they
come as I delivered the script and all went very well. Within
weeks I was given the job permanently and my ambition
was so much closer than ever before.

Everything continued to be fine at home and in 1981 our
second child, Gareth, was born in Leamington Spa on
Saturday, 12 December. I was supposed to be in London on
that day with 'Grandstand', but the country was covered in
snow and there was so little football there was no news for
me to present. Instead I was sent to Leicester to cover their
match with Watford, one of only a handful that had beaten
the weather. Thanks to that I was able to get back to
Leamington to see Gareth being born. He has turned out to
be so like me in many ways and we have much in common,
although in other ways we are different. He, too, loves
football and steam trains without any prompting from me
and has played for hours with the same push-along trains
that I had when I was a boy.

Another major event that affected me deeply in 1981, which I remember vividly during my time on 'Newsnight', was the murder of John Lennon. As a young footballer I had built up quite a collection of sixties records and I loved the music from that period of Flower Power when the message was one of love and hope, although it was spoiled somewhat by the drug scene that also emerged. So many of the sixties songs have proved to be prophetic in heralding the transformation now underway. I didn't like much of the early Beatles music, but I think their later work was excellent and I particularly enjoyed John Lennon's records after he left the group and began to question deeply the world in which we live. He and Yoko Ono showed great determination and courage to ignore the taunts of 'loonies' and 'crackpots' as they took their stand against war. The news of his death really hit me in a way that cannot be explained merely by the passing of a great singer and gutsy man. Psychics I have spoken to about this believe that we are both part of the same group of minds, or 'soul group' as some call it, who have worked together over thousands of years to restore the balance of planet Earth. They feel that his role as the physical form we call John Lennon was to help to raise human awareness through the 1960s and 1970s as part of the build-up to the planetary and human transformation of the 1990s and beyond. I am not saying that this is true, only that many psychics believe it to be so.

The big break in television came when 'Newsnight' agreed to lend me to the Sports Department for the duration of the football World Cup Finals in Spain in 1982. I was used as a reporter with the Northern Ireland team based in Valencia. They were not expected to do very well and they looked certain to be eliminated in the first round of matches. In fact, the story goes that an Irish representative who was given the job of checking out the team's hotel for the second round in Madrid had not even bothered to do so because even he thought they had no chance of reaching that stage. The hotel turned out to be pretty grotty and he was extremely unpopular!

My job was to send daily reports on the team. Everything went spectacularly well both for me and Northern Ireland. They were the shock team of the tournament and qualified for the second round against all the odds. I moved on with them to Madrid where they were eventually knocked out, but by then I had been given a stream of opportunities to produce some good work. Those in charge at the BBC in London were very complimentary and a few weeks later they offered me a full-time contract. I left 'Newsnight' to join the Sports Department, something I had set my sights on all those years before at the end of my football career in Hereford. Suddenly everything I touched was successful.

The year 1982 was magnificent for me, my best in television. In the autumn came the Commonwealth Games in Brisbane, Australia, and with so many reporters and presenters sent out there to cover the event there was a great deal of presenting to do back in London. Talk about being launched into the front line. Only weeks after joining the Sports Department I was into everything. In one week my daily schedule was to be a presenter on the early morning 'Breakfast with Brisbane' programme, to present a lunchtime programme of Commonwealth Games highlights, and then go off to Wembley to present a nightly programme of show-jumping. On the Sunday I presented a highlights programme from the show-jumping and worked with my former Coventry City manager, Jimmy Hill, on the football programme, 'Match of the Day'. I was also working for the midweek programme, 'Sportsnight', presenting a sports preview programme called 'Sportswide', and presenting the sports for a children's programme, 'Saturday Superstore'. At the same time I was writing my first book, *It's a Tough Game, Son*, a guide for would-be professional footballers. All this was happening to me just four years after leaving BRMB.

I loved presenting, but I wasn't so keen on the working environment. Only those who worked for BBC Sport will fully appreciate what I mean, and I was told it had been much worse in earlier days. I don't think I have met so many people who looked so fed-up and under pressure in one workplace. From its creation back in the 1950s it became a home for aggression, lost tempers, constant criticism and loud verbal onslaughts whenever the slightest thing went wrong. This attitude prevailed from top to bottom and so many excellent people left because they could not stand the way they were treated. Everyone seemed to shout at each other and I became caught up in it like everyone else. It was an emotional minefield although it did get more human as the years passed. Those in charge were obsessed with the idea that if you kept people constantly feeling insecure, they would work harder and better. Nonsense. All you do is wear them down mentally and emotionally. It is no way to treat anyone.

One man I liked a lot in my early days there was Mike Murphy, the 'Grandstand' editor. It was he who called me in one day to tell me the news I had waited eleven years to hear. 'Grandstand' is broadcast on Saturdays and Sundays in the summer and I was to present twelve Sunday 'Grandstands' in the summer of 1983. When I drove from my new home in Buckinghamshire for my first 'Grandstand', the tears ran down my face, but they were not the emotional consequence of presenting one television programme. They came from the realisation that, despite all the setbacks and all the disappointments, I had achieved what I had set out to achieve when few had thought it possible as I limped out of professional football. Whatever happened in the future, no-one could take away the sense of achievement, although as usual it was only later that I fully appreciated it. Those first 'Grandstands' went well and Mike Murphy promised me all the Sunday 'Grandstands' the following summer and a few Saturday 'Grandstands' in the winter as well. I was almost there.

By now I had been part of a little television history, too. I was a presenter when Breakfast Television was launched by the BBC for the first time in Britain in early 1983, two weeks before Independent Television went on the air with their version, the initially disastrous, but ultimately successful, TV-AM. I presented the sports news three times every morning. In the fortnight before the first programme we had ten dry runs, and what a nightmare some of them were. The programme was computerised. You put your scripts onto a computer and the next time you saw the words they came up in the camera lens when you were on air. That was great when it worked, as it did in the end, but all of the dry runs were chaotic to a larger or lesser degree and tempers frayed all round. I was to have a few animated discussions with the editor, Ron Neil, who I had also worked with on 'Newsnight'. But I liked Ron because he would say his piece, you would say yours and, in my case at least, no grudges were held.

The first time the programme worked without a hitch was on the first morning it was done for real. There had been a massive build-up to that day in the press and much was made of the rivalry between the BBC and ITV programmes. There were television camera crews and newspaper photographers everywhere to record this 'first' in British television and it was a tremendous success. It won a far bigger audience than the rival version which, I remember Ron Neil saying, looked like a funeral. It did, too, but ironically ITV revamped their style to resemble the BBC's programme while the BBC were eventually to change theirs to make it more serious and worthy like that first ITV effort. As a result, the mammoth share of the audience also changed channels.

My life was nearly all television in the early 1980s and when I was at home I was permanently tired. I was up at two o'clock five mornings a week for the breakfast programme and in the summer there was 'Grandstand' on most Sundays. The only other major outside interest in my life then was an organisation called Special Olympics which offered sporting opportunities for the mentally handicapped, or people with learning difficulties as they are known today. I have talked in my other books about the power of love, and what love and affection I was given by these wonderful people. They have a sense of fun and joy that I so envied and I learnt so much from them. There are many reasons why minds decide to take on a handicapped body. Sometimes they choose it for their learning, sometimes to help others around them to grow, and often both. There is always the possibility that something unplanned will happen and we become handicapped ourselves when we did not intend to be, but these cases are the exception rather than the rule. A handicap is *not* a punishment by some judgemental God. It is something we choose to help our journey to wisdom and we should remember the handicap is on the physical level so when the mind leaves at the end of the life the person ceases to be handicapped. It is only temporary. Some highly evolved minds will be incarnated in handicapped bodies all over the world today.

I was introduced to Special Olympics by a man called Bob Foxall and I worked closely with him for many years putting on sporting events and fundraising ventures. The biggest one was on the Isle of Wight when the whole Island seemed to take Special Olympics to their hearts and a great deal of money was raised to promote one of the biggest sporting events of its kind held outside the United States, where Special Olympics is backed by the Kennedy family. It was an unbelievably humbling and inspiring week, captured superbly by a BBC television programme. But it was not all sweetness and light working with the charity. There were times of enormous frustration and considerable anger when rules and regulations, petty internal politics and downright obstruction from some quarters combined to make the organisation of this and other events so much more difficult than it needed to be. The David Icke in this phase would not have got a job in the Diplomatic Corps as I moved towards the peak of my angry stage through these days of 'Grandstand', Breakfast Television and Special Olympics, but at least my inability to take no for an answer did manage to push things through against what was sometimes tremendous opposition.

Special Olympics also allowed me to lose my fear of public speaking. Chatting away to a camera watched by millions was nothing like as daunting as standing up to speak in front of a few 'real' people. As I worked on behalf of the charity I began to speak to audiences large and small to tell them what Special Olympics was about and why they should support its aims. Gradually I started to settle down and feel comfortable speaking to a live audience and eventually I enjoyed it immensely. It was excellent and vital preparation for what was soon to come and another element of my life span.

Meantime I was introduced to television snooker. This game had been brought to television in a big way by a programme called 'Pot Black' in the late 1960s. By the late 1970s, a brilliant producer called Nick Hunter at the Sports Department's Manchester office had taken this further and persuaded the BBC to cover the World Snooker Championship. The audiences simply soared and many other television tournaments followed. Three weeks or so after Breakfast Television began, the BBC's Head of Sport, Jonathan Martin, who championed my cause at this time, asked me to present a snooker event called the Masters at Wembley and it was here that I met Nick Hunter. We got on very well and it was an extremely significant meeting because he was to save my career at the BBC only a year later.

The only things blighting my life in this honeymoon period at the BBC were the arthritis, my quick temper which I hated myself for, and a throat problem that I had struggled with from the days at BRMB. Sometimes I would hardly be able to finish a sentence before needing to swallow. If I didn't my voice would break mid-word which sounded very funny. I had lived with it for so long that I learned to hide it quite well in the end, but constantly worrying about it took the shine off my work. I found television presentation so easy and comfortable that only concern about my throat threw me out of my stride. Concentrating on presenting the script when you were wondering whether you would get to the end of the sentence without swallowing was hardly the ideal way to work. It meant that I only reached perhaps seventy per cent of my potential as a presenter and I used to get so frustrated with it. Only recently have I realised what the problem has been. As I have explained, we have energy centres called chakras and one of them is in the throat area. It was an imbalance in my throat chakra that was behind the need to swallow so often and it has now gone.

Through this whole period, despite my success in television, I was permanently tense, tired and wound up and I didn't like myself very much, to be honest. My arthritis had continued to get worse ever since I left football. It had progressed into other joints and now I was getting pain or discomfort from all my toes, both ankles, both knees, the lower back, the jaw, the wrists and the fingers. Sometimes it was so bad I would have to ask people to open doors for me. With conventional medicine able to offer nothing except strong drugs, I tried many alternative forms of healing, some successful, some less so, and I was beginning to see that there was far more to the human body than conventional science had believed or understood. I always had an open mind to anything that made sense. But nothing was going to improve the arthritis at this stage because I was meant to go through this.

By late 1983, my career at the BBC had reached its peak and things were about to change quite dramatically. Mike Murphy, who had promised me all those 'Grandstands', decided to leave the BBC to start his own company. I knew this was bad news for me. He was replaced as editor of 'Grandstand' and the big events by a Scot called John Philips. I had worked with him a few times before and we seemed to get on all right, although I found it difficult to pin him down on what he wanted sometimes and this led to some confusion. It was also clear that he was going through some fundamental inner conflict as his outward emotions swung wildly between the extremes. He could be very funny and good fun, but this was often, I felt, a mask for deep depression.

Anyway, it soon became clear after he became editor of 'Grandstand' that he didn't think much of me, although he didn't say why. I was never to present another 'Grandstand' and no matter how short-handed they were he would not have me on his programme at any price. He would rather have used a canteen lady than me. They brought in another presenter from ITV and I went down the pecking order. In fact as far as 'Grandstand' went I was no longer even in the pecking order. Others in the department confirmed that John Philips would not use me at any price and that there was no rational reason why this should be. When people take an extreme view about others without any rational explanation it is often because of past life experiences. At the mind level they recognise each other and if a past experience with them has been unpleasant we take an instant dislike to a person which we can't explain. 'I don't know what it is about so and so, but I just don't like them,' is how people often put it. Perhaps this was the case with me and John Philips, but whatever the reason he was pre-programmed to stop me progressing in television because the time was fast approaching when I had to be moved on.

By now I had left Breakfast Television and 'Saturday Superstore' and I was becoming a presenter without a programme. But Nick Hunter stepped in and I was given more snooker tournaments and all the BBC bowls programmes which were produced by his unit in Manchester. I think Nick understood my situation well because he was never at home with the London set-up either. I enjoyed working with Nick and the team around him like Keith McKenzie, Keith Phillips and others. We had many laughs and it was so different from the intensity of the London-based programmes. I also liked the players, especially John Virgo who joined the BBC snooker commentary team while I was there. I could not look at him without laughing and whenever we were together in the studio the programme was a whisker away from coming to a halt in a fit of giggles. It did so on one occasion when a new player from Thailand with an unpronounceable name was playing in a tournament. We were live in the studio when I asked John how he would pronounce the name.

'Well,' he said, 'I call him number thirty-nine without noodles.' I looked at John and began to giggle. The more I tried to stop the worse I was. The camera was on John and he was trying to keep talking in the knowledge that I was in no state to say a word. Eventually, he could take it no more and he began to giggle. I was desperately trying to think of something serious, but to no avail, and I just managed to spit out some sort of introduction to a videotape item while we regained our composure.

Most of the snooker and bowls programmes were live and anything could happen. My most memorable occasion was at the Bournemouth International Centre during the World Team Snooker Championship. The rules said that the captains of each team had a maximum of two minutes to decide which of their players would play the next frame. Keith McKenzie decided to come back to me in the studio to fill the two minutes. Some captions came on the screen and I ad-libbed information about what had happened in the tournament up to that point. One caption followed another and I began to think, 'Blimey, this is a long two minutes.' I could hear on the talk-back that Keith was getting a little anxious also.

'What's happening?' I heard him ask one of the BBC staff responsible for the arena area.

'The players are in the dressing room and they won't come out,' came the reply.

I had to keep talking on and on about anything that came into my head for nearly eleven minutes before the two former World Champions, Alex Higgins and Cliff Thorburn, returned to continue the match. That's what I loved about live television, the challenge of moments like that when you either sank or swam. I continued to present snooker and bowls and a weekly multi-sport programme for several more years, but my career had begun to stand still at the

BBC. While John Philips was there I had nowhere else to go, and after presenting the same events at the same places at the same time every year I was beginning to wonder where I went from here. What was left, except to do them again and again? My mind and vision were also expanding rapidly to encompass more than just sport and television and I was increasingly dissatisfied and understimulated by my way of life. I was aching to break out into something new.

From the mid-1980s, between my television work, I was becoming heavily involved in environmental campaigning and Green politics and another stage of my life was beginning to surface. By 1990, the days of 'Hello, good evening, and welcome' were coming to an end.

6

The Politician

I have always loved the countryside and marvelled at the beauty of this astonishing planet. As a youngster I would spend hours riding my bike through the lanes of Leicestershire and I so loved the rolling landscape, the isolation, the freedom, the peace.

But by the time I was fourteen I was already seeing many areas disappearing under concrete. I used to wonder how much more green land was doomed. 'There has to be a point where this has to stop,' I thought, 'or there will be nothing left.' It seemed an obvious observation and yet all I heard in return was 'You can't stop progress.' Nor should you, but was this really progress?

I put all this to one side as I tried to carve out a career in football and later in journalism and television, but my concern for the planet was there and waiting to burst forth. In the early 1980s it simply exploded in a frenzy of anger and activity. This was triggered, on the conscious level anyway, by a Greenpeace leaflet which arrived in the post. I read it and a highly motivated environmental campaigner was born. It said:

Planet Earth is 4,600 million years old. If we condense this inconceivable timespan into an understandable concept we can liken the Earth to a person of 46 years of age.

Nothing is known about the first seven years of this person's life, and whilst only scattered information exists about the middle span, we know that only at the age of 42 did the Earth begin to flower. Dinosaurs and the great reptiles did not appear until a year ago when the planet was 45. Mammals arrived only eight months ago and in the middle of last week, men-like apes evolved into ape-like men, and at the weekend the last ice age enveloped the Earth. Modern Man has been around for four hours. During the last hour Man discovered agriculture. The industrial revolution began a minute ago and during those 60 seconds of biological time Man has made a rubbish tip of a paradise. He has multiplied his numbers to plague proportions, caused the extinction of 500 species of animals, ransacked the planet for fuels and now stands like a brutish infant, gloating over his meteoric rise to ascendancy, on the brink of war to end all wars and of effectively destroying this oasis of life in the Solar System.

Bloody hell. What were we doing? We go through our lives controlled by an economic and political system that is destroying the world as we try to make a living to survive. It is only when the consequences are put in such a simple, stark way that we realise just what the cumulative effect of all our lives is doing to this stunning planet. I felt like Corporal Jones in the famous BBC comedy, 'Dad's Army'. I had this urge to run out into the street shouting, 'Don't panic, don't panic', while doing precisely that. But, of course, this was not simply the result of reading one leaflet, it was the activation of the next stage of my life plan. It was time for events to start moving very quickly under the influence of astrological movements. The Judy Hall reading said:

In 1984, when you received the Greenpeace leaflet, significant astrological activity was underway affecting the Leo–Aquarius nodal axis. The nodal axis of the chart is our karmic purpose ... One of the Aquarian lessons all humanity is now experiencing is how to use collective power constructively and to balance out previous use, or misuses, of personal power. On the day your concern 'exploded into a frenzy of anger and activity' transiting Mars was moving through your first house, interaction with the world, and squared that nodal axis, hurling you into your karmic purpose with all the energy this impetuous planet is capable of. By the end of the year, transiting Jupiter was activating Chiron, the healer, and the Grand Cross in your chart. You simply had to begin healing the Earth.

The Tumi reading, worked out in a different way, said the same. We were now living on the Isle of Wight. I had adored the Island since I first went for a holiday when little more than a toddler. When my BBC career became dominated by the snooker and bowls outside broadcasts we took the opportunity to move there. The snooker and bowls involved travelling to the tournaments and presenting several programmes a day for a week or fortnight. So I would be away from home in Preston, Bournemouth, or wherever for the duration of the events no matter where I lived. It was just as easy to have a home on the Island as anywhere else in these circumstances and I never regretted the move. The Island is a lovely place.

When we arrived it was clear that there had been some awful developments in the 1970s and 1980s. The Island is a place of great charm with its blend of seascape, countryside and lovely old houses and cottages. But many were either replaced by cardboard box bungalows and houses or their character was being ruined by having the brick boxes built alongside them. I took the opportunity to make this point in the local paper and I attracted quite a bit of criticism, but there are few on the Island today who would disagree that many planning mistakes were made at the Island's expense in this period.

I joined all the main environmental pressure groups, but I realised you could win all the arguments, make out a cast-iron rational case for a course of action, only to see a few sweaty palms go up in the air at a council meeting to pass yet more horrendous building applications. Most of the local politicians on the Isle of Wight, indeed around the country, too, seemed to have little thought or perspective for the cumulative consequences of their decisions. The national politicians appeared to have even less. I decided that I would try to get into politics and put the other side of the case.

I was not a member of a political party although, like my father, I had a life-long interest in politics. There was no chance of me joining the Conservative Party because I could not have disagreed more with their philosophy on life, particularly the free market extremists who were running the government under the complete control of Margaret Thatcher. I had always voted for the Labour Party or, when they had no chance of beating the Conservatives in a constituency, the Liberal Party. I had met Neil Kinnock just before he became the Labour Leader, and I considered for some time working for them. I liked Neil Kinnock, but their policy on the environment was simply not credible. Indeed from what I saw it didn't exist and, given the scale of the environmental crisis, it still doesn't. But, then, they are not alone.

The Liberal Party at least mentioned the environment in their manifesto and I decided to join them. At the same time I met the Isle of Wight's then Liberal MP, Stephen Ross, when I visited a mutual friend. He said he was retiring at the next election and he joked, 'You're not interested, are you?' I had no idea until then that he was thinking of standing down, and my immediate reaction was, 'Hold on, let's think about this.' I discussed it with Linda, and later a local Liberal councillor, Morris Barton, said he would back me. Other local Liberals pledged their backing privately and as there was no obvious successor to Stephen Ross I knew at least I would not be overrun in the contest to be prospective

Parliamentary candidate. Then came a planning application for a massive complex in the Island's market town, Newport. It was totally out of keeping with the character of Newport and far too big, but the local Liberal council were supporting the development. Was I also in favour of it?, I was asked by a prominent Island Liberal.

'Definitely not,' I said. 'It's much too big.'

'You're not going to say that publicly, though, are you?'

'Yes, of course.'

'I wouldn't if I were you. Keep your powder dry, lad, until you see the way public opinion is going.'

I have never agreed with that sort of politics. A democracy works on majority decisions, at least in theory, but surely all points of view should be put before a decision is made. To keep quiet just because it is politically expedient is dishonest in my view. Anyway, I began to see how politics really works on the inside. The backbiting that goes on within the parties is unbelievable and the Liberal Party was no different. I gave some money to a local school for the mentally handicapped in Newport when I was a member of the Liberal Party and I was informed that I should not have done so because it might reflect badly on the party. I couldn't believe it. The Liberals controlled the Island County Council which was responsible for education and social services and I was told that my donation could be used by the opposition to highlight the level of council funding for the mentally handicapped. This and other experiences persuaded me to withdraw from the contest to be Parliamentary candidate and I also let my membership of the party lapse. 'If that is politics,' I thought, 'I want no part of it.'

My time with the Liberal Party led me to a group of people who were also opposing the big development in Newport. They had launched an organisation to co-ordinate opposition and the pressure eventually began to tell. The development was scaled down to a more acceptable one. When it was over I felt it would be a waste for such an organisation to fold when there were so many other destructive developments on the way. This was at the height of the phoney plastic boom of the 1980s which was built on illusions and credit. Margaret Thatcher's 'Environment' Secretary Nicholas Ridley was giving permission for developments all over the place in the name of 'economic growth' even when the local councils had turned them down. It was a free-for-all. People were making fortunes overnight by applying for planning permission to build on farmland. Once permission was given the value of the land absolutely soared and they would then sell it on to a developer. They would make their fortune simply by filling in a planning application form and waiting for a majority of the council to say yes. So this was the enterprise culture!

I put the idea to the group to evolve their temporary organisation into a permanent one called Island Watch. It would keep an eye on all local planning applications and highlight the ones it considered to be unacceptable. It would then mount a campaign against them and if it could get enough people to support its view, the council would be under more pressure to think before giving their agreement to inappropriate, unnecessary development. Enough people agreed to this suggestion for Island Watch to be formed and it is still working today. Linda and I invested a lot of effort in Island Watch over the next eighteen months and my reputation on the Island as a troublemaker continued to grow. Many local councillors and businessmen didn't like what we were doing and resented anyone having the audacity to oppose them, but I also let my anger, resentment and despair at what was happening to the Island and the planet spill over. I was far too aggressive. While some people would say a local councillor showed an unfortunate lack of judgement, I would say he was a prat. I spent half my time getting angry and the other half hating myself for it. This was all part of the plan, however, to release inner anger and frustration.

It reached a peak at a now infamous public meeting at Ryde town hall in 1988. The local Conservative borough council proposed to build a big development on a car park near Ryde town centre. The whole thing was in a financial dream world and that particular development was never built even though the council gave themselves planning permission. But what wound me up the most was the council's treatment of a lady whose house they intended to demolish for the development. I won't go into all the details, but she was treated quite appallingly. She and a number of others, including myself, began a campaign against the plan and it became very bitter. A public meeting was organised by the lady and her family at the town hall so that they and the council could put forward their opposing points of view. What a night! The hall was packed with fors and againsts. The council put their case first at some length and I was asked to speak on behalf of the campaigners and the lady who was faced with losing her house. This was particularly important for her because she had severe arthritis and her home was close to the shops.

The frustration of weeks of effort came flooding out when I stood up to speak and it was totally counter-productive. I verbally attacked two Conservatives who, I had been told by the lady, had treated her with contempt. I was way over the top, as, indeed, had been the behaviour of the council through the whole affair. Worse was to come. When the family had arranged the meeting they were told by the council they had to provide stewards in case of trouble. It so happened that two relatives of theirs were stewards at a local disco and they were big lads. When the speeches were over the audience had their say. But after hearing the council's point of view set out in the opening speeches, another Conservative councillor in the audience got hold of the microphone and began to go on and on putting the same points. I said to the chairman sitting next to me: 'Shut him up for goodness sake.' He tried, but without success.

A few minutes later the two lads, built like the side of a house, began to make their way from the back of the hall in that slow, self-assured and laid-back manner that you see in the John Wayne films. My heart sank as they closed in on

this little councillor who was still going twenty to the dozen
and ignoring all appeals from the chairman to give members
of the public a chance. The chairman had, by now, completely lost control of the meeting and his eyes were rapidly
glazing over. He had that 'How the hell did I get into this?'
look about him and his face was awash with sweat.

The councillor was not assaulted or anything, in fact from
where I was sitting the lads could not have been gentler. One
relieved him of the microphone and he was virtually picked
up like a baby and returned to his seat. To be fair they
thought they were doing the job they were asked to do, but
this was no disco on a Saturday night, it was a public
meeting in the town hall. Uproar followed. Other councillors
were screaming on about what had happened, the audience,
for and against, were screaming at each other. Some began to
leave. What a fiasco!

When the local newspapers came out a few days later I
was the focus of tremendous abuse from politicians of all
parties. I must hold the record as the only person in the
history of the Isle of Wight to unite the Conservative, Labour
and Liberal parties, albeit only for a few days. I was likened
to BOSS, the South African Secret Service, and Adolf Hitler.
They reckoned Icke had called down the bouncers to sort out
the councillor. Once my own sense of injustice at this latest
false accusation had diminished, I realised something that
was to change my whole attitude to life over the next twelve
months. Getting angry didn't work, it only attracts more
anger in return.

This was the bursting of the boil of anger and frustration.
It was the last great outpouring and the culmination of a
process that began when I joined 'Midlands Today'. My
angry young man period was almost over. The change
showed in my relationships, my work in television and
everything I did. It didn't mean I would not get angry and
frustrated sometimes because we have to let out our emotions if we are going to deal with them, but the intensity and
frequency diminished rapidly and I felt so much lighter and

calmer than ever before. It was as if a typhoon had blown itself out. The Tumi reading accurately identified these events:

The late eighties would have been a time when you were intensely angry again as you were affected by Mars' energies. Neptune energies were also triggered about this time and Neptune rules Pisces, the sign of the 'Messiah'. The Messiah is not a person, it is an energy carried by certain people. It is the energy which accepts responsibility on behalf of others, on behalf of the planet. It fights their battles, voices opinions they don't have the ability to voice. This quality would have entered you about 1988 and then Mars' energies came in at the end of the eighties to allow you to really strike out, say what you want to say. Mars is, symbolically, the questing knight, the seeker after truth and justice. Mars really carries the sword of truth.

Another reason behind that united wrath of the local politicians was that a few weeks before the town hall meeting, Linda and I had started a branch of the Green Party on the Isle of Wight and announced our intention to put up candidates at the local elections. I also proposed to stand for the Island seat at the next general election. It became obvious that the environmental movement had to challenge the politicians at the ballot box if we were to concentrate their minds on what was happening to the planet. My concern for the environment had long expanded beyond the Isle of Wight as I read more about the state of the Earth. I had heard of the Ecology Party and liked what they said on the few occasions they had been given a chance to speak. I heard they had recently changed their name to the Green Party. I sent off for some literature to their party office, a couple of cramped rooms over a building society in South London, and joined by return of post. Hallelujah! I had found a political party with common sense at last.

They had no presence on the Island and Linda and I called

a public meeting to test out local interest although my understanding of the detail of the party's philosophy was then limited. I knew they realised the planet was dying and wanted to do something about it, but that's about all I knew. The man who came from the mainland to put the party's view also seemed a little lost, but somehow we muddled through, despite the efforts of local Liberals to ruin the meeting. Because I was on television I could attract quite a lot of publicity and the Island Green Party grew so fast it soon had more paid-up members than the Island Liberals who ran the County Council.

I was also chosen by the regional party to be their representative on the national party council. This sounds rather grand, but in fact I was the only one who put their name forward! At the first party council meeting, only months after we started the island branch, I was selected to be one of the Green Party's six national 'Speakers' or spokespeople who would set out the party's view in the media. Again I was stunned by the speed of it all. It was incredible. One minute I was sending off for literature about the party, the next I was a national spokesman. Again it was typical of my life. Whenever I have moved on from one stage to another things have happened at a terrific speed. This was in the autumn of 1988 and, fortunately for me, the Green Party did not attract much media attention. There was a lot more to learn before I would be competent to tackle political interviews. I read everything that moved in the next few months and I made sure I had a complete grasp of the party's basic view. I found it so easy to understand what they were saying because it made complete sense. The more I learned the more committed I became to the party and I was constantly travelling the country between television commitments to speak at public meetings.

I felt, however, that the party and much of the environmental movement was talking in a language that most people did not understand. It is no good talking in jargon and technical language to people who do not operate in those circles. They just switch off. Some of the language irritated me because it was failing to get across the sanity of the message. I wanted to try to put down that message in a book written in a way that non-ecologists could follow. So I went to Basingstoke in Hampshire in search of a publisher called Green Print to discuss it with them. Anyone who has driven around Basingstoke will know why I went round and round in circles without finding them. But at the next Green Party Conference I was approached at a book stall by Jon Carpenter. 'Hello,' he said. 'I'm from Green Print. Do you fancy writing a book for us?'

Out of that meeting came the book *It Doesn't Have To Be Like This*. Writing and researching it was the most satisfying and enlightening experience of my life up to that point. It confirmed to me just how much the human race in general was divorced from reality. We are all programmed from cradle to grave to believe that certain suicidal courses of action are sensible and desirable and we build a prison wall around our thinking and vision. The way of life in the 'developed' countries and the economic system which supports and underpins it is, in Earth terms, the shortest suicide note in history. And yet if you dare challenge its power or its 'intellectual' basis you are either ridiculed as a loony or condemned as a dangerous extremist by the economic and political establishment. In this period I began to see the mess this system has created in stark perspective, although I saw it so clearly and grasped it so quickly that I must have a lot of past life experiences which relate to this subject.

Let us look at how this whole system works. The bottom line is its demand for 'economic growth'. Every political party, the Greens apart, is agreed on the need for more and more economic growth. Left, Right and Centre all see policies to expand production and, by definition, to expand consumption as the only way forward. This, they say, leads to more jobs, more wealth (for the few), more economic 'success'. Couldn't be simpler, could it? Well, yes, actually it could. What does this system I call 'take, make and throw away' mean for the basis of all life on Earth – the planet herself?

To increase production means:

- To increase the amount of irreplaceable resources we *take* from the planet every year.
- To increase the rate at which we use these irreplaceable resources to *make* products, the vast majority of which we don't need.
- To increase as much as possible the speed at which these products wear out or become obsolete and outdated so that people have to buy the same products again and again to generate the need for ever greater increases in production.
- To increase, therefore, the amount of natural resources, by this stage called waste and rubbish, that we *throw away* every year, the evidence for which is unmistakable.

It must have taken a genius to come up with that because it is the perfect environmental and human assassin. And yet this is the system that controls the world and the minds of its people. In short, for the system to survive and increase production every year it is essential that we rape the planet for resources and poison her with pollution. Even worse, the rate at which we do both of these things must increase every year. This, ladies and gentlemen of Planet Earth, is the system supported by every major political movement in the world, except for the Greens. This is the conventional 'wisdom' that is destroying the Earth.

But it doesn't end there. If you are going to increase production you must increase consumption and to go on increasing consumption you soon need to sell your wares beyond your own borders. You must 'compete' on the world market with every other country which is doing the same. In this way one country exports a product across the world to another country while at the same time importing that country's version of the same product and they 'compete' on the shelves of both countries with enormous amounts of resources wasted as a result.

Once you have such a global system you have surrendered control of your own destiny. If another country produces a product cheaper with new technology then you have to do the same or lose out, even though that technology may be environmentally destructive. And if you are to go on increasing production then you have no choice but to use more and more technology because there are limits as to how much you can produce manually. But if you do, countless numbers of people become unemployed and what do you do about them? Every political party except for Greens will say: 'Increase production and consumption to create more jobs!' And what of those who do have jobs? They spend most of their lives working in factories and offices producing these trinkets to earn the money to buy the trinkets that someone else is spending their life working in factories and offices to produce. The system and the culture forces this upon them. Whatever happened to living? We don't live in a free society, we live in a society in which you are free to do what that society wants you to do – that's the reality.

In pursuit of constant economic expansion you need to exploit and occupy, financially or physically, the countries that have the basic raw materials you need to ensure that you get them cheaply. In return you sell them your finished products at a vast profit to you. This was called imperialism, and the so-called 'British Empire' is a prime example of this. What is laughingly called latter-day 'independence' for poor countries has merely replaced the physical occupation by the powerful industrial countries with the financial occupation of the so-called Third World Debt. This has, in turn, forced poor people in these countries to devastate their own environment, often against their better judgement, merely to survive. This is why most of the world lives in poverty and deprivation. To say the human race has abolished slavery is an illusion. It has abolished the *word* slavery, that's all. The vast majority of people, rich and poor, on this planet are enslaved – enslaved by the system's programming and its economic imprisonment, and by their own refusal to think, question and find the liberation that comes with an open mind.

In this economic fight to the death there are far more losers than winners. While the few proclaim their economic greatness, others starve before our eyes on our television screens. It is a system which sets community against community, city against city, country against country, and trading bloc against trading bloc in brutal competition. Most importantly, it represents a declaration of war with the planet.

How can this be denied when you think that every twenty-four hours an area of tropical forest the size of the Isle of Wight is destroyed or degraded; deserts advance by a similar area; two hundred million tonnes of top soil is lost through erosion; many and increasing numbers of species become extinct; and a hundred thousand people, nearly half of them children, die through hunger or hunger-related disease? Every day.

And if you imagine the world to be one year old, then the industrial revolution which spawned the system of self-destruction has been with us, under that time scale, for less than two seconds. It is the equivalent of taking a double-barrelled shotgun to the planet and pulling the trigger.

But what is the final punchline to all this? It is the question: 'What is economic growth?' What is this annual growth figure which the whole system is geared to increasing every year? It must measure all that is good and desirable surely or the politicians, economists and industrialists would not be so obsessed with it. Well, here's the reality: economic growth measures the amount of money that changes hands for goods and services in any year. That's it. As long as money changes hands it adds to economic growth. Therefore, every time there is an accident and the emergency services are called it adds to economic growth; when anyone is ill and needs treatment it adds to economic growth – the more serious and long term the illness the more growth it creates; whenever there is an environmental disaster or transport disaster or terrorist outrage, it adds to economic growth. The list goes on and on. Think of all the negative and unpleasant events that cause money to change hands within the system and they will be adding to economic growth. And yet this is the figure that mesmerises the politics and economics of today. Economic growth is the god of the modern world.

It is because of this obsession with the meaningless growth figure that the system measures success in every area purely by volume. Asked to measure success in health care it will say, 'We are treating more patients than ever before.' Yet the only sensible and relevant measurement of the success of a society in terms of health is: how few people are ill and need treatment in the first place? We have now reached the ludicrous situation in Britain where one of the key measurements of economic 'success' is how quickly the price of a house is rising at a time when countless thousands are homeless! If it wasn't so tragic it would be hilarious. 'Have you heard the one about the Earthlings?' must be a great opening line all over Creation.

We are in such a prison of interdependency that an untrue rumour on the stock market in Tokyo, London or Wall Street can start a chain of events that can fundamentally affect the lives of people all over the planet. It all unfolds in some dream world that exists within some bubble divorced from reality. Yet every day we turn on the television news to see pictures of highly stressed people staring at computer screens in the financial centres, hysterically shouting at each other after the latest rumour or speculation, and they are wheeled in front of cameras to be interviewed by earnest newsreaders as if what they said had something to do with reality. They are all – media, politicians, economists and system promoters in general – suffering from a severe form of reality blindness. It is the ultimate hypnotic state which produces the system's version of the robot or the zombie.

Politicians and the media are obsessed with what 'the markets' think when the truth is the markets don't think. They panic and speculate with other people's lives, but they don't think. It was Margaret Thatcher who said, 'You can't buck the markets', and yet it did not seem to occur to her that if this is true there is something fundamentally wrong with the system. Most of their apparent power comes from the fact that the system is now so complicated that few people understand it, and that is how it is meant to be. The fewer who understand its increasing complexities, the fewer can call the shots and have a say in what will be. The more you can control the way people think, behave and live, the more you can convince them they are powerless to change anything and so they won't try. The system de-links people from the world that exists, or more to the point, is ceasing to exist, away from the computer screens. I feel for these money market people because most are going to be like babes in arms when there are no 'markets' or computers or means of speculation.

All the time the media plays to perfection its role as the system's propaganda machine. When do you ever hear an interviewer ask a politician or economist why growth is such a good thing and what growth really measures? They only ask how more growth is going to be achieved. It is taken as read that constant economic expansion is desirable. When do you ever hear an interviewer question the myth that an expansion of 'free' trade is desirable and any form of 'protectionism' is not. Again it is accepted without a second thought that 'free' trade is desirable when the only freedom involved is that of the strong to exploit and crush the weak. What passes for 'education' ensures that this suicidal nonsense is perpetuated through each generation. You only pass your exams if you answer the questions set by the system in the way acceptable to the system. If you don't do this, you don't pass the exams or get the job and this applies not only in schools, colleges and universities, but also in medicine, science, economics, the church and everything else.

This is the system that controls the world and they call me a loony! This is the system which is so successful that it turns out more illness, hunger, drug taking, alcoholism, stress, conflict, poverty, homelessness, depression, suicide, pain and suffering every year. And every single one of them is counted by the system as a positive contribution to economic growth. What a nonsense. The first sign of sanity is when you realise the world is mad!

Even those groups on the far left who see themselves as radical and anti-system are supporters of it in the same way as anyone else. They promote themselves as anti-capitalist, as if capitalism were the system. It is not. It is just one version of it. Take, make and throw away, growth and mind control – that's the system. And in that respect socialism, communism and capitalism are the same. They all believe we must continually increase the rate of production and so, by definition, consumption. They all believe, staggering as it may seem, that somehow having millions of people spending their lives standing beside factory machines or in the dust and darkness of a coal mine is economic success and social justice.

Most people are searching for some peace and contentment and yet the system does everything it can to stop us finding it. The last thing the system wants is people who are contented and at peace because such people don't forever want, envy, desire, and so buy, buy, buy. Most advertising is merely an effort to make us discontented with what we have and what we are. The 'fashion' industry in all its forms does a similar job. If we have a system designed to make us want, a system that judges people not by what they are, but by what they own, how can we then hold our hands up in horror when increasing numbers of people who cannot earn the money to be part of all this turn to crime as their only way to 'consume'?

The most frightening aspect of all this is that no-one controls this system – it controls us. It, itself, is a monster out of control. I'm told that the President of the United States is the most powerful man in the world. So does he control the system then? Of course not. He dances to its tune like everyone else, floundering around looking for answers that aren't there. It was during these months after joining the Green Party and particularly thanks to the writing and researching of *It Doesn't Have To Be Like This* that these basic truths about the system all began to dawn on me so clearly. We can elect who we like, it will make no difference because they won't be in control, the system will. It is a Frankenstein, a gigantic thought-form which, once created, has taken on a mind and momentum of its own, fuelled by constant 'scientific' advance.

So what is this 'scientific' advance? Most of it is not scientific at all. If it were it wouldn't be destroying the planet, would it? For instance, if *true* science were looking for a cure for a certain disease it would look at drug therapy, acupuncture, homoeopathy, herbal remedies, spiritual healing, colour healing, reflexology, and all the other alternatives and come up with the one that was most effective. But who funds most 'scientific' research? The system. And so what passes for scientific research is there to serve the good of the system, not humanity. Much of the research into illness is funded by large drug companies and so there is no way the cheaper or non-profit-making alternatives would be considered. The drug companies fund the research so the drug companies want *drugs* to be found which can increase their already enormous profits. The last thing they want is for *true* science to confirm that alternatives to drugs are not only cheaper and safer, but more effective. This is just one way that the illusion we call science does not serve humanity, but serves the system and helps it to imprison humanity. This is why the face of science serving the system is shown constantly to the world, while brilliant, visionary scientists, working to open the doors to the glories of Creation as it really is, struggle to be heard and are, almost without exception, ridiculed and condemned by their own profession.

'Science' and the system are very clever, but they are not very wise and as we can see all over the world today, cleverness without wisdom is the most destructive force on Earth.

Why is it that in Britain and around the world the apparently different political parties and movements are increasingly saying the same things, advocating the same basic approach? Why is it that politics is increasingly focused on personalities and how bad it would be under the others rather than what the politicians will do themselves to improve life on Earth? Why? Because as the system self-destructs they have less and less margin for manoeuvre and choice and so they are being forced into a corner together where they can do little but respond to events that are overwhelming them.

I am not condemning politicians and the other stewards of the system, I am not condemning anyone. I feel for them. They are just pawns like everyone else, programmed to believe and perpetuate the nonsensical view of life that passes for sanity and wisdom today.

I was amazed as I went across the country talking to all types of audiences as a Green Party spokesman. None of them could argue against the basic theme of what I said. I even had people who ran companies coming up to me afterwards to say they had not realised what the growth figure actually measured! They had been brought up through school, university and business to believe that growth was good by definition and never thought to question it. This goes for the system in general. Why does it not encourage us to think for ourselves and question its 'truths'? Why does the system want us to hand over our responsibility for how we should live to politicians, industrial leaders, economists and the church? Because it knows that if we think and take responsibility for our own lives we will see the system for what it is, a house of cards that is now tumbling down. As Albert Schweitzer said: 'It will ever remain incomprehensible that our generation, so great in its achievements of discovery, should be so low spiritually as to give up thinking.'

That is how the system gets people to accept the unacceptable without question. It convinces them there is no other way and discourages them from thinking and realising that there is. Billions of people have fallen for it and continue to fall for it. The system aims to keep our heads down, working, working, working, so we have no time to think. It seeks to keep us working and wanting, producing and buying, and it has inbred the work ethic that basically says we must work full-time at least five days a week and if we don't we are lazy and unworthy of respect. We are not even called people anymore – we are called 'consumers', which is how the system sees us. What a lot of baloney, but it is clearly very persuasive and effective baloney if you allow it to control you.

I also began to read about the native cultures at this time, the so-called 'primitive' peoples, who clearly do have the desire to think. One particular piece of wisdom affected me deeply, not least because it was such an immense contrast to all that I was observing in the system. In 1855 the United States Government made an offer for an area of Indian land. Under the rules of the system, the Indians should have tried to squeeze every cent from the government. Instead, Chief Seattle of the Dwamish Indians told them:

How can you buy or sell the sky? We do not own the freshness of the air or the sparkle on the water. How then can you buy them from us? Every part of the Earth is sacred to my people, holy in their memory and experience. We know the white man does not understand our ways. He is a stranger who comes in the night and takes from the land whatever he needs. The Earth is not his friend, but his enemy, and when he's conquered it, he moves on. He kidnaps the Earth from his children. His appetite will devour the Earth and leave behind a desert. If the beasts were gone, we would die from a great loneliness of the spirit, for whatever befalls the Earth, befalls the children of the Earth.

That, remember, was said in 1855. Look what has happened since.

It was in this same period that I became a vegetarian as I began to realise how the system treats animals. They are not seen as fellow members of Creation, but as commodities to be got as fat as possible as quickly as possible on as little food as possible. Nothing sums up the soulless system more than the way it treats animals and it knows it, too. Why else would the food industry try so hard to hide the reality of meat and other flesh production? As someone once said: 'If slaughterhouse walls were made of glass we'd all be vegetarians.'

When I realised what happened to the animals before they became those neatly packaged slabs of meat on the supermarket shelves, I did all I could to pass on that information. This included a report for the BBC programme 'Countryfile' which did not go down well with the farming establishment or their publication, *Farmers' Weekly*. You can always tell when you are having an effect because those who benefit from the status quo start having a go at you. The programme producers were so pleased with the report they asked me to appear on a regular basis, but then suddenly the offer was withdrawn. I have no doubt that pressure from the farming lobby was involved here. What made the whole thing so silly was that anyone who looked closely at the way farming was being organised could see that it was such a ridiculous mess that in the end the biggest losers would be the farmers themselves. It was a cruel and barbaric system for the animals and an economic time bomb for the farmers because their way of farming was simply unsustainable both financially and ecologically. So it has proved. Yet again the Greens were ridiculed and attacked as cranks who didn't know what they were talking about, only for what they said to be proved correct. For example, many chemicals which the

Greens protested against have since been banned, while some farmers have developed related illnesses. It is now accepted, too, that the vicious circle of exploitation and over-production has bankrupted many farmers.

But I didn't become a vegetarian only because animals were badly treated. I felt it was quite wrong to take the life of an animal, full stop. What arrogance to think we 'superior' humans have a right to take life and what hypocrisy to think that if you wring the neck of a chicken that's fine, but if you strangle a dog it's a criminal offence. The difference is that society lives with dogs, we see they are individuals with personalities and feelings, but we don't live closely with chickens or pigs or cows and so society can close its collective mind to the fact that they, too, are individual personalities who feel pain and fear.

We should also remember that emotions generate energy and all the extreme negative energy created by the pain and fear of the slaughterhouse is in the meat that people eat. They absorb that energy and it can have serious effects on all levels of their being.

I began to campaign against vivisection and blood 'sports' as well, something that had always appalled me from when I was a child. I even received a letter from a solicitor threatening me with legal action for remarks I made about the Isle of Wight Hunt. Nothing would have given me greater pleasure than to have appeared in court and exposed the barbarity of fox hunting, but, unfortunately, no further action was taken. Those who try to justify our treatment of animals invariably point out the cruelty in the animal world with one killing another to survive. For me two animals being cruel to each other does not justify us being cruel to them. Anyway, as I was later to learn, the animal kingdom has also been scrambled by the imbalances that have affected humanity. The constant fear and cruelty in the wild was not how animals were supposed to live. It is another manifestation of the imbalances plaguing the Earth and when the transformation is over animals will no longer live in this way.

Another thing I learned from my involvement with the animal welfare movement was how two apparent opposites can be, in reality, the same. I spoke at the Central Hall, Westminster, on the World Day for Laboratory Animals and I made the point that meeting violence on animals by vivisectors with violence on vivisectors by animal rights activists was not the way. The overwhelming majority of the audience loudly supported this, but a handful of youngsters from the Animal Liberation Front began to shout abuse. Afterwards they informed me that if that was my view I could not possibly care about animals. One said that I should watch out because one day they would hang me! If only they could see that the imbalances within those who harm animals are also present within the tiny minority of extremists in the animal welfare movement. Violence is violence, and those who try to justify violence on people in response to cruelty to animals are just kidding themselves. Both are two sides of the same coin.

When I went into the environmental movement it was still just below the surface in terms of public awareness. It was growing and bubbling away, but not yet in the political mainstream. But the case it was presenting was indisputable, and it was only a matter of time before even the stewards of the system could ignore it no more. In the autumn of 1988, Mrs Thatcher, the head of one of the most un-Green governments of all time in Britain, made a speech which tried to take the Green high ground. It didn't work because her words and her actions did not add up, but what she did was put the environment and the word Green on all the television and radio bulletins and in all the newspapers. If even she was admitting there was an environmental problem after once condemning environmentalists then there must be something in this Green lark. Maybe it was not just a bunch of bearded, sandal-wearing cranks after all.

Interest in the Green cause in Britain began to pick up significantly after her speech and as we entered the spring of 1989 the Green Party was making more progress than at any other time in its history. At the local elections we won around eight per cent of the vote and on the Isle of Wight the first Green Party county councillor was elected. It was an incredible achievement only months after the party was formed on the Island. We chose to put up only two candidates and really go for it in those wards. If we could get one or both elected it would be a tremendous boost which would shake off the idea that a vote for the Greens was a wasted vote because they could not win. The tactic worked superbly. One candidate, Paul Taylor, was elected and the other, a local woman, Val Adams, came in a good second. The other parties on the Island began to attack the Greens and this was confirmation of how well we had done.

It was the first election I had been involved in and it was fascinating to see how it is done. First of all you try to knock on every door in the ward or constituency and ask people if they will be voting for your party. Depending on their reaction you put a mark next to their name on the electoral roll to indicate yes, no, probable or possible. You write down on little tickets the names, addresses and electoral numbers of all those who have committed themselves to your party. On election day, the parties have a 'teller' at the door of the polling station and when each voter comes out they are asked for their number. They don't have to give it, but most do. These numbers are sent back to the election headquarters throughout the day and the numbers are ticked off on the name and address tickets to indicate who has voted. This means that by the evening you know how many of your committed supporters have actually been along to vote. Those that have not are then 'knocked up' and offered transport to the polling station or at least reminded that it is polling day and the polls close at so and so. From these returns a good election agent will know how the party has done even before the votes are officially counted.

The efficiency of the work and the number of people you have available to do the 'knocking up' can win or lose an election. This is what the parties call 'getting the vote out'. At ten minutes to nine in the evening on that election day on the Island, I went out to knock on the door of a family who had said they were going to vote Green.

'Yes,' said the man who answered the door. 'I'm going to vote with my wife after the news, don't worry.'

'What news?' I asked.

'The nine o'clock news, it's just about to start.'

'You know the polls close at nine o'clock?'

He didn't. He quickly called his wife and they headed for the polling station just down the road. They can only have arrived with a minute or two to spare. An hour later the result was announced. Paul Taylor won by *one* vote.

There were significant planetary sequences during 1988 and 1989 which were adding to this increasing awareness about the dangers to the Earth. Planetary energies don't just affect us as individuals, some can also have a collective effect on humanity as a whole, or rather produce the potential for a collective effect if enough people are willing at a deep level to tune in to them. The Judy Hall reading set out the background for this period:

During 1988 the whole world was experiencing the effects of Saturn conjunct Uranus moving through Sagittarius. The seeds of freedom were being sown – and of revolution. Sagittarius seeks meaning, and whilst Saturn energies would dearly love to hang on to the status quo, rebellious Uranus makes sure that the vibrations are speeded up so that everyone becomes aware of the need for change ... During 1989 much was being stirred up beneath the surface. On a global scale, Saturn and Neptune were moving through the heavens together, and Uranus would shortly catch up. This is the aspect which led to the Berlin Wall coming down, the end of the Cold War, and the release of the communist countries. These planets, which describe the battle of the old order against the new, were in Capricorn, the sign of law and established convention. It is an Earth sign and so Green issues would be a fundamental part of the changes being brought about. The successes of the Green Party at this time were a reflection of this aspect, but, as you say, unless the system could be replaced there could be no solution.

Through that summer the Green cause was also helped enormously by a series of prime-time programmes on British television highlighting the damage to the planet caused by our way of life, and there were many news stories to back up this information on an almost daily basis. The subject was really at the centre of public attention and this growing concern burst through into support for the Green Party at the European Election of 1989, helped by a brilliant election broadcast. We won fifteen per cent of the vote, although, under the anti-democratic first-past-the-post voting system in Britain, no Green was actually elected. But two million people voted Green and suddenly my role as a party spokesman was transformed.

Up to then our press conferences were attended by one or two journalists, sometimes none at all. A public meeting would attract a handful, although the numbers had been growing. As for television coverage of the Green Party, forget it. But we were invited on to all the television election programmes that night because the polls had shown that we had attracted massive support and I sat in the studio at Sky TV as I watched the fantastic results come in. Sanity, at least temporarily, was breaking out all over Britain. The following morning at the Westminster Central Hall I sat with another party speaker, Sara Parkin, and before us was a sight that no other Green Party representatives had seen before in Britain. There were so many journalists and television crews there was hardly room for them all. We were constantly blinded by a stream of flashing camera bulbs. Outside there were more pictures with the Houses of Parliament in the background – next stop the first Green MP!

These were heady days indeed, but I remember walking

away from the Central Hall that day thinking: 'Well, that's it, the honeymoon is over.' It was obvious that the other parties would now retaliate in the usual way and so it was. The Conservative Party had leaflets printed for all their local branches suggesting ways of discrediting the Green Party and so did the Liberals who had suffered most of all from the big Green vote. This explosion of support for us was also very fragile. The public had voted in the same frame of mind that attracted me to the Greens in the first place. They were worried about the environment and they knew the Green Party were, too. Now the reality of the Green case would come to light and life was bound to get harder for us. We were challenging the very basis of the system on all levels and the very foundations on which the modern world was built. People could see there was a problem with the environment. But would they accept that the problem could never be solved, indeed could only get worse, unless the system was replaced with another that was gentler and non-destructive? The answer, I felt, would be 'No', and that is how it turned out.

There was very little chance of getting across the sanity of our message because the medium for that message, the newspapers and their like, are part of the system we wished to replace. It is take, make and throw away, that pays for the advertising that keeps them going. This is another way in which the system controls us all. It makes us dependent upon it in almost every area of our lives. I have to smile when I hear talk of the 'free world'. Look at what you would really like to do with your life and see how the system is designed to stop you at every turn unless you are willing to play its game.

Stories about the 'loony', 'extremist' Green Party abounded in the media after those European Elections and yet there were few opportunities to get across our wider analysis to show that if anything was extreme it was the economic and political system that was destroying the world. Most of the news media is not interested today in looking deeply at a subject. It deals in one-line quotes or 'sound bites' as they are called in radio and television. How can you get across the magnitude of the Green analysis in a quote of twenty seconds? For example, we were dubbed the 'No growth party', a description that was misleading and very damaging. Rarely did we have the opportunity to explain the alternative, an economy which takes no more from the Earth than she can replenish and throws no more back at the Earth than she can safely absorb. In other words we stood for the way of life that did not depend for its 'success' today on destroying tomorrow. No growth economics for the Greens means no growth, and indeed a significant annual decline, in the rate of use of natural resources until this sustainable level is reached. The other parties hi-jacked the word sustainable and invented the impossible – sustainable growth! There is no such thing because the economy cannot go on growing forever without destroying everything else with it. But even the Green view of economics I have outlined has been overtaken as I have learned more and more of how Creation really works.

To be honest, the Green Party became an embarrassment for television. It was much easier for them on a political story simply to quote the Conservative, Labour and Liberal Democrat who all spoke the same political and economic language and supported the basics of the present system. In 1989 after our election result they couldn't quote the Liberal Democrat without quoting the Greens because we were well ahead of them in the polls. Rather than quote us they often dropped the Liberals as well and quoted only Conservative and Labour.

The Green Party did itself no favours, either, however. The party's membership increased massively through that summer, but its ways of working were so complicated and primitive that it could not respond to the changing circumstances. It had become so used to being in the political wilderness that its organisation was sloppy and self indulgent. No-one was allowed to make a decision and all this

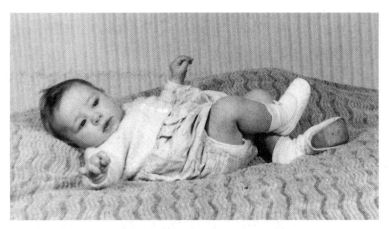

My first picture. Welcome to Planet Earth in 1952.

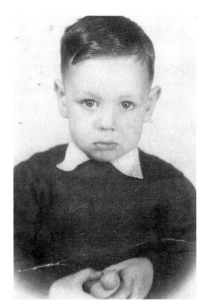

Aged three. Smile please!

Whitehall Junior School football team (I am standing, third from the right). The start of a new self-confidence.

The fourth year at Whitehall School (I am in the back row, fourth from the left) with the 'fossil' teacher. 'Was it broken when it got to you, David?'

My first year at Crown Hills in 1963. (I'm second from the right in the first row of boys.)

Left to right: Father, Paul, Mother and me, in the mid-sixties.

Leicester Boys Under-15s, 1967. (I am standing, third from the left.)

Left: Aged fifteen and on the way to Coventry City. *Right:* Playing for Coventry City at Tottenham Hotspur, in the FA Youth Cup Final, 1970.

Made for each other.
Lin and me a few days
after we met.

30 September, 1971.
Just four months after
we met we were
married at Leamington
Spa, Warwickshire.

Hereford United prepare for their first year of League Football and, as it turned out, my last. (Here I am in the middle row, third from the left.)

All change. Permed hair and a ruthless ambition as I join the BBC.

Made it! 'Grandstand' presenter, early 1980s.

All dressed up for Dame Edna, alias Barry Humphries. BBC Children in Need Appeal, 1988.

My mother and father. Such different characters, but both essential to my life plan and personal development.

produced was a shambles. The rules that governed the party seemed to me and others to be designed to stop anyone doing anything. 'This must be a matter for the conference to decide,' was a line I kept hearing. I was sure that one day I would ask a meeting if they wanted tea or coffee and someone would stand up and say: 'Point of order, chair, this is a matter for the party conference to decide.' What made it even more ridiculous was that the party conference was thoroughly undemocratic in that they did not have delegates voting on behalf of the local parties. If you turned up at the conference and you were a member of the party you could vote. That meant the party's policies and decision-making process were based on who could get to the conference. If you couldn't afford to go or did not have the time, you were disenfranchised.

The cumbersome internal workings led to so many opportunities being missed. Some in the party did not like having two high-profile speakers in Sara Parkin and myself who were being asked to do most of the interviews. They were suspicious of anyone who looked likely to be seen as a party leader. The Green Party did not have a leader because, among other things, they felt it was undemocratic to have someone at the top with more power than anyone else. I understood that and I did not want the party to have a leader in the conventional sense, either – and certainly not me. What the party needed, however, was efficient, simple structures that provided leadership on a more collective basis. Anything would be better than the maze of committees, sub-committees and working groups that generally came to no particular conclusion or, if they did, could not implement much of what they decided.

It was so frustrating because the general analysis of the Green Party was so obviously right and light years ahead of the rest. Two distinct camps developed – those who wished to re-organise the party and, to an extent, present a more acceptable front to the public, and those who wished to continue with the shambles of organisation and hold back on none of the party's policies, no matter how hard it was for people to accept them in the short term. These camps have been called the realists or realos and the fundamentalists, or fundies. It was the very situation that destroyed the success of the German Green Party and has caused conflict within many others around the world. Tolerance of the other's view was sadly missing in both camps. I found myself in the middle as a sort of 'fundie-realo'. I wanted to see the party organisation sharpened and the message made easier for people to understand, but I also wanted the party's view put across with nothing held back. What was the point of telling people what they would rather hear, if it was not what was necessary to check the destruction of the planet? And if I had been forced to choose, I would have stood with those who did not want to dilute the message.

The first party conference after the European Election success was perhaps the greatest missed opportunity. For the first time the conference had terrific media coverage. What the party should have done was clear the decks of much of the business that had been planned before the election triumph and replace it with a series of debates and speeches highlighting the Greens' foundation views and principles. We needed to expose the present system to the spotlight and set out the Green alternative in a simple, easily understandable fashion. But to do that was impossible under the archaic disorganisation that continually held the party back in those days. I used my speech in one debate to expose the reality of economic growth, even though that was not exactly what the debate was supposed to be about. But much of the conference was unreportable, so bogged down did it become with internal party argument.

The conference was, though, an unforgettable experience for me. I was interviewed so many times on so many different subjects. This was encouraging because it helped to explode the myth to some extent that the Greens are a one-issue party. This was the angle taken by the other parties after the European Elections, but it shows how far from reality the system had become. The environment is every-thing and so affects everything, and is itself affected by everything. You simply cannot protect the environment without a fundamental shift in economic policy, energy policy, foreign policy, transport policy, and so on. That was something even the traditional parties began briefly to pay lip service to before it was quietly forgotten as the truly Green revolution began to blow out rapidly.

As 1989 became 1990, the signs were that the British people's flirtation with the truly Green had begun to pass. They had been sold a line that the environmental problems that everyone now accepted existed could be overcome by tinkering a little with the system of self-destruction. You know, a bit of a clean-up here, a touch of recycling there. Oh yes, and much stricter laws on dropping litter: 'Use a bin, the Earth is dying you know!' It was a compelling argument when you consider how programmed people are to believe that the system is not just the best way to operate, but the *only* way. 'There is no need for the extremes of the Green Party,' the others would say. 'We'll fix it with more growth so we can spend more money on protecting the environment.' No, they won't, you know, but enough people were taken in for the Greens' support to plummet.

I knew then that if it was left to the scientific and political system, not just in Britain, but throughout the world, we were on our way to oblivion and a great deal quicker than anyone imagined. Politics by its very nature thinks only in the short term and yet what was needed was a vision that would be shared by every country at the same time, a vision that looked beyond the next election for centuries to come. This was simply not going to happen through political action and change brought about by the ballot box. The programming of the people was too entrenched. The Green Parties may be the most sensible political movements in the world, but they are not going to save the planet because they will not get elected soon enough, or in sufficient numbers, to make the changes necessary. Think about it. To do what was necessary in the time we have left would have meant a truly Green government being elected immediately in every major country. It obviously wasn't going to happen in this country, let alone in America and everywhere else. Even if this political miracle were to have happened, the system would have brought them down.

The much heralded, but predictably irrelevant, Earth Summit in Brazil in June 1992 has since confirmed that the answer to the survival of this wondrous, glorious planet does not lie in the hands of politicians controlled by the system. It was the then President George Bush who uttered the greatest summary of the situation I have yet heard. Asked about the Earth Summit and what America's contribution might be, he said: 'I will agree to nothing that will harm America's economic growth.' Those words might have been spoken by any leader in the industrialised world and increasingly those in many developing countries also.

It was a very dispiriting time as the Green Party faded. I was still travelling the country talking at public meetings, but there was no way the system was going to evolve to sanity. It had spun such a complex web of control and dependency and I began to realise that unless there was some other unknown force out there in Creation that could intervene in this nightmare, then it would soon be all over for the planet. But was there an unseen force that could intervene? I didn't know, I had rarely thought about it before.

In the spring of 1990, that question was to be answered in the most extraordinary way.

7

The Earth Healer

This next stage of my life is described in detail in *The Truth Vibrations*. It was the start of an astonishing experience that was to set before me the basic truths about Creation and who we really are.

My Green book, *It Doesn't Have To Be Like This*, was published in February 1990, and I went off around the country for a series of radio interviews and public meetings. One of the cities I visited was Nottingham and I stayed overnight with two Green Party members who I had met several times before. I knew they believed in the afterlife, spirits and suchlike, and the conversation quickly turned to that subject.

I was interested because my own thoughts and attitudes had been going through a change for a year or two, especially, as I have described, over the previous few months. I just had this overwhelming sense of being guided by some force I didn't understand and I became convinced of this when I was made a Green Party national speaker in such a remarkably short time. Throughout my life I had set myself targets and reached them quickly, only for something else to suddenly come up and move me on to the next challenge, the next experience. It was such a regular pattern of ambition, achievement, change, that it could no longer be dismissed as coincidence. Nor was it that David Icke was a genius capable of achieving all he wanted so quickly with no outside help. It had to be that there was another force of some kind opening doors and closing them to keep me going forward along a particular road. By the time I was chatting that night with the couple near Nottingham, I was sure that this was the case. But who? What? And, in particular, why me? My awakening that had been gathering pace at deeper levels through my life was now becoming conscious.

The couple told me that spirit guidance was indeed real. They said we come into physical incarnation for a series of experiences which we choose to increase our understanding and wisdom, and speed our eternal evolution. These guides on the unseen levels of Creation, I was told, try to lead us into the situations and experiences that we had chosen. That was why, if we listened to this guidance in the form of intuition and a 'gut feeling' of what is right or wrong for us, we would be guided smoothly in and out of many experiences, just as I had been. I now know that these 'guides' are mostly higher levels of our own minds, but these were early days.

I was open to all this because it was the only explanation that made any sense. I had rejected the traditional Western church and 'scientific' view from an early age. People have every right to believe what they wish and there are some wonderful men and women who either work within the church or support it. You do not have to believe in reincarnation to live a positive life and many individuals working through the church do a magnificent job in their communities. Not all by any means, but many. What I have always challenged is not a person's right to believe everything in the Bible, Koran or whatever, but the way the religions of the world so often impose their beliefs on others in subtle or less subtle ways and seek to stop debate if it departs from rigid dogma.

This is what the religious crusades (wars) were all about: removing violently those sources of challenge that could not be overcome intellectually and spiritually. That is what the law of blasphemy is about also. It is a means used over the centuries to stamp out alternative views of life and Creation which exposed the nonsenses and contradictions of the church and threatened its power. The church knows it is vulnerable to challenge, so dogmatic has it been. This is why people like the Bishop of Durham are jumped upon so forcefully when they dare to question whether some parts of the Bible should be taken literally. There must not be the tiniest leak in the dyke called dogma, because they know it would soon be a flood. The astonishing fact that many churches still resist the right of women to become priests shows the scale of this dogma and spiritual arrogance.

The church is held together by a fraying thread that is about to snap. You only have to ask a few questions before the dogmatic stance of the church is in serious trouble. If God is all loving according to one part of the Bible, why does He threaten eternal punishment and damnation if we don't do all He says? If we are judged on one single physical life by this all-loving God, why are some judged on lives lasting a few seconds and others on lives of a hundred years or more? Why are some people handicapped, poor or constantly ill, while others are millionaires and constantly healthy? And why are we being judged at all when one of the key messages attributed to Jesus was don't judge each other? You could fill a book with basic questions about the Bible and the church view of life, which cannot be answered. The reason why there are no answers, I have believed since childhood, is that the foundations of religion are built on claims, stories and myths that are, in whole or part, simply not true. I believe there was a man with great knowledge and understanding who has become known as Jesus, but most of what he stood for and most of what he said has been lost or distorted and much has been attributed to him that either never happened at all or was done by others.

That is not to say there is no truth in the Bible. There are many themes of truth and many truths described symbolically that have been taken literally by the dogma of the church. This dogma has been used throughout the history of the church to increase its power and control through the manipulation of those highly destructive emotions, guilt and fear. I was handed a leaflet once by a group of Born Againers depicting the Biblical view of Noah and the Ark. It said the Great Flood was God's way of dealing with the wickedness of the people at that time. After that flood, it went on, God promised He (it's always 'He', isn't it?) would never destroy the Earth in that way again and He gave us the rainbow as a sign of that promise. The leaflet continued:

> Today, we as people are no less wicked than the people of Noah's age but the good news is that God's way of dealing with us is far different. Our sin still deserves God's punishment of death, but through His love for us, He sent His only son Jesus Christ to die on the cross for us. He took our place of punishment. This act of love means we can now experience God's forgiveness and His promise of Eternal Life. We just have to acknowledge before Him our sin, believe and accept Jesus as our saviour. God did all this for us in His word, the Bible. That is why we as Christians can sing, shout, and say 'God is good'.

I had to read that a few times before I could believe it was not all meant to be some kind of joke. People are entitled to believe whatever they like, but when I read things like that I never fail to be staggered by the naïvety. To claim that you only make it to 'heaven' if you believe in Jesus Christ has always been to me just plain silly. We are asked to accept that no matter how positively you live your life or how much you care for others, you won't get to 'heaven' unless you believe in Jesus as your 'saviour'. But live a selfish or destructive life and you'll still be all right for a ticket to paradise if you believe in Jesus on your death bed. And what kind of loving Jesus is it who says, in what would be the ultimate arrogance, that only if you believe in Him will you have eternal life? It is, of course, a nonsense, but a nonsense that controls the minds of millions of people.

Far from adding to human appreciation of Creation, religion muddies the waters of enlightenment and understanding, much to the delight of the system of which it is a crucial part, particularly in the areas ruled by Roman Catholicism, extreme Protestantism, Islam, Judaism and the other homes of unthinking dogma that seek to control by guilt and fear. It is a form of brainwashing and you only have to look at the audiences on those American religious television channels to see that. Yet all this is outrageously imposed upon children in schools, and in Britain the BBC, which claims to be independent, has a whole religious affairs department turning out programmes day after day from, primarily, the Western church view of the world. Indeed the Western church view is woven into the very core of the structure that rules the United Kingdom with the Queen at its head. It is the same elsewhere. What would happen to any United States Presidential candidate if they dared to challenge religion?

The church view of life survives because of this influence and propaganda, and because each generation is born into a world in which the church and its views already exist. Imagine how different it would be if those same views and much that is in the Bible were put forward for the first time today as literally true. Think of the reaction if someone came out and claimed that a man took a few loaves and fishes and fed thousands of people with them, and that God created woman from the rib of a man, that a book full of contradictions and written by who knows who, who knows when, in who knows what circumstances, was a hundred per cent accurate. But that is what we are asked to believe and if anyone dares to challenge such a view openly, they are accused of blasphemy. Look at how many have gruesomely lost their lives over the centuries because they had a mind of their own and the courage to say what they thought.

Religion is another excuse for not thinking. The Bible, for all its contradictions and omissions, is seen by many as a hundred per cent accurate because those people want to believe that all the answers can be neatly packaged between two covers. They want to hand over the responsibility of how to think and live their lives to a book, a God, or a man called Jesus. It's easier that way. Taking responsibility for your own thoughts and actions is much harder. Some people believe in the church view so much that when they leave the physical form they actually see the classic representation of Jesus waiting for them. Jesus is not really there, it is a manifestation of their own imagination, but a very powerful one such is their belief in what the church has told them.

The other conventional alternative view of life and death which again I had rejected since childhood is that the lights go out forever when the physical body dies and that, according to mainstream science, everything can be reduced to the level of a machine with no overall intelligence, creating and guiding. That's the saddest and most far-fetched of all the theories, I feel. But if you put forward these two ideas expounded by the traditional church and science, it is perfectly acceptable in our society. The system wants you to believe that it is a straight choice between intellectually untenable religion and system-serving 'science'. This is why it seeks to shut out talk of reincarnation, karma and all that goes with it, and portrays you as mad or dangerous if you try. You have to laugh, really.

Science can answer some of the questions relating to physical matter, of course it can, but until scientists open their collective minds to the non-physical or sub-atomic levels they will never answer the big questions of who we are and why we are here, or indeed, the true nature of physical matter.

Surely people have a right to hear all the alternative views so they can have access to all the information available before deciding what they wish to believe. But the most logical explanation of life has been suppressed by the established system and people have been fed the views of science and religion. It starts in the schools and continues into adulthood. The Western church has guaranteed air time for its view every day, and there are many other programmes and news bulletins reflecting what the church and science believes and wants us to believe. Where in the United Kingdom and so many other countries is there even one regular programme a month about reincarnation, karma and the nature of life from this viewpoint? Nowhere. It is another way the system controls us – by letting us hear what it wants us to hear, and keeping from us what it does not.

All my life I had rejected those church and 'scientific' views without looking seriously for an alternative explanation, but that was about to change. By early 1990 as I sat in that couple's home near Nottingham I was convinced that there were other levels of life which we could not see and that we were eternal beings who moved on at the end of a physical life to another level or, as I was later to learn, frequency. I was also sure that forces on these other levels were in the process of trying to sort out the mess that humanity had made of this planet. It was a relief to know this because without that outside help it was over. It is strange looking back at how I moved into these areas so quickly and confidently because I was terrified of ghosts as a child, and the whole idea of having spirits around us had given me the willies well into adulthood. Now, suddenly, it seemed the most natural thing in the world, which, of course, it is. I began to say out loud: 'Look, if you really are there, let me know – contact me in some way.'

My life changed fundamentally after I visited a medium and healer called Betty Shine on 29 March 1990. I tell the story in *The Truth Vibrations* of how I was drawn to the book shelves in a local newsagent. It was as if there were magnets pulling my feet. I saw Betty Shine's face on the front of a book called *Mind to Mind*. I read it in twenty-four hours and wrote to her. I wanted to see if her healing could help my arthritis and, more than anything, I wanted to find out if I really was being guided by unknown forces. I went to see her twice for healing and nothing happened, except that my health improved. But on the third occasion a series of messages came through her for me. I could feel the atmosphere in the room change quite suddenly and Betty visibly shuddered. 'Oh,' she said. 'This is powerful – I'll have to close my eyes for this one! 'She said she could see a being who looked like a Chinese mandarin. He gave his name as Wang Yee Lee and added, 'Socrates is with me.' He then gave Betty a number of messages to pass on to me and among them were these:

There will be great earthquakes. These will come as a warning to the human race. They will occur in places that have never experienced them.

Taking oil from the seabed is destabilising the inner Earth. The centre of the Earth will move and the poles will change. The sea spirits will rise and stop men taking oil. The sea will reclaim the land and humans will see they cannot do these terrible things. They cannot abuse the elements. They have to be treated with respect.

In the country in which he lives there will be a cultural revolution in five years' time. He was chosen as a youngster for his courage. He has been tested and has passed all the tests. He was led into football to learn discipline and training, but when that was learned it was time to move on. He also had to learn how to cope with disappointment, experience all the emotions, and how to get up and get on with it. The spiritual way is tough and no-one makes it easy.

He is a healer who is here to heal the Earth and he will be world famous. He will face enormous opposition, but we will always be there to protect him. He is still a child spiritually, but he will be given the spiritual riches. Sometimes he will say things and wonder where they came from. They will be our words. Knowledge will be put into his mind and at other times he will be led to knowledge.

We know he wanted us to contact him, but the time was not right. He was led here to be contacted, not to be cured, but one day he will be completely cured. He will always have what he needs, but no more.

When he is at home he must do family things and keep the family unit together.

If he abuses the gifts, the gifts shall be taken away.

I suppose such an experience should have left me dumb-struck, but it didn't. I felt relieved more than anything that I had not been imagining the guidance I believed was responsible for so much that was happening in my life.

'Who was Socrates?' Betty asked. 'He was a healer, wasn't he?'

'I haven't got a clue,' I said. 'I just know he was famous for something.'

Eventually she found Socrates in a book of quotations and we realised he was a Greek philosopher who was killed for corrupting the young by indulging in the most heinous crime known to those in power: he told them the truth.

I rang Linda to explain what had happened and tell her the nature of the messages. She was remarkably unfazed by the whole thing as well, although we were both a little confused about what we were supposed to do with the information. Four days later there was an earthquake on the England–Wales border of 4.9 on the Richter Scale which was a big one for Britain. The day after that I was drawn to the books in a health food shop and café in Ryde. The experience was the same as with Betty Shine's book, again it was as if a magnet was pulling me. There I found myself looking at an American book called *We Are The Earthquake Generation.* I was obviously interested in anything about earthquakes, but what really caught my eye was the word 'psychics'. Jeffrey Goodman, an open-minded American scientist, had gathered information together from respected psychics with proven records about what would happen to the world up to the end of the century. They had all told the same basic story – the 1990s would be a decade of massive earthquakes, volcanoes, and tidal waves. Some of the quakes would be 12 on the Richter Scale and depending on how close to the surface they were, that could make them five thousand times more powerful than one of 8.4. This was a sobering thought when you realised that the most powerful earthquake recorded by modern instruments was 8.6.

The book also highlighted the predictions of America's most famous psychic, Edgar Cayce (pronounced Cay-see) who also told a story of fantastic geological events in the last decade of the century, the locations of which he passed on in some detail. Cayce was known as the 'sleeping prophet' because he went into a sort of trance as he tuned in to the frequency of another level so information could be passed through him in the form of thought energy. He was a keen student of the Bible and yet the evidence of his own work was so overwhelming that he had to accept the reality of reincarnation and karma. When he died in 1945, he had completed fourteen thousand readings for people while in his trance-like state. He would tell people some of what they had come to learn and pass on advice about their health and lifestyle. The accuracy, apparently, was phenomenal and I was led to many of his books. At my next visit to Betty Shine, more messages came through from Wang Yee Lee:

Don't try to do it all alone. Go hand in hand with others so you can pick each other up as you fall.

One man cannot change the world, but one man can communicate the message that will change the world.

The written word will be there forever. The spoken word disappears on the wind.

He will write five books in three years.

Politics is not for him. He is too spiritual. Politics is anti-spiritual and it will make him very unhappy.

He will leave politics. He doesn't have to do anything. It will happen gradually over a year.

So now I knew what these communicators were asking me to do. They wished me to pass on the truths to the public through books and other means. There was never any question that I would agree. I had seen enough of the consequences for the planet and humanity of the economic assassin we had created to know that walking away from this was not an option. The Green Party, Greenpeace, Friends of the Earth and others have played a big part in raising awareness of the environmental crisis, but only forces outside this frequency of ours could stop us destroying the planet. If they were asking me to pass on information needed for this operation then I would be delighted. When I look back I am astonished at how Linda and I accepted all this so easily. It just felt so right. The Judy Hall reading said there was a lot of highly significant astrological activity during these months that was affecting me and a pattern was emerging in relation to eclipses:

I looked back through your life to track the eclipses and the effect on your development ... Because of the way eclipses are distributed around the heavens, there will be many people who never really feel the powerful effects they can have. And yet, in your chart, the eclipses regularly triggered something major through contact with a planet. This has opened up a whole new area of study for me. I can only assume that your chart was even more carefully chosen than most. I have never, in all my experience, seen a chart that reacted so perfectly to astrological influences. Whenever a planetary sequence has had the potential to affect you in some way – it has!

This, I feel, was the power of the Grand Cross at work, those tense and taut lines of energy interacting to keep me right on course with the life plan and make sure everything happened when and how it was meant to. Many strange 'coincidences' began to happen to me. I remember standing at Waterloo Station and I couldn't stop singing the hymn 'How Great Thou Art' to myself. Why this should suddenly come to me I couldn't imagine. On my way home that afternoon I bumped into a friend of mine, the Reverend Walter Fanncut, who was making a rare visit to Ryde. He invited me to go with him to a church service in Newport that Sunday. It was the first time I had been to a church service for years except for weddings and funerals and indeed it turned out to be the last time, too. Walter is a wonderful person and so is his wife, Amy. He spent much of his early life working with those suffering from leprosy. He had now retired as a minister and we sat together waiting for the service to start.

'What is your favourite hymn?' Walter asked me.

'"How Great Thou Art",' I replied without hesitation, although I had only heard it twice in my life.

'Lovely hymn,' he said. 'But we don't have it in this church, it's not in our hymn book.'

At exactly the moment he finished the sentence, I turned over the page of the sheet giving the order of service. There, with the words typed out on the sheet, was the main hymn – 'How Great Thou Art'. It was specially printed on the service sheet because, as Walter said, it was not in their hymn book. Walter couldn't believe it and neither could I, but I think these 'coincidences' are set up sometimes to help convince us that we are being contacted and it's not all an illusion. Such 'coincidences' have become part of my life now. They happen all the time. On one occasion I rang a friend to ask if she knew a healer who could help Paul

Vaughan who was having some health problems. She didn't, but she said she would ask around. She then had a call from someone she had never met, but who had heard of her through a mutual friend.

'I am a healer and I just have this overwhelming feeling that I have to ring you,' said the voice on the phone. 'But I have no idea why.'

'I think I do,' said my friend. 'You are going to treat David Icke's agent.'

The healer then gave my friend her address. It was a small village in Worcestershire. Paul had moved his business to that same village two months earlier! They were so close that only two digits in their phone numbers were different.

I was led to many books on reincarnation and karma in this period. By 'led' I mean that I would be drawn to a bookshop and of all the books on all the shelves, my eyes would be able to see just one. Everything else would be a sort of blur and only that one would be in sharp focus. I was asked at this time to speak at the opening of the first Green Show at the National Exhibition Centre in Birmingham and I chatted to a woman on the *Kindred Spirit* stand. *Kindred Spirit* is a magazine that deals with spiritual matters like reincarnation and so on. I said I had received communications about earthquakes and she said that a woman had been at the stand earlier in the day saying something similar. What's more she knew where to contact her.

In fact at this stage the woman had not received communications about earthquakes. She had received her first communication on the *day* of an earthquake – the one on the England–Wales border. But by the time I contacted her at her home in the Midlands some weeks later, she was indeed getting communications about great geological events. Her communications came through what is known as automatic writing. This is when someone tunes in to thought forms sent from other levels and converts them into the written word. Often you write about subjects you have no idea about and this was the case here. The woman was as shocked as anyone at what she was writing on her typewriter.

Her early messages had talked of the Earth's energy system which is made up of 'ley lines' as some people call them. Just as our bodies have a network of non-physical energy channels or lines which acupuncture calls meridians, so does the planet which is the physical body of a mind in the same way as our bodies are. It is these lines that carry the lifeforce energies which keep us and the planet alive. All over the Earth there are also energy centres which are basically the same as the chakras and acupuncture points that we have. The ancients knew of this system, it was part of their everyday life, and the stones, stone circles and mounds we see all over the world, like those at Stonehenge, Avebury and Glastonbury Tor in Britain, are situated on these points and lines. Stones were used like an acupuncture needle to balance the flow of energy. All the native cultures know of these lines. Some call them dragon lines and in fact the ancient myths about dragons and serpents are symbolic of these energies. The automatic writing asked the woman to gather some friends together to begin the process of repairing the ley lines in her area of the English Midlands.

I was still in the very early stages of my understanding of all this and trying to fathom it out was a bit like finding your way home in a thick fog. All that I knew for sure after reading the books and talking to those involved in this work was that reincarnation and karma were true and that this energy network I have just outlined also spanned the whole of Creation, linking up all the planets and stars. As time went on I began to see, through the communications, that the Earth's energy system was in a terrible state and threatened the very survival of the planet.

To be at their most effective the energies need to have a positive–negative balance, but because of the negative energy created by humanity's thoughts and actions over thousands of years the energies around this planet are dominated by the negative. When this happens in a ley line, it has the same effect as a blockage in the arteries of the human body. The blood supply, energy in this case, cannot get through, or not in sufficient amounts. So these negative energy blockages must be removed if the planet is to avoid catastrophe.

This can be done by going to the point of the blockage and sending out positive thoughts and bringing in positive energies to disperse and balance the negative energy. This can often even be done without going to the site because you can send thought energy across to the other side of the world in a fraction of a second. But it is sometimes necessary for energies to be passed through a physical body and into the Earth at these sites. When this happens, it feels like a warm glow or even an electric shock in some cases. The body works as a transformer to step down the energies from other frequencies of life to the wavelength of the physical Earth. This sort of work is going on in every region of the world. It involves many thousands of people and that number is growing with every passing day. I knew little of all this when I first met this channeller, but it will help you to see the significance of her communications and others if you know the background at this stage. What struck me about her writing was that it confirmed the basic information I had received through Betty Shine, information the woman knew nothing about. Among her communications were these:

The world is changing and the North will become South and the East, West ... We shall come in the thunder and the wind shall blow across the land. The sea will rise and there is much to be cleansed ... There have been many prophets, but the warnings have gone unheeded. We speak and the land becomes silent waiting for the work to begin ... Men have not understood what is the nature of life on Earth. Much has been forgotten and wisdom has taken the wrong path ... The Earth has become weak under the burden placed upon her and the power must flow again ... At this time, many changes are occurring in the Earth's core and the volcanoes will soon erupt as the pressure becomes unsafe under the surface. You should look to the East for the first signs. The earthquake cycle has begun and many will be triggered by the movement that has already occurred.

In this same period a man came to my house to talk about an environmental project and yet within minutes we were talking about earthquakes and volcanoes because he was having visions of such events. We widened the conversation to reincarnation and he suggested I contact a woman called Judy Hall who specialised in recalling our past lives and relating them to what we have come to do in this life. Again Judy knew little of what had happened to me, but when her taped reading came back, she confirmed other parts of the basic story I had already been given:

From the moment I picked up your astrological chart I was aware of tremendous psychic energy which I feel was sent to help me with your reading. Your purpose in this life involves the collective power of humanity and working to bring in change. Your role will be to help to bring about a spiritual revolution and you will become a cosmic parent to the planet and humanity. Your birth chart indicates that you have enormous power to get things done and stand up for what you believe. I would imagine if you put your mind to doing something that nothing on Earth will shift you. You will go on when others give up and you get there in the end. If you harness your mind with that will for change then literally you can do anything ... Your purpose is to go out into the public eye and be seen to stand up for what you believe in, and to convey a new understanding.

You have taken on quite a task – nurturing the world mentally and physically. But you have plenty of help. Psychically I think you are just surrounded – there is a huge host who are there, ready and willing to help. Your task is what is important.

The whole astrological chart is powerful in terms of where you have been and where you are going. You have the potential to be incredibly psychic with the ability to channel information down to the Earth.

She also saw a vision while she was working on the chart of a spider in the centre of a web. She felt this was symbolic of many things relating to me, including a previous life working in a sort of secret service. She believed it was in Elizabethan times and that I had been close to Sir Francis Bacon. A few days later I was looking through a book in the local library about Queen Elizabeth I and it talked about a man who set up a 'spy' network with Sir Francis Bacon and the Earl of Essex which, it turns out, had been a front for the passing on of information about reincarnation, karma and the energy system at a time when the promotion of such things would have meant instant death. The man's name was Anthony Bacon, brother, or at least step-brother, of Francis.

A later reading said that Linda, Kerry and Gareth were also here with big tasks to perform and Linda's would become clearer about 1995 or 1996. It was all rather a lot to take in. For goodness' sake, I was a sports presenter and here I was being told I would communicate the message that would change the world and that all my family were involved in the great transformation! Mind you, I would not be a sports presenter for much longer. When I left the Crucible Theatre in Sheffield in the spring of 1990 at the end of the World Snooker Championship, I just knew I had presented my last programme for the BBC. I had already lost my job presenting sport for BBC News because of my Green Party role and soon I was in the papers for not paying my poll tax. This tax was so deeply unfair because it was asking rich and poor to pay the same. Any tax that is not based on the ability to pay loses its right to be respected, and I decided to make a protest against it by refusing to pay. Even many of her own side told Mrs Thatcher it would be a disaster, but she would not listen. It eventually cost her the premiership and that was her karma. It was rather indicative of the political system that we had politicians who clearly thought the poll tax was ridiculous standing up and defending it because they thought 'party unity' was more important than natural justice.

The country was in uproar over the poll tax and there was tremendous interest when the first non-payers and couldn't-payers came to the courts. And of all the courts and all the councils in all of England and Wales, the first people to appear before the magistrates were on the Isle of Wight – and I was one of them. What a sight greeted me at the entrance to the court in Newport! I had never seen so many photographers and television cameras in one place, apart from the Green Party news conference. Questions came from every direction. It was wonderful to sit in court and see so-called 'ordinary' people take the system apart. They had worked out a series of delaying tactics which the courts could not handle and then came the final embarrassment for the whole poll tax fiasco.

Late in the afternoon I was standing in line facing the magistrates with about nine others when one of the defendants, a man I had met before at poll tax meetings, began to question the council official about the timing of the poll tax bills and the subsequent summonses for non-payment. In a short time you could sense the atmosphere change and after some discussions the magistrates left the court. When they returned it was announced that the council had sent out the summonses too quickly and therefore all the convictions for non-payment that had already been dealt with that day were invalid, and everyone else who was still waiting to appear was free to go. I made the point to the court that if the council had sent out the summonses too early, then everyone who had appeared that day had a right to compensation for transport costs and loss of earnings. The court had no choice but to agree. I had arrived at the court that day to face a summons and I left with Mrs Thatcher's poll tax made to look ridiculous and my bus fare of £2.50 paid by the council.

As events and communications gathered pace over the six months that followed, I had to pay the poll tax because there was no time to spare to spend three weeks or so in jail. It was an agonising decision to pay, but by then I could see the wider picture and, anyway, such was the scale of the protest across the country that the Conservative Government was forced to abandon the tax as soon as they had replaced Mrs Thatcher as Prime Minister. There is no point in taking a protest beyond what is necessary to bring about change. What the poll tax protest showed is just how little power politicians really have. They only have the power that we allow them to have, mostly through apathy. In fact there is, in a sense, no such thing as power. What we *call* power is merely one group of people persuading another group that they have power over them. Power is only a thought form, a state of mind, yet another illusion. The system seeks to persuade us there is nothing we can do to change things and yet non-violent non-co-operation, in large enough numbers, can bring about fundamental change and expose the truth that the only power the system has over us is the power we are prepared to *believe* it has over us. As Gandhi said of British rule in India: 'One hundred thousand Englishmen simply cannot control three hundred and fifty million Indians if those Indians refuse to co-operate.' Exactly.

Soon after the court appearance and all the coverage in the papers and on television, I was asked to meet with a BBC Sport executive. I had an idea what was happening. I had only recently received a letter to say I was being replaced on the athletics coverage through the summer and now the executive was telling me that the Friday afternoon programme I had presented since it began was also being given to someone else. 'This will obviously mean less money,' he said.

'OK,' I said. 'I don't want to stand in the way of someone

else having the chance and I accept you can't pay me as much if you are not giving me as many programmes.'

He was most insistent that the poll tax protest and my work for the Green Party was nothing to do with this decision. He said he would not discuss money with me, he would talk to Paul, my agent. A few days later Paul rang to report the outcome of the meeting. Far from offering me less money, which I had accepted, the BBC were offering nothing. There would be no work between July and the start of 1991 and even then there was no guarantee that I would be offered any programmes after that. My contract ran out at the end of July and it would not be renewed. In four weeks' time I would have no income after working for the BBC for the best part of twelve years. What made it worse was that Paul had asked six months earlier about the renewal of the contract so that I would have more warning of impending unemployment, but they had said it was too early to discuss it. I have never received a credible explanation as to why I was dropped and although I now know such things were meant to be to move me on in another direction, I was very disappointed with the way it was done after twelve years with the Corporation.

We had built up enough money by living well below our means for many years for me to continue with the first book, *The Truth Vibrations*. It wasn't a fortune and would not last forever, but at least I was much better off than someone who loses their job with nothing in the bank. As it was it was vital that we had that money because there were going to be a lot of expenses. It was in this same period that I began to ease back on my work for the Green Party. I had made the closing speech at the Spring Conference in the April, just after those first communications. I set out the Green vision of a world without war, hunger and environmental destruction, and urged the party to be more professional in its organisation without diluting the message that the present economic system had to go. But once again as I walked from that stage, I knew I had made my last speech to a party conference as a national speaker.

I had to be true to what I believed in and it was clear that the Green movement as such could not by itself prevent planetary suicide. It was great that more people were becoming concerned about the planet and making an effort to change, but recycling a few cans was, while desirable, a mere drop in a very deep and turbulent ocean and enough people were not going to vote for the fundamental changes that were necessary. To emphasise the point, the Greens were at one per cent in the polls when I joined them, then they rose dramatically to fifteen per cent at those European Elections, but by now they were heading back to two per cent and lower. The planet was still being dismantled at an ever increasing rate, but Green fatigue had set in, the novelty was wearing off, and public attention was turning to other things. Real change had to come in another form and if we, as a human race, would not take the measures necessary to save the planet, then outside forces would have to step in, as indeed I now knew was happening.

I had no wish to harm the Greens in the short term with the ridicule I knew I would attract when *The Truth Vibrations* was published the following spring and I began to withdraw from my work with them. I wanted to fade away quietly over the year, but it was difficult because they wanted me to continue to speak on their behalf. I was in a dilemma because on the one hand I wanted to step back from the front line for the party's sake, but I could not, at this stage, tell them exactly why. I did tell three people about the first communications, including Sara Parkin, but they didn't seem too impressed to say the least. After that experience I felt it better to keep it to myself for the time being.

So, in a matter of three months my life had taken yet another dramatic turn. My television career was over and, in all but name, so was my work for the Green Party. A door to a whole new world had opened before me and I knew the time was right to step through.

8

The Solidifier of Thought

I continued to meet many other people who were receiving information for me. Through the channeller in the Midlands, I met another sensitive in Northamptonshire who was taking automatic writing supporting the same basic themes.

Her source gave the name Attarro and her information confirmed everything that I was getting from elsewhere. The world was certainly about to go through an immense transformation and if that transformation did not take place there would be no Earth. The planet was so imbalanced, with far more negative energy than positive, that the spirit or mind of the Earth was close to disincarnating and if that happened her physical shell would die just as our physical bodies do when our minds leave. The channellings said that humanity had not understood that all the 'resources' we take from the Earth and fritter away should be left where they are. Oil, coal, crystals, minerals and everything on and in the Earth were there for a reason. They each had a role to play in the workings and health of the Earth spirit's physical body. Imagine what state we would be in if bits of our bodies were just taken away. The channellings also said the damage to the ozone layer was far worse than humanity had yet realised, something that has since proved perfectly accurate. All these things had caused enormous pain and anguish to the Earth spirit and she was in emotional turmoil. Her cries for help had appeared, the channellings said, in the form of what have become known as crop circles. In fact, they should more accurately be called crop symbols because symbology is the universal language of Creation and these messages in the corn fields of England and elsewhere could be understood by the rest of the universe and other frequencies. The messages explained that the crop symbols, or at least many of them, are formed by the thought energy of the Earth spirit. The symbols have a terrific impact deep within people who are awake or awakening because they trigger their eternal memory. The communications said of crop symbols:

> These rings are of great importance ... the energy is transmuting and the symbols rise from the voice of the Earth. Just by taking shape they reach our inner eyes and memories and for those who glance, or are aware, reach deeply to send the quiet messages of Mother Earth ... She tries to reach us in many ways, but now is the time to communicate her deeper level of consciousness. Her messages are simple, her language complete. It just needs decoding. Through the absorption of her symbols, so the message, like beautiful music, plays deeply within our souls. These symbols have been etched many times on stone walls throughout civilisation, and it is not the first time they have appeared on nature's canvas. They are necessary to rock human awareness as it becomes self absorbed and not part of the divine family.

The crop symbols have done just that for many people, despite the efforts of the hoaxers and the forces of government disinformation, both of whom are seeking to suppress interest in this phenomenon. The disinformation is felt necessary because the crop symbols have shown clearly, to anyone with a mind they can call their own, that contrary to what the system wishes us to believe, it can't explain everything. The scientific claims that they are created by the wind are so incredible that they only confirm that here is something that cannot be explained by Earthbound science. I believe the symbols are created, not only by the Earth spirit, but also by energies from other levels who also wish to communicate with us. Some could be formed by misguided negative forces who know the power of symbols and create them to speak to humanity at a deep level for negative reasons. We should beware of this and learn to identify the difference. The 'feel' of the energies within the symbols is the way to discriminate.

The Northamptonshire source also had writing about me personally just before I went to meet her. It said she would know me by my eyes, my voice and the shape of my fingers (swollen through arthritis). She might see other things around me and be aware of my unusual energy pattern. 'He is a solidifier of thought and helps the Word to surface with those he meets.' The writing also said that I would become involved with literature about the Incas of Peru. I would be 'drinking of holy water soon' and meeting people of great importance through my work. Many mystics would gather, a new group would be born and I would travel to all ends of the Earth. It said that Linda was just as important to the task as I was: 'You are the roses and she is the rosebowl.' A later communication for Linda said:

> Tell his wife, Linda, she is much appreciated by the world of spirit and a gift of a child will become hers, though not in the way she expects. But let her know we watch and guide her always. She is not alone in her daily tasks and although she becomes tired of the mundane, her job is of equal importance to that of the roses. Let her polish her rosebowl and look deeply at her reflection to open up her inner consciousness.

Another communication for me said: 'There might be a time when you are led on. Watch the time, it will be around the daffodils. Watch your signature on the page and know the dealer and the dealings.' Another intriguing message said:

'The time is approaching when you will be tested by a woman.'

This sensitive channelled a lot of information on many subjects including a communication which said that what humans called a comet would be seen in the night sky and that this would be significant to the changes the Earth was about to go through. She also said she thought I should decide on a symbol or sign which the other levels could use to communicate with me in a yes/no fashion when alternative communications were not possible. She said I should ask them to show me this symbol to say yes or no to a question or confirm that something had been completed as required. As she was speaking I was looking over her shoulder at a pottery fish ornament on a shelf behind her.

'My symbol will be the fish,' I said. Well, some of the ways they have conjured up a fish in answer to questions have been extraordinary since then. I asked them to show me a fish while driving along a motorway, once thinking there was no way it could be done. Almost immediately I found myself looking at a fish and chip van in front of me. On another occasion I was out on an isolated country lane and within seconds of asking for the symbol a wet fish van came over the hill towards me. It was the only vehicle I saw on that whole stretch of road. I then met a sensitive in the West of England who channelled information from a source called Magnu and again this supported the themes of all the others. Magnu said the energies surrounding the planet, the energies in which we live, were changing. Positive energies of enormous power were being introduced to restore the negative–positive balance and this would bring a fundamental change on all levels:

I feel you are sensing now the energies coming in, the energies surrounding your planet. This is causing you to ask questions. It is causing many of you to re-evaluate completely your way of life, where you feel you wish to go, what you want to do. It is causing tremendous upheavals. Some of these upheavals are very confusing, very distressing, very disturbing. Some people in relationships are finding they can no longer continue in those relationships because their partners cannot tune into what they are tuning in to. It is causing a great deal of disturbance. And as I have said to this sensitive on more than one occasion, you must organise yourselves into groups to support each other.

This channelling also revealed to me for the first time that some sort of emergency measures were taken at the end of the Atlantis civilisation around twelve thousand years ago to stop the planet being destroyed. Subsequent communications through another channeller said that the one who had become known in the legends as King Arthur was involved in the process of closing down very powerful energies that encircled the Earth at that time. The legend of King Arthur was symbolic of these events and the person involved was not a 'King' in the human sense, but an Atlantean.

The civilisation called Atlantis was the most evolved this planet has yet seen because the Earth was then on a much higher frequency with access to far more powerful energies and knowledge. We have been falling down the frequencies ever since. Each time you go down a frequency, you have access to less knowledge, wisdom and understanding. This fall down the frequencies caused by an ever-increasing negative imbalance is the real meaning of the phrase, 'The Fall of Man'. The Magnu channelling said:

In the Atlantean period there were many energies being used and information and knowledge being used which were, for particular reasons of safety, withdrawn, shall we say, to prevent complete catastrophe, to prevent the total destruction of your planet. One could say these were emergency measures if you like, to prevent the inhabitants of this planet from an untimely destruction.

As the energies around your planet quicken, so these

latent energies which were withdrawn will be phased back in. They will gradually be awakened. As the consciousness level of your planet raises itself, those of you light workers who are working together to raise your consciousness will be able to hold more and more refined vibrations, and so we will be able to use you as a catalyst. As more of you raise yourselves to meet the challenge, so we can awaken more of these energies. Now energy is consciousness and the energies themselves contain the knowledge and information which is beginning to surface again in your consciousness, so that many of you will remember the Atlantean times. You will remember that you communicated with, say, dolphins and whales. You understood these sentient creatures. You could levitate. You could cause quite significantly large objects to levitate. You could manifest things. You could cause spontaneous combustion by not miraculous means at all. Once you know what you are doing, these things follow. It is a matter of order.

These channellings also explained a little more about my own role in all this. In fact they put it very succinctly when I look at what has happened since. I should say that the thought energy passed through a sensitive during a channelling is turned into words by him or her. They will interpret the thought forms in their own everyday language and this, as you will see, was the case here:

Those of you who are in the forefront of this, you are rather like a snow plough. You are the thin end of the wedge. You really have, how shall I put this? To a certain extent I suppose you have the shitty end of the job. You have got to do an awful lot, but nevertheless you are capable of doing an awful lot. That is why you have chosen to come, that is what you are here for, to really shovel some shit and therefore make some space to make it easier for the others. [For 'shit' read extreme negative energy.] There are many of you for whom the Earth is not your indigenous evolutionary home, shall we say. There are many of you on this planet who come from other spheres of evolution. I think these have been called 'star children' by some of your writers, that is a good enough expression. More evolved beings came to your planet and manifested on your planet in Atlantean times. This was the biggest impulse in bringing in the new knowledge to Atlantis which caused it to grow into the civilisation that it was. New knowledge was brought into this system from universal sources from highly evolved spirits, bringing knowledge into the planet. And you're going to bring it back, basically.

It has always amused me how many people find it impossible to believe that there is any other life in Creation outside of this planet. More than that, they find the very suggestion to be hilarious. But what is more incredible: That there are planets as havens of life all over the universes, or that they are there for no particular reason at all and somehow, by a series of flukes and accidents, life has evolved on this planet and no other? Of course there is life on other planets, although it can be on another frequency or wavelength which we cannot see, or even in another time frame because our concept of time with a beginning and an end is not the same as that which exists elsewhere in Creation. What we see in the night sky is a tiny, tiny fraction of all that exists even on our frequency, let alone all the rest, and what we call humanity is only one small part of the family of Creation.

Another woman I met in the course of writing *The Truth Vibrations* was Joan from Wales. It was through her that I was first contacted by the one known as Rakorski. Some spell the name in other ways, but I spell it the way it is pronounced. This is the mind or group of minds, it was emerging, who has overall responsibility for the transformation of the Earth and one of its most famous incarnations it is widely believed was as Sir Francis Bacon. Rakorski's first communications to me said:

> The diamonds can be found even in the mud – the waters wash them clean. Nuggets of gold (philosophy) are not for you. Seek diamonds, sparkling truth, the clarity, perfection of the Word. The whirlpools of life carry you to where the diamonds are. Resonate to the perfection of the crystals. Arduous seeking is not necessary. The path is already mapped out. You only have to follow the clues.
>
> The race against time is of some importance, but the standard of the work is of greater importance. If any urgency arises, you will be told. Do not worry. Learn to relax – there is always tomorrow. Every physical life needs pleasure and enjoyment. Don't forget the humour. We are guiding you along a set path. You are learning according to our teaching of you. It was all organised before you incarnated.

Another psychic in the room said he was seeing a vision of Linda, Kerry, Gareth and myself together, then came great turbulence, symbolised by turbulent water, before we were all together again on the other side of the turmoil. This made me very concerned about my family and whether I would be parted from them for long periods. I was very down at the thought of that. Rakorski said:

> No need to worry about your wife. She has a job to do. Leave her free to do it without any worries, any strings, any attachments, so, like a bird she can fly off whenever she will and back to you whenever she's able, and you to her.
>
> Your son is his own self and must go his own way. He has his path and it is no concern of yours. You are merely his custodians while he is young. One day your daughter will see her star and go for it.
>
> None of you realise how much the love of the Godhead

enfolds you. It cares and guides. Not one single being is left alone, uncared for. All is gathered in at the end of the day and not one sheep will be left in the field.

True love does not always give the receiver what it would like to receive, but it will always give that which is best for it. So welcome everything you receive whether you like it or not. Ponder on why it is necessary. Acceptance will then be very much easier.

Shortly after this, I had a letter from Calgary, Canada, from a channeller called Deborah Shaw. She had left England to take up a job as a teacher of the deaf in Calgary some months earlier and I had met her at the home of the woman in the Midlands who took the automatic writing. The woman had rung me at home late the previous night to say she felt certain I had to meet a friend of hers who was over from Canada. I went the next morning and met Deborah and some others. We chatted for a couple of hours or so about what we all thought was going on and came to no particular conclusion except that something very big was about to happen to the Earth. For some reason I knew the meeting with Deborah was significant although I had no idea why. I thought no more of it and by the time her letter arrived I had forgotten all about her.

The letter said she had received her most powerful communication yet. She had been busy on the phone with one call after another when she felt an enormous push. She was left in no doubt that she was being asked to leave the phone, sit down and take a message. This she did through automatic writing and it said that I was to go to Canada and an area south of Calgary near the construction site of the Old Man River Dam, which local Indian communities had opposed, unsuccessfully, because it involved flooding their sacred burial grounds. She also said she saw a vision of an Indian who was in a boat and he had with him the body of a woman. He shot an arrow in the air and it was guided by the Great Spirit to a special place where the woman was to be laid to rest. The vision was one of great contrasts between the Indians who were clearly from another age and the surroundings which were how they would be today. I was going to the United States a few weeks later to speak at an animal rights conference at Raleigh, North Carolina, and after checking out the letter with other channellers, I arranged to stay for a week in Canada.

The Truth Vibrations tells the full story of what happened in those five days, but the most astonishing incident was at the Old Man River Dam. On the way we stopped at many places to remove karma and negative energies which it seemed we had both created during lives as Canadian Indians. I had been Setting on an Eagle Tail, chief of the Peigan Indians. Their lands were taken over by the white settlers in the last century and Eagle Tail was one of the signatories to the peace treaties, or at least what were claimed to be peace treaties. The white settlers saw them as a real estate contract. Linda, Kerry and Gareth had all been with me in that incarnation.

It was a spectacular night as we approached the dam, which was still under construction. It was crisp and clear with nearly a full Moon casting its brilliance across the water and the landscape. As we drove over a bridge that spanned the river near the dam, Deborah said: 'This is it – this is the scene I saw in the vision.'

The river was low and we walked across the expanse of stones and mud to the water's edge. When we stopped I saw a large stone shaped like a diamond, then another and another. We collected eleven and the words of Rakorski came back to me: 'The diamonds can be found even in the mud – the waters wash them clean. The whirlpools of life (those Indian incarnations) will lead you to where the diamonds are.'

A psychic communication asked us to take the stones to a point on Nose Hill, a one-time Indian settlement which looks out over Calgary. There we made a circle with them and allowed the energies they carried to be passed on to that site. By now I knew that everything carries, absorbs and generates energy and if you move stones from one place to another you are moving the energies they carry and generate. This can help to balance out and harmonise the energy flows around the planet.

We did a tremendous amount of repair work with the energy system in that part of Canada during my stay, as well as removing karmic imbalances created in particular by the conflict and resentment generated when the white settlers took over Indian lands. Once you create negative energy through wars, conflict, resentment or whatever, it stays at that place, disrupting the energy system until it is balanced by the positive. It is this extreme negative energy imbalance that makes a place feel 'eerie' or 'evil'.

I had been doing similar energy work in England and on the Isle of Wight which, it was becoming clear, is a very important area within the global energy grid. The channellings from several sources indicated that I had some sort of energy pattern which had a significant effect on the energies. Incidentally, another interesting 'coincidence' emerged regarding Deborah Shaw. When Linda and I were married, the reception was at a small hotel in Leamington Spa owned by Deborah's family.

I returned home from Canada and the United States and completed *The Truth Vibrations*. This was an incredibly frustrating time because there were so many questions which I could not answer. I got a little angry on occasions and said to no-one in particular: 'How the hell am I supposed to do this if you won't give me the information!' But I realised that there were definite times for this information to be made known and there was much that we would never understand in the confines of this dense physical form. So the first stage of this spiritual journey was over. Just nine months after that original communication through Betty Shine, I had written a book, left the BBC and ceased to be active in the Green Party. The speed at which it had all happened was once again unbelievable. But it would soon become clear that I had only just begun.

Although I didn't realise it, I was now fast heading for some very rough water.

The scene was set for the monumental year of 1991, a year that so very nearly destroyed everything I had ever held dear. I knew nothing of this at the time because we are never told what is to come if it would affect the experience. I was like a little boy sitting in the dark looking at a speck of light in the distance. I was soon to realise that the light was attached to an oncoming train.

9

The Channeller

When I raised my glass to say goodbye to 1991, I could not have been more delighted to put that year behind me and bid farewell to the nightmare it had visited upon me and my family. It was a year of great emotional pain and turmoil, underpinned by much confusion.

Yet the year had begun so well with the book accepted and at the printers, and with my understanding of the ways of Creation continuing to grow. There were communications from various sources which said I was to go back to Canada for another week and then on to Peru to work on the Earth's energy system and gather material for the next book.

I left for Canada on 29 January in a virtually empty plane. The Gulf War was underway and because of the fear of terrorism very few people were flying. I was once terrified of flying, but since I had realised the true nature of life this had disappeared and I began to enjoy it. Most if not all the unexplained phobias and apparently irrational fears we have can be linked with past life experiences and I am told my fear of flying had a past life connection.

The Gulf War had been mentioned many times in communications, some of which I had included as an addition to *The Truth Vibrations*. There was clearly something very underhand about the whole Gulf operation and the messages said this would eventually come out, although I didn't know exactly when or what it would be.

Deborah Shaw had now changed her name to Mari Shawsun because she said she felt that was the right one for her. The few days I spent in Canada moved me forward rapidly in terms of activating the psychic gifts which we all possess. Up to this point my own communications had been confined to using a pendulum. This can swing one way for 'yes' and another for 'no', in response to energies passing through the arm and hand. But it is very easy to influence the answer with your own thoughts, even unknowingly, and it can be a primitive way to communicate unless you are highly skilled and experienced. This all changed when I went to see a woman Mari had met since my last visit. She specialised in helping people remove blockages on their psychic skills. These blockages can be caused by energy imbalances carried over from previous lives or created by experiences in this one. She took me through various periods of my life to acknowledge the emotional disturbance that certain experiences had caused within me. As we have seen, what appear to be minor incidents can have a major impact.

Once these blockages were acknowledged and removed I could feel the difference immediately. I was so much more sensitive to the energies and the thought forms being passed to me from other levels. The woman helped me to develop another type of yes/no communication. When I asked a question my right or left arm would push inwards against my body depending on the answer. It was a weird sensation and very funny to see. I also started to hear a sort of voice which was, in fact, the process of my brain decoding the thought forms and turning them into words I could understand. There are endless people in mental institutions because they can 'hear voices' or see spirits when there is nothing mentally wrong with them at all. They are just very sensitive at decoding thought form communications and changing their own vibrationary state to see something of another frequency. But unless someone explains this to them they think they are going crazy and they are often encouraged in this view by the psychiatric profession.

The most memorable experience for me on this Canadian visit was when I began to channel information from other frequencies. I cannot adequately explain how it feels at these times. The whole room fills with energy and you can feel it pour through you, full of warmth and love. It is like being wrapped in a blanket of love and the feeling is indescribable. This energy builds up and you feel your own self begin to float back into another state of being. This allows energies from another frequency to take over your conscious level and the physical body, although you can choose to pull out of it whenever you wish. It feels as if you have had three stiff gins. Eventually, your mouth begins to speak, but they are not your words. They are the words, or rather thought energy, of the communicator. I channelled Rakorski and Attarro for a group of people in Calgary.

I also began knowingly to channel energy into the Earth. Energies needed by the planet are passed through you, as I have explained, so they can be transformed into a mixture and frequency which the Earth can absorb. I had seen others doing this on my travels during the writing of *The Truth Vibrations*, although I had never felt anything myself on these occasions. This was about to change in a very big way. I went with Mari on to Nose Hill on a wonderful, crisp, sunny day, and we stopped at the site of an Indian medicine wheel, which was their version of a stone circle. I was standing facing the Sun when suddenly this force just burst through me with the most incredible power. My arms were thrust outwards to make a cross, then upwards above my head, before being pushed out in front of me with my palms facing downwards. As this happened a tremendous burst of energy poured from my hands and down towards the Earth. At no time was I in control of what my arms were doing and I just grunted every now and again and tried to stay on my feet. When it was over I felt like a sponge that had been squeezed dry.

Later that day, at the home of Mari's friend, the same thing happened. The gathering of psychics there also had information saying I had been channelling energy all my life without knowing it and I had been led to many places to channel energy when I thought I was going for my own reasons. Saudi Arabia was one example. Many other people are going to realise that they have been doing the same as this decade unfolds. This was different, though. There was no way I could have channelled energy of this power without realising it! This energy channelling is going on all over the world in every country every day. The process of cleansing the energy field or sea in which we live involves not only taking out extreme negative energy, but also bringing in positive energy from other frequencies.

I began to channel energy most days and the rest of the trip to Canada was spent repairing energy sites and ley lines. The overall picture was still shrouded in mist, but a few things were now clear to me. I had come to pass on the truth about Creation and what was happening to the planet; I had an energy pattern that had a significant effect on the energies; these energies were seriously imbalanced by negative energy and this was encouraging humanity to think negatively and create yet more negative energy, so making the imbalance still worse all the time; when this imbalance reached a certain point, the mind or spirit of the Earth would disincarnate and her physical body, the planet, would disintegrate and die; that point was getting very close.

On the last night before I left for Peru something happened that was to prove highly significant. It had been a long day and I fell asleep on the floor in the lounge of Mari's apartment. It was a deep, deep sleep, I remember that, and when I woke up things were very different somehow. It was almost like being hypnotised. I will never be able to put it into words, but it was as if someone had flicked a switch. It just wasn't the same world that I had been aware of when I fell asleep and nor was it, somehow, the same me. Only someone who had experienced it would know what I mean.

Astrologically the deep sleep coincided with planetary

movements which would have brought about a transformation within me as new energies were activated or brought
in. Combinations and interactions involving the Sun, Moon,
Jupiter, Neptune, Saturn, a lunar eclipse, and particularly
Uranus, the awakener, set off massive changes in my own
energy field and allowed a higher dimension of myself to
manifest through the physical body and make things happen that needed to happen even if, on this level, I would
have wanted to avoid them. 'It was a quite extraordinary
combination,' Judy said in her reading, 'producing amazing
results as the whole of your Grand Cross was kicked into
action.'

I left Canada for Peru a few hours after that deep, deep
sleep. I walked down the stairs from the aircraft at Lima
Airport at about a quarter to six in the morning. I had no idea
what I was to do first in what was, to say the least, rather a
large country. I felt strongly, however, that I needed to get to
Cusco, high up in the Andes, and the departure board said a
plane was leaving for there at half past six. 'Si,' was about the
limit of my Spanish and everything looked chaotic with
people pushing and shoving everywhere. There was no
chance of making myself known in time to catch the plane.
Suddenly a Peruvian man walked up to me and asked in
pretty fair English where I was going. 'Cusco,' I replied.

'Do you have a hotel?'

'No, I don't even have a plane ticket.'

'Leave it to me.'

He then proceeded to book my hotel in Cusco, for which
he received commission, of course, and he by-passed the
queue to speak to his friend at the ticket counter. By twenty
past six, just thirty-five minutes after walking off the plane
from Canada, I was walking onto the plane to Cusco. This
was to be a situation that would repeat itself again and again
in my travels around the world.

The former Inca city of Cusco is situated at twelve
thousand feet and the lack of oxygen blows you away for
twenty-four hours. I spoke no Spanish and I sat in my cold

and damp hotel room wondering what on earth I was doing here. I did, however, have one contact to follow up. I had met a friend of Mari's in Canada who knew a Canadian woman who had settled in Cusco. I took her name and address because even then I felt I would need to visit Cusco at some point on the trip. The address was a tourist office and somehow I made my way there after several detours. She was not at the office, but one of the staff gave me her telephone number. That afternoon we made contact and I went to her home where she gave me cups of coca tea which is supposed to help with altitude problems. I told her what I knew, which wasn't much. My own communications had told me that I needed to visit Machu Picchu, the ruins of an Inca settlement not far from Cusco by Peruvian standards. Also I had to visit Sun Island which was a considerable distance to the south, just over the Bolivian border on Lake Titicaca, the world's highest navigable lake. 'How do I get to all these places?' I asked her.

'Well, you will need a guide,' she said. 'And if you are going to do everything in the time you have, you must be on your way by tomorrow.' She was leaving for Chile the following morning and if she was going to help me it all had to be organised within a couple of hours. She wasn't hopeful. 'What a mess,' I thought. Then she had an idea and she picked up the phone. A good deal of Spanish later, she said she had found a guide who was free for the week I needed him and we should go over to meet him. At the same time she asked a friend at the tourist office to organise a ticket to Machu Picchu for the next morning.

I got on well with the guide who could speak quite good English. He was involved in a vegetarian café and environmental project in Cusco and made his living showing tourists around the country. We arranged to leave for Puno and Sun Island two days later and I went on a day trip to Machu Picchu.

What a fantastic journey. There are no roads through the Sacred Valley of the Incas and you can only travel by foot or by train. The line winds its way through the soaring hills and mountains alongside the waters of the Urubamba or 'Holy River'. You can travel by bus from the station up a switch-back track to the ruins, but as I got off the train I had this overwhelming feeling of staying in the valley and going down to the riverside. While the buses passed me on their way to Machu Picchu I walked along another track and found a quiet spot next to the water, hidden by the under-growth. I stayed there for hours channelling energy, paddling and drinking the beautiful water. 'He will be drinking of the holy water soon.' Later I was told that the Urubamba is a sort of special energy line which carries particularly powerful energies. Over the years this ancient knowledge has been distorted by the various cultures and religions and so you get names like 'holy river'.

Water is the most effective carrier of these sub-atomic energies and so rivers, particularly where two meet, and islands are always powerful unless they have been weak-ened by negative imbalance. It is also why most of the Earth is covered by water and why most of the physical body is water. The pollution of the planet's waters is therefore suicidal because pollution is, and is constantly generating, negative energy and destroying the flow of the lifeforce energies.

Early the next day I met up with the guide for the trip to Puno near the shores of Lake Titicaca. When I arrived he asked me if I had had any dreams during the night. I was surprised to be asked that question and even more so because I had indeed had a very vivid dream about one of my middle front teeth falling out.

'Have you got a father or grandfather?' the guide asked.

'Yes, I have a father,' I replied.

'Well, the dream you had is symbolic of the death of a father or grandfather.'

When I next made contact with Linda she told me my father had died while I was in Peru after suffering from the effects of a stroke and stomach cancer over the last six months.

The journey to Puno was both one of the best and worst of my life. The scenery was simply indescribable, but the train would have been at home with the string of old bangers I used to own. It must be the only place on Earth where you can get seasick on dry land at fourteen thousand feet. The journey took thirteen hours. The tourist coaches of the train are locked to prevent robberies. There are many who travel the line looking for ways of parting tourists from their money. When the train stopped for a long time at one point and people went out for a walk I was robbed. I knew who had done it and they could not get away because we were in the middle of open countryside, but I let it go. 'It's your karma for the future or mine from the past,' I thought. I was finding it much easier to forgive and see everyone as people at different stages of the same journey, although I emphasise the word is *easier*, not easy. Also, while I don't condone stealing you can understand why some people are tempted by crime when you see the grinding poverty that so many in Peru have to endure.

The tour company had booked us in a hotel in Puno called the Sillustani, named after a large Inca burial site an hour's drive away. I felt sure that I needed to go there the following day. It was a magical place. The stone burial towers, called Chullpas, are built on a mound surrounded on three sides by the Umayo Lagoon and it is one of the most beautiful places I have seen. I charged up the energies there and channelled in more. To charge up the energies you walk around a site, usually in a circle or circuit, and your energy pattern interacts with the energies around you. This whips up the power similar to the way an electrical coil works.

As we left Sillustani I saw two large mounds ahead of us a few minutes up the road. I knew I had to go to the one on the right. I can't explain what happens, but you just know you have to do something or go somewhere. I left my guide and the driver at the van and climbed to the top of the mound. There I found what was left of a small stone circle. It wasn't like Stonehenge or anything – the stones were only about knee high. I walked around the circle to charge up the energies and soon the power was like nothing I had experienced before. The atmosphere was thick and, my goodness, what power I felt all around me. I channelled energies for a while, but I soon had the feeling that something big was about to happen. My feet could not move. It was as if two giant magnets were pulling them down and suddenly my arms were thrust to the sky. My feet were vibrating, almost burning, as energy of incredible power poured through me from head to toe and vice versa. Then it began to pour out through my hands.

I was looking back towards Sillustani and over to the distant mountains. I could see on the horizon the rain from a gathering storm. I heard a message very clearly which said this would be over when I felt the rain. If that was true, I thought, this was going to take some time because the storm had some way to travel, if indeed it was coming my way at all. For well over an hour I stood there, arms to the sky, my feet never moving an inch, as the power built up. My head was pounding and it was like a piece of music getting louder and louder. By now I was drifting away somewhere and I had almost lost contact with my physical self. Then I felt the first drops of rain and it was like a switch had been turned off. The power diminished and I stumbled, hardly able to stand. I was shivering with the cold, something I had not felt until now, and I was gasping for breath. My hands and feet were vibrating as if they were plugged into an electrical socket. It was twenty minutes before my hands returned to anything like normal and my feet took nearly twenty-four hours to settle down.

The next morning we left Puno for Sun Island. I had channelled Rakorski down by the river at Machu Picchu using a small recorder to tape the words and I was told that I would be visiting Sun Island, although the guide would say it was not possible and try to talk me out of it. A reading by the psychic in Northamptonshire before I left England had also said I should stand my ground in Peru and go with what

I felt was right, no matter what others said. This turned out to be true because the guide said it was not possible to get to Sun Island and stay two nights as I wanted but I refused to take no for an answer. It was quite funny because the guide was trying to take me on the usual tourist trips while I was trying to tell him I was being guided by others about where to go and when. He never really accepted that even though everything I wanted to happen was happening every day.

Sun Island is a two-hour journey in a small boat from the Bolivian mainland at Copacabana, which is a Roman Catholic shrine dominated by a massive cathedral. The water was rough, but the scenery breathtaking. Sun Island has no electricity and is very sparsely populated. There are few settlements and the people make what living they can from fishing, a little farming and whatever they can sell to the tourists who stop over for forty-five minutes on their hydrofoil tour of Lake Titicaca.

As our boat approached the little harbour I saw a blonde girl on the shore. Again I knew she was significant, but I didn't know why. With me were the guide and the man from the Puno tour company which had arranged the trip to the Island. We climbed the old Inca steps from the beach and stopped to drink at a spring. The waters pour out of the hillside and down a gully alongside the steps into the lake. It is called the fountain of eternal youth and the water has to be tasted to be believed. There we met the girl I had seen on the shore. I realised that something must have happened to me at that mound the previous day when I shook her hand. I could see a look of surprise on her face and she was reluctant to let my hand go. It was not an effect I usually had on people! She didn't speak a word of English, but through the guide she said she was on holiday from Argentina. She had been in La Paz, the capital of Bolivia, when she felt the need to be on Sun Island that day.

She was clearly very spiritual and in touch with other frequencies. She had arrived some hours before and found the only accommodation available on the Island, a run-down old building high on the steep hillside. On the way she was telling my guide to warn everyone about a ferocious dog which lived at the building. She had been attacked earlier. When we approached, the dog appeared and was indeed extremely aggressive. The others stopped immediately, but for some reason I walked towards the dog with the palms of my hands pointing towards it. What made me do that I cannot imagine, but after a few seconds this vicious, barking, growling animal went quiet, dropped his head and whimpered away wagging his tail. On one level I couldn't believe the sudden change, but on another I just knew that was going to happen. Very strange.

Later I walked with the girl to the site of an old stone circle, similar to the one near Sillustani, and channelled some very powerful energies. Sun Island is not only one of the most beautiful and peaceful places on Earth, it is also a key point on the energy system of the planet and I did a great deal of work there.

The most important event came early next morning. I was hearing messages which said basically that there was an energy circuit to re-link which had been broken for a very long time. This had to happen before the end of a certain planetary sequence and if it did not happen it would set back considerably the work going on to repair the planet's energy system. It had been raining during the night and the sky was still full of clouds. The Sun appeared over the lake and threw into silhouette another island nearby called Moon Island. It was a wondrous scene with the pale sunlight dancing off the rain drops hanging from the leaves. It was also a scene described perfectly by the psychic in Northamptonshire before I left England! She even got the time of day right.

I walked along a path high above the lake until I came across a circle made up of small stones left by who knows who. I walked around the circle many times until it was pulsating with energy. I stood in the circle and looked out across the lake to Moon Island and the rising Sun. I heard a voice saying that I would know when the job was complete

The family group. Left to right: Dad, Mum holding baby Gareth, Paul, Lin
with Kerry in front, and me.

Sporting children. Kerry the record-breaking athlete, and Gareth the goalkeeper in a picture that brilliantly captures his personality.

A new direction. Green Party Conference, 1989. *(Syndication International)*

A wry cartoon in the *Daily Mail*, August 1990. *(Daily Mail)*

'I think we've found David Icke's successor. He doesn't give a stuff for the environment and could be persuaded to pay his Poll Tax . . .'

Left: Sun Island, Bolivia, looking out to Moon Island at the scene of an extraordinary energy channelling in 1991.

Right: Glastonbury Tor. Heart Chakra of the British Isles and part of the Heart Chakra of the Planet. No wonder it is surrounded by myth and legend. It is one of the most powerful energy points on the Earth.
(Syndication International)

Before, during and after the 'turquoise period' in the spring of 1991. In the centre is the person I simply did not recognise when I later saw the pictures. *(Press Association; Today newspaper)*

Crete, 1992. So much pain behind the smiles.

Jaymie Alexander Icke, aged two days.

The bond that nothing can break. The roses and the rosebowl. Always together. *(Today newspaper)*

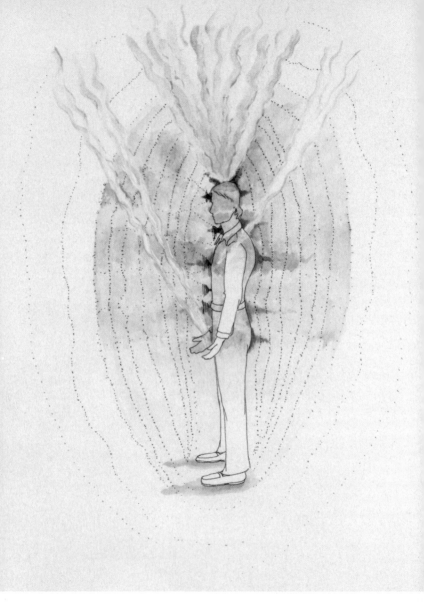

On the unseen levels around the physical body are the many energy fields that make up our eternal selves. The chakras pass energies between the levels so that an imbalance in one energy field can affect the others and eventually cause physical dis-ease. *(Ann Davies)*

because the Sun would cast its rays across the whole area between Moon Island and where I was standing. At that moment this looked a long way off because there were many clouds in the sky and the sunshine was confined to odd spots on the lake.

I stood there for an hour and a half with my feet again fixed to the spot. The energy became more and more powerful, but I sensed a kind of opposite force pulling the other way. I was well aware by now that there are extreme negative forces seeking to destroy the Earth because of the damage that would do to a much wider area. These forces feed off negative energy and they want humanity to go on producing more. A smooth transformation and the end of humanity's suicidal ways is the last thing these imbalanced and misguided forces wish to see.

The clouds gathered and became darker until it began to rain. The Sun was nowhere to be seen. The voice said I should rest and try again later, and I returned to the accommodation to recover my strength after standing there for so long. When the rain eased off I went back and walked the circle of stones. For another hour and a half I stood there, the palms of my hands facing out towards Moon Island, and the power of the energy became so overwhelming I was struggling to stand. My whole body was shaking in the end and it was just like having a mighty electric shock. This went on for what seemed like hours and all I can remember in my kind of semi-conscious state was repeating the words 'More power, more power,' over and over again. With my strength all but gone, the clouds parted and the Sun's rays filled the area between Moon Island and myself for the first time. Just as with the rain drops at the mound near Sillustani, the flow of energy stopped and I collapsed on the floor. At that exact moment the girl from Argentina appeared to say goodbye before she left for home.

I was to learn later that the group in Canada had been channelling energy on Nose Hill at the same time into a ley line which linked up with Peru and Bolivia. Precisely what had happened I didn't know for sure, although it seemed to have something to do with reactivating a triangle of energy lines linking Sun Island, Moon Island, and Copacabana.

While reading this story Judy Hall had a psychic vision which related to the incident on Sun Island:

> I had a brief picture of you somewhere at a point which was a 'control centre' for the energy grid, dressed as an Inca priest and wearing an ancient feathered cloak which had been yours centuries before. You were standing with your arms thrown out and then you brought them down to seal the energy system closed. There seems to be an urgency to this experience, as though you have foreseen the imminent arrival of the conquistadores and could see the disasters this would bring, but no-one listened to you. Everyone else, whipped up by the priests, was awaiting the 'second coming' of the god, Quetzacoatl, which had been foretold and this was why the Spanish were able to walk in and take over Peru. There is tremendous ridicule hurled at you by the other priests and there is a sense of terrible punishments being inflicted on you to try to make you reverse that closure of the energy grid, but you resisted. My sense is that, having died as a result, you then hurriedly incarnated in England as Anthony Bacon in the hope that you could work from a different angle to minimise the damage being inflicted on the Earth. Bacon, of course, was a 'magical' initiate and understood much about the esoteric levels of Creation, although he, in his turn, I understand, suffered much ridicule in his latter days.

I continued to channel energies in many parts of this fantastic country of Peru and so many times it happened in or near churches. It is the same in every country I've visited because many of the first churches all those centuries ago were built on sites held sacred by the so-called 'primitive' peoples who preceded Christianity. These areas had been held sacred because they were energy sites, a truth that has been increasingly lost since that time, though not completely. Many early Christians saw the Earth energies as something evil which had to be suppressed and they felt that building a church at the key points would have this effect. From this have come the myths and legends about 'defeating the dragon'.

Negative energy has been poured into the system at many of these points because so many churches are obsessed with death, guilt, fear and sadness. It is so ironic that I and countless others have been led to churches to remove negative energies that are harming the Earth. On the other hand those churches that are joyful and fun are putting positive energy into the network, which is what it desperately needs.

The last channelling on that first trip to Peru was just before midnight inside the Inca ruins at Machu Picchu, a glorious place that makes your soul sing with inspiration at the beauty of the Earth. It is awesome, just awesome. I then returned to Lima and home. I had problems all through the trip getting money from my credit card because it was not very widely accepted in Peru. But these problems led me to places I would have missed otherwise as I searched for a bank that would take the card. On the last day in Lima I ran out of money, so much so that I didn't even have enough for the taxi to the airport. I sat in the hotel room wondering what I was going to do when there was a knock on the door. It was a taxi driver called Henrique. He said the hotel receptionist had told him of my situation. He would take me to the airport for free, he said. In the end I gave him a radio for the fare, but at least I got to the airport.

My problems were not over. I had stayed in Peru longer than I envisaged and I missed my original flight home via Toronto. The next one was full and I arrived at the airport at three o'clock in the morning hoping that enough people would not turn up to give me a seat on the plane. My ticket was not transferable and I had to fly by Canadian Airlines or buy a whole new ticket at considerable expense. This flight only went twice a week and when I arrived at the check-in desk I was told there were so many others in my position that it was highly unlikely that I would get on the plane. The flight a few days later was also full with forty on the waiting list. I asked Rakorski and those guiding me again and again if I would get on the flight that morning and each time a voice replied, 'Don't worry, all will be well.' One message said: 'You will get on the plane and we have found you a seat by the window with plenty of leg room!' I dismissed it as me talking to myself, but half an hour before the flight left the check-in supervisor told me I was on the plane. I was so relieved to walk up those steps and I was shown to the seat I had inherited from the person who had failed to show. It was by the window and there was an emergency exit between me and the seats in front. I have never had so much leg room on an aircraft before or since.

I've lost count of the number of times something or someone has appeared at exactly the right time to help me out whenever I am in trouble or need help. The Tumi reading identified a significant combination in the birth chart involving Jupiter which basically shows that the universe is constantly looking after you. As the reading said: 'You could be in the Sahara Desert dying of thirst and you'd find an oasis with a spring of ice-cold water. The universe looks after you with this Jupiter placement.'

Back in England, I spoke of my experiences for the first time in public. It was on a programme called 'Through the Keyhole' in which a panel of three are shown the inside of a person's house and they have to guess who lives there. When this is done, the person comes into the studio to be interviewed by David Frost. I'll never forget David's face when he asked me about my new book and I said the information had come from elsewhere in Creation. The programme was recorded for broadcast a few months later, but the time when all this would be known to the public was fast approaching. While I was away on my next trip abroad, the letters arrived at the Green Party locally and nationally with my resignation as a party speaker and as Parliamentary candidate for the Isle of Wight. I said my book was due to be published two months later which took the concept of life and Creation further than the party was ready to go, and it would be wrong for me to continue to be a high-profile member of the party while expounding views they would not yet accept.

The papers made some further inquiries and stories began to appear about me being contacted by Socrates. As if that wasn't startling enough they still had to exaggerate and they had me having a vision of Socrates manifesting in front of me at Betty Shine's house! I have no doubt that if the extreme sections of the media were faced with a true story of a pig and an elephant flying over Buckingham Palace singing 'God Save The Queen', they would find some way of exaggerating it. They seem to do it by reflex action, a fact that would be confirmed again and again in the weeks and months ahead.

10

The Son of the Godhead

I arrived home from Peru to life without my father. A year
or so earlier I would have been devastated, but now I felt
pleased for him. He had been confined to a hospital bed for
many months after a serious stroke which disabled him, and
tests he had for a stomach complaint revealed that he had an
advanced cancer. Add to this a heart weakened by a
coronary a year or so earlier and you had a man who was
always clinging to life by a thread in the most distressing of
circumstances.

I was glad his suffering was over and he had left his pain
behind. I also knew that what I was about to say and do
publicly would have destroyed him. I missed him, and more
than I realised at first. Despite all the aggravation between us
which it was part of the plan to endure, there was a close bond
that I suspect goes back a very long time. He is still around me
on the unseen levels quite often. After a television programme
a year later when I was in the depths of despair a psychic in the
audience asked me afterwards if I had lost someone close to
me because of something wrong in the stomach area. 'Well,'
said the psychic, 'when you walked on the stage this energy
came over me which had enormous love for you. I sensed there
had been a problem with the stomach in the last lifetime. The
message I was given for you was to keep going and keep doing
what you believe to be right.'

As my father deteriorated he became more angry and bitter at the world and he used my mother to vent his frustration. Not many people would have put up with what she was asked to endure, but put up with it she did. During those months in hospital, and indeed in the period before that, my relationship with him was the same as always. Sometimes we would be very close and sometimes there would be mighty rows as I challenged the way he was treating my mother. This contrast also showed itself when I tried to help him prepare for his physical death by explaining about Creation and how we lived forever. On some occasions he would listen and take comfort from what I said, while on others he would question my sanity. My father was a victim of the Bible-based religions. The Bible and the teachings of the church made no sense to him, especially after what he had witnessed during the war. If there was a loving God, how could He let such things happen? And if these things were supposed to happen then how could such a God deserve any respect? So many people have switched off any thoughts of a spiritual dimension because they confuse the spiritual with the religious. Spirituality and religion are not the same thing.

My father's death released me from some restrictions of action because often I would do, or not do, things after assessing the effect they would have on him. My subconscious need for his approval which went back to football and childhood had created a prison of guilt around me and with his passing this came tumbling down. I am now convinced that my father's attitude and behaviour were designed to prepare me for what was and is to come. He came to teach me sometimes harsh lessons about life and myself and I am very grateful for what he did. It was all part of the plan and, it is now clear, he left the physical body at precisely the time envisaged before he was even born and behaved towards my mother and me in just the way we had all pre-arranged: 'True love does not always give the receiver what it would like to receive, but it will always give that which is best for it.'

Communications indicated that I should return to Canada in early March 1991 for more energy work. By now the change in me that I had experienced so strongly after that deep sleep on the floor of Mari's lounge was gathering pace all the time. I just didn't feel like me anymore. As I have said, it was like being hypnotised. We accept it is possible for one person to hypnotise another, but it is also possible for our conscious level to be hypnotised by our sub-conscious and upper-conscious levels, if (and this is the point) all levels are in close enough synchronisation. In my case, that part of us I call 'the brakes' which sees things coming and says, 'I can see where this will lead – no thanks', was no longer part of the decision-making process. It was the same as when you channel information. Your own personality takes a step backwards to allow other energies to come in and use your body as a vehicle to bring information down to this physical level. This is how I was feeling most of the time and it was the higher levels of my mind preparing to 'take over' and make sure some extraordinary but necessary situations would unfold in a very public way. A great deal of energy channelling was done around Canada and I just got higher and higher and further and further away from the driving seat. I took some automatic writing which said I was a 'Son of the Godhead' which even at that time and in that state, I found astonishing. What exactly was meant by a Son of the Godhead I had no idea, but I accepted it because by now I would have accepted almost anything.

Astrologically, a lot was happening. Neptune energies, which are extremely strong in my birth chart, were affecting me. These dissolve barriers between the different levels of our being. The more Neptune energies affect us, the more the divisions between the higher and lower mind, the mental level, the emotions and the physical body fall away and all begin to merge to bring about what we call 'oneness' – all levels in sync and working together as one. Neptune is one of the three 'outer' planets along with Uranus and Pluto and all three were beginning to influence my energy field, as was

Jupiter. The Tumi reading said:

> Most people are not affected too much on a personal level by the outer planets unless they have begun to wake up spiritually and their own vibrations have reached a stage where they can cope with the power of these energies. They tend to work more on humanity as a whole, the collective mind of humanity, where their power can be diffused across a large number of people and not affect directly those who are not ready for them. Even so, the power of Uranus, for instance, can still hit some people so hard that it can start revolutions and mass riots. Yet here were you, one person, taking on and channelling the power and intensity of this energy. It's no wonder you felt blown away at first. But the key planet at this time was Jupiter, the 'Messiah', the 'King', and during these early months of 1991 its energy was flooding your vehicle, your energy field. This is the 'Christ' energy that will transform the world and when this, in the form of Jupiter, came into relationship with Saturn (symbolised by Satan), you had the combination and balance you needed to do your work. Your energy field, flooded by these 'Messiah' energies, would have recognised what was happening and it manifested on the physical level with 'I am a Son of the Godhead'.

It also came through on that visit to Canada that Mari was being asked to return with me to live with my family in England and channel information for the next book, *Love Changes Everything*. Mari's job had just ended and she had been refused resident status by the Canadian authorities, which surprised everyone. She hurriedly arranged to leave Canada and she flew back to England with me. When we arrived at Gatwick Airport we were met by Linda and a few journalists who were following up the story about the 'Socrates vision'. I had taken some automatic writing, backed up by Mari, which said I should announce to the world that

I was a Son of the Godhead. The David Icke I had come to know would have said, 'Up yours, sunshine', but by now he was at the back of the bus trying to make sense of what was happening at the front. My voice of 'reason' was not in control. So I told them and the die was well and truly cast.

I, and others, had also received many communications about the Gulf War which I also passed on. I still don't know what that war was about, but I am sure that a tremendous amount will come out about the background which will put the conflict in a new light and expose the Allies as less than the innocents they claimed to be. Indeed this is already beginning to happen. A channelled message for *The Truth Vibrations* had said:

> Here we have a war of economics, money, materialism, but most of all greed. The monies do not go to the people, but into the coffers of only a few because of corruption and secrecy. As the walls fall on the economic crisis, so will dishonesty come to light. It will involve those that you trust as well as those you do not trust.

More communications said we should call a press conference and tell everyone what was going to happen to the world. We were also to be dressed in turquoise all the time! I knew that colours had an effect on the energies and that turquoise was particularly effective so, again, I went along with it. The 'take-over' of the rational me was now at its peak and it needed to be, I can tell you, to stand up in front of a room of tabloid journalists and announce not only that you were a Son of the Godhead, whatever that meant, but also a long list of fantastic geological events compiled overwhelmingly by Mari Shawsun. All this would happen, I said confidently, before the end of 1991. Standing there was a weird, unreal experience. I was speaking the words, but all the time I could hear the voice of the brakes in the background saying: 'David, what the hell are you saying? This is absolute nonsense.'

It made no difference, though, and the words just kept coming out. This was in line with that early communication which said: 'Sometimes he will say things and wonder where they came from. They will be our words.' The lower self, the 'brakes', the personality called David Icke, stepped aside and the higher levels of the mind came in to make things happen that needed to happen for the plan to stay on course. If the higher self had not intervened in such a powerful and extraordinary way, I would not have done all that was to follow in the early months of 1991.

My feeling is that when you take on work on behalf of the whole, you have agreed to that before incarnation and our free will is somehow more limited than when you are here to deal only or mainly with personal karma and evolution. This is understandable when you think of the critical state the Earth is in and how little time there is to prevent a catastrophe. What needs to be done must be done by those who have agreed to come to trigger and ease the transformation of people and planet. In my case the Grand Cross ensures that the show stays on the road.

The press conference was splashed all over the papers the next day and I was the laughing stock of the country. Part of me could not have cared less, but the brakes, the lower self, by now shouting from the wilderness, most certainly could. I felt like I had a big lump of lead in my stomach. I ached with anguish and confusion, and that feeling was to stay with me without a break for the rest of the year and beyond. The ridicule reached its height when I appeared on Terry Wogan's chat show and the audience spent much of the interview laughing. Again the part of me doing the interview could not have cared less, but the brakes were saying: 'David, tell me this is not happening. How did you get yourself into this? Let me go home and quietly die.' The ridicule from press and public was enormous. I was laughed at in the street wherever I went and often in front of my children. It is staggering how those three little words, Son of God, can get humanity's collective knickers into such a twist, even among those who say they don't believe in the Bible.

I understand that the producer of 'Wogan' was criticised for inviting such a 'madman' on the programme and that Terry Wogan was criticised by others for the way he handled the interview. He was seen as being highly biased against what I had to say. But it was quite right that I was asked on the programme in the light of the publicity at the time and although Terry Wogan played to the laughing audience, there were far more biased and less hospitable hosts than him in this period. There was one man I had once worked with in television who launched into a series of highly aggressive questions in one of the most biased interviews I have ever seen, let alone experienced.

Getting a fair hearing proved impossible anywhere in the media, except for one article and two radio interviews which showed a balance painfully absent elsewhere. But then did anyone expect me to get a fair hearing in these early days? Of course not. Getting a hearing at all was what it was about, for the reasons I will come to shortly. If those of us who are challenging the system are only prepared to go out into the media when they think they will get a fair hearing they might as well hoist the white flag now and be done with it. The media in general, with rare exceptions, is the propaganda machine for the system and they are always going to be hostile to anyone who challenges its thought control or says anything 'different' from the norm that the media is so committed to worship.

The basis of everything I said at that time was true – but truth taken to the extreme. Yes, wearing certain colours can be good or bad for you depending on the person involved but you don't have to wear turquoise all the time. Yes, the Earth was preparing to go through incredible changes on all levels, but whole islands and countries were not going to disappear within a few months. This didn't matter, however. What the plan demanded was massive publicity for the basic themes of what will happen, that's all. The extremes of the press conference were so different from what I had written in *The Truth Vibrations*. This was a book compiled with the brakes on and so many people have said what a difference there was between how I appeared and what I had written in the book. In fact, if you look at pictures of me in this period and compare them with ones before and since, you can see the difference in the face and the eyes. I don't even look like the same person. A year later when I appeared on the Pat Kenny programme in the Irish Republic, they played in a clip of an interview I did in Ireland at this time and I was really shocked when I saw myself. I kept my composure and laughed it off, but I was very shocked. 'Who was this guy dressed in turquoise?' I thought as I looked at the screen. 'I don't recognise him.' What you are seeing in the eyes of that temporary personality is the energy that surged through me to bring about certain extreme events necessary for the life plan.

When people I knew met me in this period they had two reactions. Some said I didn't seem like the same person while others said they were amazed because I seemed like the same guy they had always known – so different from the man they had seen on 'Wogan' or in the papers. They were both right. What appeared to be happening was that another level or whatever would take over at key times like press conferences, television interviews, etc, whenever it was necessary to suspend the brakes, and in between the old me would return to take the consequences of what had happened. These times were sheer agony as I would survey the wreckage of my life, blown apart in less than two months. Talk about confusion. But there was no time to sit and think and try to work out what was happening. Always there were communications saying, 'Go here', 'Do that'. There was so much information it was impossible to process and analyse. It was like being blown along in a typhoon.

There was a rush by individuals and organisations to distance themselves from me as urgently as they could. A Special Olympics group dropped me as their president, an organisation which had been instrumental in giving me an award for services to animals only a year earlier dropped me from their list of patrons, and at least two prominent environmentalists went into print and the broadcast media attacking me as a loony. None of them felt it necessary to pick up the phone and talk to me first or write to ask for an explanation of what I was doing. What was also interesting, I was later to discover, was that all those psychics who knew me were either told directly or had the overwhelming feeling that they should leave me to go through this experience and work it all out for myself. Judy Hall was one of them. She wrote a letter to me, but it mysteriously disappeared before she could post it. They might have upset the whole plan if they had intervened, not that it is likely that I would have listened. People also commented on how exhausted I looked in the papers and on television. This was because the energies working through me were so powerful my physical body was working flat out to cope.

The 'take-over' energies reached their peak, as I have said, about the time of the press conference and the subsequent media interviews in the March, April and May, but gradually through the summer the old me was re-emerging. This coincides with astrological changes that would bring this about. There are no words adequate to describe the agony I began to feel. In a matter of weeks, indeed in one short press conference, I had surrendered every ounce of credibility I had spent my life creating. I could not understand why, if all those different psychics were right and I was here to pass on truth, I had been put into a situation where that credibility had been shattered into millions of tiny pieces. What the hell was going on? What was happening to me? My greatest agony was to wake up every morning and look into the eyes of Linda, my best mate for twenty years, and see her pain and confusion at what was happening. Only a relationship as incredibly strong as ours would have survived.

Further channelled communications said there was a need for Mari and me to visit many countries through that spring and summer to work with the Earth's energy system. These included Egypt, Italy, the United States, Canada, Germany, the Netherlands, Denmark, South America and many parts of the United Kingdom. Again, as I was to learn much later, this period of intense travelling coincided perfectly with astrological sequences in relation to my birth chart that suggested a time for long-distance travel. It was hectic and there was little time to think and assess.

There were so many 'coincidences' on these trips that allowed things to happen. If we arrived late at an airport there were always two seats left on the plane, and time after time we were told that something the messages said was impossible, only for it to happen. We were leaving the Inca ruins at Machu Picchu in Peru on one occasion and the only way out of that part of the Valley of the Incas is by train. The communications had said we should get the train that afternoon. When we arrived at the station we were told the train was fully booked and we had no chance of getting on. The train was a special for tourists and standing up was not allowed. At that very moment who should I see but the guide who was with me on my previous trip to Peru. He knew the railway officials and persuaded them to sell us some tickets. But instead of standing for the three-and-a-half-hour journey, we had the seats of two people who didn't turn up – and the seats were at the front of the train with a panoramic view through the front window!

The lowest point for me was that trip to South America. I didn't want to go, I didn't want to leave Linda and the family again, and my mind was in a turmoil. I went because I knew it was necessary, but they were the longest three weeks of my life apart from the time I spent away in Saudi Arabia. By late summer I had made contact again with Joan, who channelled information for *The Truth Vibrations*. She told me how she had wanted to contact us at the height of the publicity after the press conference, but her communications had asked her to stay out of it. She helped me to focus some of my thoughts on what had happened. She herself had been through an horrendous situation, similar in some ways to ours, earlier in her life. As she told me her story the parallels were remarkable.

Joan came to the Isle of Wight in the autumn to help to check the information in *Love Changes Everything*, which I compiled from information channelled by Mari over a period of three months, plus some other communications. When the book was complete Mari left to continue her life elsewhere and when she left, something left me also. Almost within hours of her departure I could feel my old self return in full. The brakes were back, the mist had cleared and the veil had lifted. I might have put this down to imagination, except that all my close friends were saying to Linda how nice it was to have 'the old David back'. Others said how I was even looking like my old self again. On reflection, that was the moment the experience came to an end for both myself and Linda and coping with the consequences of it were now to begin.

The change was timed perfectly to finish *Love Changes Everything*. The first draft was frankly awful, far too long and suffering from a total lack of balance. Mari's channelling was sometimes very accurate, but on other occasions it was far less so. Like all of us, channellers have good days and bad days and they can be influenced by their own emotions and wishes. I feel that some of the information was lost or added to as it passed through Mari and there were sections that described situations in the way she wanted them to be rather than the way they were communicated. This is not a criticism of Mari because this problem is not uncommon. I mention it rather as a cautionary note to all those who channel or receive information from channellers. It is so easy to allow personal wishes and emotions to get in the way of the true message, even unknowingly, and that will happen in most cases to some extent. All the best channellers know this and they always make it clear to those who hear the information they pass on. Neither should we underestimate the power of negative forces to disrupt and confuse, especially at the opening-up stage when people are most vulnerable to delusion and misunderstanding before they become spiritually 'streetwise'.

When Mari left I set about an immediate and massive rewrite, trying to eliminate as much as I could of the information I felt had been affected. The rewrite produced the final published version. Many sections are symbolic rather than literal, but that symbology triggers reactions deep within those who read the book, as I know from the letters I receive. Some of those who wrote the Bible also used much symbology, but these symbolic truths have been lost as religious dogma has chosen to take them as literal truths. Nor do I ever claim any book to be a hundred per cent accurate, because this is simply not possible with channelled information and it is important to remember that. *Love Changes Everything* contains a great many sparkling truths, but in some areas it also reveals the confusion of the opening-up stage that everyone goes through and must go through if they are to find the balance point and reconnect with the higher levels of the mind. I feel the writing of that book and the processing of the information was as much a learning experience for me than anything else. It was through that book and the turquoise months that I began to learn discernment, picking out the truth from the fantasy. It was also part of the fine tuning of the psychic 'antenna' which is vital today with so much information being channelled, much of it either some way off the mark or simply nonsense. We constantly need to analyse and question channelled information from whatever source until we find what we feel is the truth. Sometimes you can get it perfectly right as with the 'Diamonds in the Mud' channelling by Joan in *The Truth Vibrations*, but this is rare and it is best to look at the main themes that are constantly coming across while keeping an open mind on detail. The most important thing to remember about any channelled information is that there is *always* more to know. There is, I have no doubt, a great deal more to know about the life and times of the man we call Jesus before that whole period can be given a true perspective.

Also, human minds are programmed to individualise

everything and so many channellings tend to refer to energies and forces as 'beings' to help us understand the basic themes. Then, when we are ready, they stop talking of 'beings' and talk of energies and consciousness. I believe, for instance, that names like Lucifer and the Devil are symbolic names for the extreme collective negative energies that are encouraging humanity to act in negative ways. Some of these forces are misguided minds, others the negative energies we generate, and still others are the negative side of ourselves which we can either choose to control or allow to control us.

The symbology and channelled information is open to interpretation and anyone, like me, who tries to pass on these communications to the public is always putting their head on the block. But despite all these difficulties, which it is only right to point out, many of the channellings for *Love Changes Everything* and *The Truth Vibrations* are already proving remarkably accurate as I write these words.

After Mari left, Linda and I began to pick up the debris of the previous eight months. Kerry and Gareth had come through it remarkably intact and so had the bond between Linda and me. We had always tried to bring Kerry into everything we could so she was aware of what was going on and she had tremendous support from her friends. She managed to laugh at the ludicrous stories about her in the press. One article in a Sunday newspaper said she had left school early to become my 'disciple'. In fact she left at the earliest opportunity because she had always intended to. She simply didn't like school and never had. Nothing would have made her stay on and she began an excellent job in the dental profession. But that is not a good story to a tabloid newspaper and so yet another fantasy appeared on the printed page. Gareth, fortunately, despite being a sensitive lad, is a very confident, happy-go-lucky boy and this helped him come through the sometimes harsh ribbing from his school friends as they repeated the unthinking prejudice of their parents. It is this same process which perpetuates the prejudice, pain and division in places like Northern Ireland and the Middle East. Both Kerry and Gareth were followed to school and questioned by 'journalists'.

We began to live as the family we had always been and it was just wonderful. It was a time of rest and restoration. All I wanted to do was walk away from everything that had happened, live quietly away from the public gaze and help my children make their way in life. But even then I knew deep down that if I was given the opportunity to walk away I would turn it down. Linda and I would walk and talk, walk and talk, day after day, trying to make sense of everything, and we have ended up with a relationship even stronger than before if that is possible.

My mother and brothers Paul and Trevor were also subjected to the media and yet although they, like all of us at that time, did not have a clue what was happening to me, they stuck by me through everything. They were just superb and so were Linda's parents and brothers.

Only the love of and for my family kept me going and once again the game of football came to my rescue. Kerry began to play football for the Isle of Wight women's team and Gareth was becoming an outstanding young goalkeeper. He began to play for a local club and eventually the Isle of Wight at both youth and school levels. The time that Linda and I spent together seeing him play and practise gave us respite from the pressure. Also the people we met at the games and at one club in particular, Ryde Sports, gave us 'normal' conversation to balance out the one topic that dominated everything at home – i.e. 'What the hell was all this about and what were we supposed to do next?'

Of all the fairy stories about me in the press in 1991, the untruth that stood out most was the claim in a Sunday magazine article that I was a remote figure who did not care about my family. If anything has ever been written that is further from the truth I have never seen it. From the moment I walked into the room to meet that journalist I knew what he had come to do. He was sweating profusely, his hands were shaking and he just generated aggression and negative energies. I have rarely come across anyone who looked quite so on edge and uncomfortable. After two hours of asking a series of largely unrelated questions in an often confrontational style, he left to write pages and pages of the sort of extremely negative abuse he was always going to write. I know of another person he interviewed for the article who was also subjected to his aggression and his almost obsessional attitude that everything I said about the nature of Creation had to be wrong. Only he will know when his physical life is over if that is what he came to do or whether he made an unfortunate decision not to have an open mind to what he did not understand. Judy had a vision of him in a previous life as a churchman of high status who resisted with all his might a new understanding being passed on by me and others, probably during the Anthony Bacon incarnation. Karma was giving him the opportunity to react differently this time, I think.

It was not until the start of 1992 that I really began to appreciate what the previous year and the 'turquoise period' were all about. We are not told why we are going through certain situations until they are over because it would reduce the power of the experience. First of all the pressures of this period were part of the development of the lower self on its journey to the state of being and understanding necessary to complete the life plan in the years to come. When part of our mind incarnates and works through a physical form it has to lower its frequency, its vibration, to synchronise with this level. You could think of this process as being symbolically similar to the locks on a canal. On one side of the lock gate the water is high and this can represent our higher self, the subconscious and super-conscious levels of the mind, which do not incarnate. On the other side the water is low and this can be seen as the lower self, the conscious level, that part of the mind that incarnates and works through the physical brain. It is 'lower' in terms of its understanding because of all the limitations of the physical body and the imbalances of this planet, all of which results in a 'lower' vibration or frequency to that of the higher self. The experiences set out in my life plan are designed to increase the understanding of the lower self, to raise its level up the side of that symbolic lock gate so it reconnects with the higher self. As the lower is getting closer to the higher the full potential of the whole mind is increasingly able to manifest its eternal wisdom at the physical level. It is not so much a case of 'learning' through experience as 'remembering' through experience what the lower self already knows but has forgotten because of the limitations of the physical world. If the life plan unfolds as it is pre-programmed to, then the moment will arrive when both the higher and lower will be totally in sync. At that point the lock gate can open and the higher and lower levels will be as one working on this physical level. And if the lower self can synchronise with its even higher level – the 'True Self' – wow! Goodness knows what will be possible then. That's the plan and all those horrendous experiences in the 'turquoise period' were part of that and much else besides.

One reason for that experience was the need to overcome any fear of what people might say about me and to trigger the full potential of the will. This will be vital preparation for the future when the opposition will turn from ridicule to condemnation as the system in general sees that the information I am passing on is having the desired effect – i.e. making people think and question what we are all urged to believe and accept as conventional 'wisdom'.

After that desperate year I have no fear of ridicule or of anything people might throw in my direction and I have true freedom. That is a state of being in which you do not care what people say about you, do about you, or think about you, as long as you can justify your actions to yourself. Most people in this world do not make decisions based on what they think is right or on what they wish to do, they make them on the basis of what others – the neighbours or the people at work – will find acceptable. I am free of that imprisonment of thought and action and I recommend it. Anyone who has ever said anything worth hearing has been first ridiculed, then condemned and later acknowledged as an expander of human understanding, often long after their physical life was over. Ridicule and condemnation have always been the precursor of accepted wisdom and we all have to go through this if we wish to take human knowledge forward.

The ridicule also taught me so much about those who were doing the laughing. I could see that the way we react to others is a mighty statement about ourselves. People would do well to try to acknowledge the imbalance within them that derives pleasure from laughing at others and seeing them ridiculed. Often it is a defence mechanism to shut off areas that we don't wish to think about or, in many cases I feel, indicates a deep desire not to think at all. That was certainly the case with most people who laughed at me. They would rather get their views from a tabloid newspaper than seek their own truth and think for themselves. How we treat others is the outward manifestation of what we think of ourselves. If we don't have respect for others, it reveals a lack of respect for ourselves and in the same way some of the most outwardly violent and aggressive people I have met have been people who, deep inside, really hate themselves.

The second reason for the 'turquoise period' was that the experience showed me clearly how we are guided in and out of less than pleasant situations that we would normally see coming and avoid. If we are open to this guidance the 'brakes' can be removed from the decision-making process for long enough for us to walk into the situation. Then the brakes return and our eyes open. How many times have we said about people we know: 'Why can't they see what they are doing, why can't they see where that will lead?' And yet how many times have we got ourselves into difficult situations and said: 'How did I get into this – why didn't I see this coming?' We feel terribly guilty at these times, especially if others have been involved, but much of the time we were not meant to see things coming. We were meant to experience the aftermath, the consequences. The subconscious level sets up the experience and the conscious level learns from the experience. This is just one reason why we should stop judging each other. We don't know why people behave in certain ways, so how can we judge them?

My amazing behaviour at this time also relates to simple necessity. The people who are here in the vanguard of minds to help to trigger the transformation have been pre-programmed to open up at certain times. This was the time chosen for me. If I had been 'activated' earlier in my life I would never have gone into journalism and television because I would have rejected both as a career from the perspective I have now. I would have wanted to take a spiritual and environmental direction immediately. But I needed those experiences both to develop the communication skills I would need and to give me the public face that would create a platform of publicity when I donned the turquoise shellsuit. That meant that when I was activated it had to be very quick and overwhelming so I would go in a matter of weeks from television face and politician to a 'Son of the Godhead'. I did not have the luxury of a long and gradual preparation period that many others enjoy. My higher consciousness and those working through me just opened the top of my head, the crown chakra, and poured in these unbelievable energies. For many weeks I was staggering about like some spiritual drunk, hardly knowing what planet I was on! This was used to show people very publicly how these energies affect you until you have balanced and integrated them within yourself. Again this was done to help people through their own transition. I know from the thousands of letters that began to arrive after I went public so dramatically that a great many find comfort and understanding from seeing what happened to me and how I came through it. When strange things happen to them, they can now look at my experience and understand theirs better.

What happened to me in the spring of 1991 was a little like

pouring water, or in this case energy, into a bowl of calm, still water. The more you turn on the tap the more the calmness and balance is disturbed. When the tap is on full the water in the bowl is thrashing about in total turmoil, chaos and confusion, until the tap is turned off and the calmness returns at what is, by now, a much higher level. That is what happened to me at this time and the key moments were that sleep in Mari's apartment and when that energy poured into me on the mound in Peru. But the chaos and confusion which followed until the new balance was found was used by those on other levels working for the transformation of the Earth in ways that would only become clear later. It was all part of the plan.

One way it was used was to attract enormous ridicule to me, for reasons I will explain in the next chapter, and enormous publicity. It was the means by which this whole subject could be blasted through the wall of suppression and on to the centre stage of public attention. Most, though not all, of the information I have passed on since the start of the decade has been available in specialist bookshops and in ancient folklore for a very long time, but it could not get into the main public arena.

We are constantly given the church view of life and Creation and that of 'science', but trying to get even a mention in the mainstream media of the sort of things I and millions of others are saying was impossible. The media constantly complains about 'censorship' when the greatest censor of information is the media itself. They were simply not interested in looking at this from a serious point of view, which was the way I would have chosen to bring this to public attention given a choice. So sometimes you have to act in an outrageous fashion, in a way that cannot be ignored, to get through the suppression and deliver the information in a high-profile way. Once that information is in the public arena, whatever the initial reaction, it will grow. It is like planting a seed.

The media played a vital role in this during 1991 without

realising it. They thought they were simply crushing yet another victim when, in fact, they were helping to promote the operation that will eventually remove the system of which they are part! As long as what I said attracted massive publicity and carried the basic themes, then the job was done. The information was out there, the genie was out of the bottle, and the other levels had orchestrated a massive publicity stunt that would lead to so many opportunities to pass on the spiritual truths later in a more conventional manner. It was an excellent way around the suppression of information relating not only to the Earth changes, but also to the true nature of life and Creation.

This suppression is one way the system controls humanity. It seeks to hold back the rising tide of true understanding by letting us hear what it finds acceptable and not hear what it does not. The church is no threat to the system and what passes for science is a vital part of the system, so both are given a free rein. But the attitudes encompassed by the thinking I am passing on challenge the very foundations of the system's control of human minds and will bring an end to that control. For this reason the information is either suppressed, doctored before it reaches the public, ridiculed, or condemned as 'dangerous'. If you are seeking to control people, it is easy to see why what I and so many others are saying is considered dangerous. Ladies and gentlemen of the world, you are being conned. You are being allowed to hear only what is acceptable to the system and all the vested interest groups and not allowed to hear, as much as possible, what is not acceptable to them. One increasingly disturbing dimension to this is the number of television channels and media organisations being created and taken over by the religious right who make fortunes peddling fear, guilt, and mind-controlling fundamentalism.

Because of this suppression, millions of people are frightened of their 'strange' experiences and question their sanity when really they can be explained very easily as a natural and desirable part of life. People are mutilated through surgery and devastated by drugs when gentle, more effective, methods of healing are often available. They are frightened of death when death in terms of the mind does not exist. They are frightened to tell even their closest relatives what they think and experience because they fear what the reaction might be. This is just what the system wants because it controls through fear ... fear of ridicule, of condemnation, of poverty, of unemployment, of being 'different' in any way to the standard issue, off-the-peg 'norm'.

Behaving in the way I did broke through the suppression because it simply could not be ignored. Coming out in the way I did, wearing my turquoise shellsuit and saying what I did, led the establishment into a false sense of security. They didn't condemn what I said or seek to stop me initially because the last thing this apparent lunatic appeared to be was a danger to anything or anyone except himself. He would surely disappear and end up in a mental home in the not too distant future. Poor old Ickey! He had always seemed so sane and sensible before, now he had gone completely around the twist.

I was a comedian's dream. Jasper Carrott did a piece about me. 'Well, one thing's for sure,' he said at one point. 'He won't find three wise men and a virgin in Leicester!' I was even mentioned at the Royal Variety Performance at the London Palladium when presenter David Frost announced that I was to star in a remake of the film *Postcards from the Edge*! It all added to the profile, the interest and the curiosity so necessary for the next stage.

The most important three words in terms of publicity and profile were 'Son of God'. I said I was *a* Son of the Godhead and this was immediately repeated in the media as *the* Son of the Godhead. What I said was true. We are all expressions of the energy that is everything, what I call the Infinite Mind, and what others individualise under the term God. Therefore, if you want to use symbolic language, we are all Sons and Daughters of God, all part of the Infinite Mind of Creation. But because society programmes people, even those who don't believe in religion, to think the words 'Son of God' mean the biblical version of Jesus, the media predictably linked me to that whole concept of 'messiahs' and the 'second coming'. The result was someone who was fundamentally challenging religion and the Bible view of Creation being dubbed in the media as someone who had discovered religion and was promoting the Bible! You could only laugh at such blinkered, unthinking nonsense. It didn't matter in the short term, though. As much publicity as possible and the themes of human and planetary change were all that mattered at this point.

By the start of 1992 we were into stage two. The turquoise had gone and I began to speak at universities around the country. It was time to use the interest created by the 'Son of God' publicity to get over what I am really saying. If I had only written a book the interest would have long disappeared. Far from attracting large audiences, I would not even have been invited to speak. When over seven hundred people turned up on a cold Thursday night in Bangor, North Wales, at my first engagement I realised just how vital the events of the previous year had been to all this. Granted, they were attracted there by sheer curiosity or because they thought they would be in for a great laugh. It didn't matter, they came, they listened in silence and respect once they realised what I was really saying, and it made so many of them think and question. The same thing happened all over the country. It was so different from what they expected to hear. I remember when I turned up at Bangor I was told not to worry because anyone throwing beer glasses at the stage would be ejected! No glasses were thrown, but many seeds were sown.

The quality of the questioning in a few areas of the media also began to improve a little. The 'Icke's a loony' angle was getting tired, blown out by uninspired repetition by both the media and 'comedians'. At last the opportunity to make serious points was growing, albeit slowly. Increasingly I was also able to explode the myth that I had 'discovered' religion and become a sort of religious 'freak'. What I was saying had nothing to do with religion. Indeed religion is part of the problem, not part of the solution.

The very fact that I was still around, still unbowed by all that had been thrown at me, added to people's interest and curiosity. It is a sad reflection on the world communications industry that you have to act in ways you would like to avoid to get a message across, but unfortunately it is true. One man wrote to me saying that he was frustrated that I was getting all this publicity when he had been saying the same thing in a conventional way for many years and could not get anyone to give him air time. What he needed to understand was that we have to react to things as they are, not as we would like them to be. One communication said very early on that the system would be used to bring down the system. The communications network had been used to spread the religion of take, make and throw away around the world, and that same network would be used to spread the truth that would help to end that whole self-destructive way of life.

You can see parallels with the way John Lennon made his protest against war by having a 'sleep-in for peace' with Yoko Ono in a hotel bedroom. There they were dressed in long white gowns, John with his bushy beard, and the media came to take the micky. 'Lennon's cracked,' they said. 'He's gone crazy.' But his message went around the world as a result and by the time he was killed years later there were few who thought he was anything less than totally sane. Dangerous, yes, from the system's viewpoint, but certainly not crazy. What I did in 1991 will be seen from the same perspective; in fact it already is among those with an open mind.

Not that all the 'potty prophet' and 'mad messiah' stories disappeared, nor that journalists stopped coming along being nice to your face, saying how much they are interested in what you say, only to go away and write the usual boring, tedious, predictable accounts of their meeting with the loony

'Son of God'. One incident sums up the way the media work. I did a radio interview about that astonishing year and at no time did I say or indicate that I was mad or had ever been mad. The following day, however, the London evening newspaper ran a report of the interview saying just that. The national tabloids saw that report and repeated it the following morning. The broadcast media then picked it up from the tabloids and forty-eight hours after the initial interview in which I had not said I was mad, I turned on the local television news to see a picture of myself on the screen and the newsreader informing the viewers that I had admitted I had been through a period of madness! 'It must be true that you said it,' people told me, 'because it was in all the papers. They can't all be wrong.' Oh yes, they can, particularly when they are all repeating the same single, untrue source, and this is how untruths become accepted as fact day after day all over the world. Letters began to arrive telling me I wasn't mad and saying how distressed people were that I was retracting all that I had said about what was happening. I wasn't. If people don't believe anything at the extreme end of the media, they will be much nearer the truth! Even my old paper, the *Leicester Mercury*, spurned every opportunity to give me fair hearing and report accurately what I was saying.

Another outstanding example of how the media is a vehicle for disinformation, and therefore mind control, was a report sent out to the British media by the national news agency, the Press Association. I made a speech in which I listed a long series of ridiculous situations and ways of working in the world today and said if that is what passes for sanity, then thank God I was a loony because I didn't want to be that sane. On my way home from the speech, I heard the news on the radio which announced that David Icke had said: 'Thank God I'm a loony because I don't want to be sane.' That was it. None of the rest of the speech reported, no effort to put anything into context, just basically David Icke has admitted he's crazy and says he doesn't want to be sane. One reason why the media and many others were so desperate to write me off as a loony was fear. If they accepted that I could possibly be right in what I was saying, it would mean taking a whole new look at themselves, their work and the world around them. It was much easier just to hang a 'closed' sign on their mind and dismiss me with a laugh.

The communications industry is one of this planet's biggest tragedies because it could make such a positive and key contribution to her survival. Instead, large areas of it are in a perpetual state of fear. Journalists fear – some to the point of terror – their editor, that god they must worship back at base. The editor fears the proprietor, who in turn fears the financial institutions and the stock market who must be kept sweet if this whole cycle of fear is going to survive. It is a tragedy for the media, their victims and, crucially, for the truth.

What I say about the media both here and later is not meant as a condemnation of those journalists as individuals. If that had been my intention I would have named them all. They are as much slaves and victims of the system they serve as anyone else, more so in fact, and we should not underestimate the number of journalists trying to do the right thing within the strict limitations of thought and action their system-serving industry imposes upon them. I have highlighted the way the communications industry works to make the wider and far more important point of how humanity is constantly mind-controlled by the media. If you want to control the way someone thinks and behaves then the most effective way of doing that is to control the information they have access to. Make sure it's only the information you want them to have and invariably they will think and act the way you want them to. Tell them Icke's a loony, for example, and deny them any information that points the other way, and you will persuade large numbers of people that Icke's a loony. This process is happening day after day in relation to endless people and events. If the public only realised how much the disinformation of the media is controlling the way they perceive people and events they would be outraged. Most of the print and broadcast media should carry a health warning: 'Danger – not to be taken seriously.'

But something I began to realise was that the words I speak or write are only part of the story. The most important effect upon people comes from energies that are being generated through me and many others. Indeed the written and spoken words are also generating an energy and it is at this level that the biggest changes take place. It is these energies which stir and awaken the lower self's sleeping memory of the true nature of life and what it is doing here. This memory, once awakened, continues to expand until it manifests on the conscious level. Sleeping within everyone is all the knowledge we require at this time. We know all we need to know about this physical life. We know that reincarnation is a fact and the basic nature of the transform-ation humanity and the planet is now going through. We chose to come to experience it. Getting that knowledge to the conscious level is the problem, especially on this troubled and imbalanced frequency.

Most of what I and others are doing is kick-starting this memory. With some people this can bring the knowledge to the conscious level in some form almost immediately and with others it can take a long time, but once the eternal memory is awakened it will make its presence felt in some way. I had letters a year after the 'turquoise period' from people who said they thought initially I was completely bonkers, but there was something about what I said that they simply could not let go. Over the months, they said, the feeling just grew and grew that there was some truth in it. Now they just knew that the basis of it was correct, but they could not explain why. This was the process of awakening the eternal memory. It is done on two fronts. The actual words work on the conscious level while the energies being generated through the communicator work on the deeper levels where the eternal memory sleeps. These energies can be generated through media interviews into the rooms where people watch their televisions or listen to the radio, and they can be generated through books like this one. People are being affected and triggered all the time without them realising it, even if, on the conscious level, they are laughing at what they see and hear. This is what was meant by the Magnu message: 'He is a solidifier of thought and helps the Word to surface with those he meets.' I am not telling people anything they don't know already, I am helping them to remember. As another Magnu communication said:

> I am not looking to a time when this knowledge will be for a few, but when your whole planet will be awakened to this understanding which you have simply forgotten. It is not a matter of new information, it is a matter of remembering who you are and where you come from.

It doesn't matter how people perceive me and others like me initially because the most important interaction is taking place between our energy fields. While I am speaking the words or people are reading the books, the real awakening is being triggered on the deeper unconscious levels by the transfer of energies. The conscious level is almost like a battle ground between the information coming from the higher self and the information coming in all the time through the eyes and the ears from the system. It is a question of whether we allow our actions and responses to be guided by the eternal wisdom of the higher levels of the mind or by the programming we receive from the world around us. Anything that can re-link people with their eternal knowledge and remove blockages to their higher mind can have an enormous effect on the way they see life. This energy being generated through me and others is helping to do that, whatever the reaction of people on the conscious level.

I knew none of this at the time as I was transformed overnight from being a respected television presenter and Green campaigner to a figure of fun of quite monumental proportions. Living it without understanding it was crucial to the experience I needed to go through as part of the journey of awakening. But then, just as we were starting the painful process of coming to terms with all that I have described and much more, the next stage in the story was about to be thrust upon us. How much more could anyone take? It was like drowning in a turbulent sea of pain and emotion, but somehow I was determined to swim.

11

The Scapegoat

Throughout more than two decades together I have always believed that the bond between Linda and myself could survive anything. Now I know it to be true. Several psychics and astrologers have said that exceptionally strong energies are linking us together, and they needed to be for our unit to stay intact in the face of the mental and emotional onslaught that faced us in 1991 and 1992. But then, of course, this unit was not put together by accident. It was all planned before incarnation in the knowledge of what it would have to survive.

I must take you back to that moment when I awoke from the deep, deep sleep on the floor in Mari Shawsun's apartment on the last evening of my second visit to Canada. I said that when I opened my eyes the world looked very different and so it did – in every way. It was like being hypnotised. I thought no more of it and I left a few hours later for the long trip to Peru. While I was there after that incredible event on the mound I started taking automatic writing and time and again I was being told that I had to have a physical relationship with Mari. It was part of the plan and it was very necessary, indeed vital that this happen. The writing said that it was something to do with the effect on energies.

'What?' I remember saying as I looked at the page. 'You must be bloody joking! I have heard some excuses for it, but affecting energies is the best yet. Where is this coming from?' But the writing kept on flowing. 'You will not understand the significance of what we are asking you to do for some time, but believe us it is necessary.'

'No.'

So it continued until I received a communication which said: 'David, it has already happened on the etheric, so you had better get used to it.'

As I explained at the start of the book, everything has an etheric energy field, a non-physical version of a physical body or object. The etheric energy field is the template and the organiser. Everything that happens on the physical level is the result of what has happened in the etheric field. A frequency as a whole also has an etheric level on which events first take place before they eventually manifest on the physical level. Once something has happened on the etheric, it will happen on the physical at some point because the decisions have been made at that higher level and the physical body must respond to that. I felt after receiving that automatic writing that the decision had been made at a much higher level of my being, leaving this conscious level in some emotional turmoil. I felt guilty about Linda and yet I felt guilty about not doing what was necessary, if that indeed were the case. On the one hand the guilt over Linda was obvious, and you can imagine from what I have said throughout this book how terrible I was feeling at the thought of her feelings. But the communications had constantly urged me and others to 'see the wider picture'. I felt guilty, too, at refusing to do what was apparently necessary for the greater good, not that I understood at that time how the greater good could possibly benefit from what I was being asked to do.

I decided to wait and see what happened. I discussed the communications with Mari and after considerable deliberation, it happened on my third visit to Canada. Mari received similar messages. There were certainly massive energy changes within me in the days and weeks that followed. There was one amazing incident when I looked at Mari and her face kept changing to someone else and then back again, and she saw the same happen to me.

Throughout this period I was sort of floating around in some kind of spiritual mist with my feet some way from the ground. The word 'hypnotised' keeps coming back to me. I have talked about the brakes being suspended and some force taking over, a process that began with that deep sleep. It was now that this gathered pace and the earthly personality we call David Icke went on holiday somewhere else in the great unknown. The turquoise press conference came about three weeks later. I still didn't understand what on Earth was happening to me. The confusion was total.

Talking to Linda about the situation was just agony for me and her; I really can't tell you how much. Nothing I ever do in this life could ever be so painful. I put off the moment as long as I could, although she is a highly intelligent woman and knew all along really. You don't have a relationship as close as ours and not know these things. One of the reasons I put it off, apart from the pain I knew it would bring, was the hope that I would get at least a reasonable idea of what this was all about.

In the end, the press forced the issue in precisely the way I always knew they would. Linda stayed with it for many reasons; the magnetism, harmony and pre-programming of our energy fields; her love for me and the love she never once doubted I had for her; and the knowledge that whatever the rights and wrongs of what had happened eventually turned out to be, my motivations were a wish to do whatever was necessary for the good of all. As I often said, I would walk naked down Oxford Street if I knew it would help this planet to survive. Linda also knew that at least the basis of what we were being told about the Earth was correct. She has never had a problem with that and, looking back, she knows that part of her consciousness was suspended through that period also. The Linda Icke before would never have stood for what happened or was to happen. It was against all she believed in.

I felt sorry for Mari too. Here she was stuck in a spare room-cum-office at our home with her life in limbo. It was very difficult for her and I felt terribly guilty about the situation she was in. Unfortunately, a side to Mari began to emerge once she arrived in England that was to turn a very difficult situation into a nightmare. She was to appear, to my conscious level, as the most unpleasant and destructive person I had ever met. Even going for a walk alone with Linda could bring tears or enormous rage from Mari when we returned. I did not intend to mention any of this when I wrote this book and I have no wish to do so now. I wanted to say nothing in public because what happened was a learning experience for everyone concerned and should have been quietly accepted as that, I feel. But for reasons that will become obvious shortly, some misrepresentations need to be corrected. Linda and many others began to feel that Mari was trying to force Linda out through various means. I didn't see that in the beginning, not least because the very thought of life without Linda never even entered my head. Now, as you will have seen from my life so far, the earthly personality called David Icke a few chapters back would never have stood for this and Mari would have been asked to leave. But instead I talked with Linda and we agreed that people had a right to have the information the book *Love Changes Everything* would make available, and that the book was meant to be channelled by Mari. We would, therefore, put up with the situation until the book was completed and then many decisions would have to be made by all parties about the future. This was the period symbolised by the turbulent water in the vision seen by the psychic many months earlier, a period of enormous confusion, turmoil and pain on all sides, Mari's included.

The more it became clear to Mari that the bond between Linda and me was not to be broken, the more angry she became and life became increasingly difficult. At the same time Mari was channelling information about unconditional love for the book. There would seem to be a contradiction here, but there is not. Channellers are vehicles for others to speak through them, they are not the source of the information. I know that some people think all channellers must be very wise people, the fountain of knowledge, but it is important to understand this is not necessarily the case. Just as some people come into incarnation to be footballers or musicians, so others come into incarnation with a particular gift to channel if that is in their life plan. It doesn't mean they might not have great karmic imbalances that they have come to remove in the course of their work and life. Everyone has.

By the time of the trip to South America, it had reached such a pitch that the mere mention of my family was sometimes enough to move Mari either to tears or incredible rage. Yet, at other times, she could be the most delightful person and great company. You never knew from one minute to the next. As spring became summer and the brakes were slowly returning, I decided that the situation must end. 'I don't care whether it's necessary or not, it's over. No more,' I remember shouting at the sky one day in frustration at what was happening to my life and those around me, Mari among them.

It was like waking up from a dream and finding it was a nightmare come true. How my family held together I will never know. Mari always said that Linda was a weak person. Mari, like most of humanity, mistakes strength for the loudest voice or the most dominant personality. That is not strength, it is often a cover for weakness. Linda personifies strength and only someone with immense inner reserves could have coped with what had happened and with what was to come.

When Joan arrived to help us to check *Love Changes Everything,* she told me of many communications she had been receiving about the situation. They said it was time for Mari to leave as soon as possible. I had taken some automatic writing a week before saying Mari's time with us was rapidly coming to an end and she would be invited to travel abroad alone to Canada. I had said nothing to anyone at the time, but then Joan received the same information and Mari accepted it and flew off to Canada and the United States. It was like turning the release valve on a pressure cooker, bursting a balloon of pent-up emotion that had been getting bigger and bigger with every day. Life became so much more peaceful. Then, after several weeks of trying to work it all out and find some kind of meaning for what had happened in the past year, we had a phone call from Mari late one night from Canada. 'I'm eight months pregnant,' she said. 'And it's your child. I am coming back tomorrow and I am going to tell the world.'

Well, imagine the scene. You are sitting watching the television with Linda and Kerry one minute and the next you are faced with that. Mari, for some reason I couldn't understand, told the newspapers several months later that I knew she was having a child from the start. Anyone who saw my face after that phone call as Linda and Kerry did would laugh at the very suggestion. Obviously we were all in a state of considerable shock. But why, you might rightly ask, was it such a shock? Surely we could see what the situation was before Mari left, when she would have been around seven months pregnant? First of all that's not necessarily so even in normal circumstances, because some women give birth to children without even knowing they are pregnant, and second don't kid yourself for one minute that it is not possible to switch off so you can't see even the obvious. That happens all the time so that either karmic situations are set up for the lower self to experience or to ensure that what needs to be done for the good of Earth is done. If I were reading this as you are, I would find it ridiculous that anyone would not realise the situation, but the power of the sub-conscious over the conscious is far, far greater than people imagine. Just look at what hypnotists can make people do and yet when they wake up they can remember nothing about it. The suspension of the brakes is a similar, but much more complex principle. Paul Vaughan came for a weekend not long before Mari left and had no idea she was pregnant; the same with Joan and others. Linda had her own thoughts, but kept them to herself, hoping that she was wrong. No doubt others on the edge of the situation also had their opinions.

It was only when the channelling for *Love Changes Everything* had finished and I had completed the rewrite that everything began to move rapidly. As the song says: 'There is a time to every purpose under heaven.' The timing of everything in this whole story has been impeccable all along the way to allow everything to happen in the correct sequence. As I keep saying, when things are meant to be, everything falls into place quickly and easily because it's all pre-planned.

Obviously it would have been difficult for Mari to return to our home because there was no room for what was to happen and the emotional consequences for Linda would have been too much to bear. But if an alternative had not been found, Linda had already said that Mari would have the baby here. Early the next morning I went to see the two healers who had become very close to Mari. They were magnificent. They said she should go there to have the child and they would go to the airport to pick her up. They did not want me to be involved because they didn't want to be besieged by the press. What's more, one of them had recently learned the art of natural childbirth, which is just the way Mari wished the baby to be born. They also persuaded her that perhaps announcing it to the world and having the press camped outside would be rather less than sensible.

Mari said the child was mine and I accepted that without a second thought, although whenever I was ready to say so publicly something happened to stop me or the words simply would not come out. It was most strange. Later, on the advice of many people and for my own personal reasons, I ensured that everything was genetically confirmed so there could be no doubt in anyone's mind. I wrote to Mari offering to bring up the child with Linda if she wished. She said that she wanted to start a new life with the baby and wanted me to have no access. It was an extremely painful decision for me to make, but I agreed because what was needed now was a period of quiet contemplation by everyone and what was best for the child. Many times in our lives we are all faced with situations in which it is impossible to do what is a hundred per cent right for everyone. This was one such occasion. All you can do is what you think is best overall, taking everyone into consideration. None of this ever appeared in the 'Icke abandons baby' stories that Mari was to tell to a newspaper. Rebecca was born on 14 December 1991, at the healers' home. I made a decision not to see her because I felt it would increase the pain of not being able to see her in the future. But one night I had a tearful phone call from Mari asking me to go over and see Rebecca. I did and she was a gorgeous child. When I asked to see her again soon after that, Mari strongly objected and I was not to see Rebecca again until she appeared in a double-page spread in a Sunday newspaper. Mari stayed with the healers for some months. In the end, however, she was taking control of their lives. She left and eventually bought a house on the English mainland.

Now before people start accusing me of putting Mari in a bad light, let me repeat a major theme of this book. We don't know why people act towards us in certain ways. It could be free will, but it could just as easily be part of what we had wanted to experience either for personal or collective reasons. My father's treatment of me is a case in point. I didn't like it, but it was essential to what I needed to experience. I ask you to look at everyone, Mari included, from this perspective. I am setting out what happened from where I was standing, not judging or condemning. How could I without knowing the background? And what right have I or anyone else to judge another, anyway? The same applies for what follows.

I have said many times that the way we see events and people around us can be so different from the way we see them when we are not in a physical body. This is relevant in terms of Linda. When the other levels are communicating information to psychics they often do it by manifesting a symbolic vision of a scene we can relate to and understand from our physical perspective. Judy Hall was given a psychic picture of a large number of people sitting around a table before the present incarnation. Among them were myself, Linda and Mari:

> What I find interesting about what I am seeing of that meeting is the amount of input that Linda is putting in. She is much more active than I've seen her, much more confident of being able to handle what is to come, knowing her own strength. She has got much more than she recognises now and that is always available. It's really going to develop quite soon, I think. She really is commanding and impressive in her contribution to the meeting, not overpowering or anything, but just so competent and sure of what is happening ... As for Mari, I think that this act of creation was something that for her, at the time of this symbolic meeting, was very 'iffy'. There's something very karmic in her chart about motherhood. It's something that a very deep part of her wanted, but another part of her didn't want anything to do with. And so I feel that it was built into the plan that it may or may not be her who was the vessel for this child to come through.

Meanwhile, back on this level and without knowing any of the background, Linda and I tried again to work out why so much had happened to blitz the lives of so many people. Less than a year before we had been a family doing all the things that families do. Now, a matter of months later, all this had happened. We were blown away totally and utterly, but we were going to stand up and come through this no matter what. There had to be a good reason why everyone was going through such great pain and confusion. I was damned if I could think of it, but I was sure we would find out eventually.

My first reaction when I had the phone call from Canada was that everything must be kept quiet to avoid all the pain that would ensue. And what effect would this have on the truth I was trying to pass on? But after that initial shock, I thought, 'Hold on a minute, this *is* the truth', and I began to understand more about the workings of Creation with regard to all of these things. I felt it was right that if it would help others to understand events in their own lives then I should write about it all in this book which I was beginning to put together. But under no circumstances would I do that without Mari's agreement because of the implications for her. She said that she did not want anything written on the subject whatsoever. I accepted that, but I just knew that it was irrelevant anyway. For some reason I knew all this was going to be played out in public and that it would happen in time to be included in this book.

For five months after Rebecca was born not a word appeared in the press and yet throughout this period I only had to cough in public to get in one newspaper or another. Even me playing for the dads against an under-tens football team was considered 'news'. But here was Mari going about the Isle of Wight and the mainland quite openly with Rebecca and the press knew nothing. I had to laugh when I later read stories about Rebecca being 'secret'. The press might ask themselves how this could be. The answer is that the time had not come for this to be revealed and so it wasn't.

Then Linda found that she was having a child. She was nearly forty-two and we thought our days of producing children were over. News of this reached the press very quickly and one morning a Sunday newspaper reporter, who had become obsessed with us over many months, arrived to ask questions about Linda's pregnancy. We could not think what interest this could possibly be when there was so much the public needed to know about all around the world, and we would not speak to him. He should hardly be surprised when he stops a woman in the street and asks, 'Was it planned or was it an accident?'

The press coverage was typical of the cliché-ridden, black and white world in which most of the media permanently lives. It did not matter to that end of the industry in which thinking is considered a distinct disadvantage that I had already written two books challenging religion and the Bible's view of history, and that both books said the idea that Jesus was born on the Christian Christmas Day was a myth. In this barely one-dimensional world, if you are talking about spirituality and life after physical death, then you must be talking about religion and religion = the Bible = Jesus = Christmas. Therefore it was considered highly significant that the 'Son of God's' child was due to be born in December. If I had announced that the baby was due on 25 December as opposed to 2 December it would have been the final orgasmic experience for them, I guess. In fact some of them, I understand, even invented quotes from us saying that we hoped the child would be born on 25 December. I feel for such people because their cocoon is about to be shattered by events as a whole new world they have constantly suppressed for themselves and others comes bursting through. What is significant about December or any other month are the planetary sequences and how they relate to the life plan of the incoming mind. But to talk about that you need to break free from the cliché and the obvious and this means thinking and inviting your readers to think. That is not considered good for business.

Once the news of Linda's pregnancy became public knowledge, she was convinced that the other story would break and she was right. Linda can read Mari like an open book and she felt that she would talk to the papers eventually. Astrological readings of their birth charts have picked out Linda's ability to see right into Mari's heart and mind after many incarnations together. Unknown to us around this time Mari was telling the story to a Sunday newspaper.

Both Linda and Kerry said the story would break while we were abroad in Crete. The British papers arrive in Crete a day late and on the first Monday of our stay I walked across to the news kiosk. I don't normally buy papers, but again it was like I was hypnotised and drawn to the display of newspapers. I just knew what I would find. I can't tell you why, but I knew. There it was shouting at me from the front page of the Sunday paper. My first reaction was to think of how my mother and Linda's parents would feel, but almost immediately this great surge of relief burst through me. 'Thank goodness, now we can get this whole thing out in the open,' I thought.

The story had many inaccuracies with the 'Kerry left school to be his disciple' nonsense repeated. Mari was quoted to indicate that basically I had abandoned her and Rebecca which people like the healers, who knew the truth and the background, found staggering. It also said our friends had deserted us because of what had happened since 1991 and yet we had more friends than ever before and that number is growing all the time. Then there was the line that sums up this kind of newspaper. Whenever you see an unnamed 'friend' quoted it is often not a friend at all, but the reporter putting the slant on the story that he or she wants. The line was something like: 'A friend said, "It comes to something when a man has to invent a whole new religion in order to get a blonde into bed."'

Now you have read the whole story since that first visit to a psychic. You may have many differing opinions on what has happened since, but to say that I went through all of that, gave up everything, stood up in the way I did to make myself open to enormous ridicule and all the rest, just to get a blonde into bed, is absolutely beyond belief. But, you see, such papers have to explain it away in such ludicrous terms because to do anything else would require them to break out of their mental cocoon and actually think and open their eyes. That, however, takes vision and courage and both are in short supply not only in the tabloids, but also in the broadcast media and in the so-called 'quality' press. The 'quality' papers are just as blinkered as the tabloids in their own way. They simply come to the same basic conclusion using bigger words and longer sentences. They are all mind-controlled by the system to play their essential part in mind-controlling everyone else.

But let us not forget that the papers do not work in isolation from society. They help to create that society to some extent but they also reflect it or at least the part of it they are aimed at. If they didn't they would not sell in such numbers every day. They merely reflect the prejudices against women, homosexuals, foreigners and anyone who is remotely 'different from the norm', that pervades the whole of society. Yes, they treat their readers like morons, but then the readers are giving them permission to do so every time they buy such a paper.

The tabloid press is a wonderful barometer of the society in which we live. But while it exists and holds the attention of so many people, the other levels will continue to use them to play out karma and promote interest in the message, bizarre as this process has to be sometimes. As so many communications have said: 'We are going to use the system to bring down the system', and the media is the face, the propaganda machine, of that system.

But we should not allow the behaviour of some journalists to colour our view of everyone in the media. They are not all assassins of the truth. There are many trying to do the right thing, but they are restricted in what they can do by the limitations imposed upon them by the collective closed mind which controls most of the communications industry.

After the Sunday paper article, other journalists started looking for us and some eventually found out that we were in Crete. We spent many evenings at the Panorama Taverna at Kalo Horio just along the coast from Agios Nikolaos. It has a glorious view across the bay. We became very friendly with the owners, George and Andreas, and they produced a cake for Linda's forty-second birthday. A few minutes after we left that night, some journalists arrived there from

Britain. Over the next few days circumstances prevented us going back to the Panorama and when we did go again we were told the journalists had been waiting for us virtually all day and night, but they had given up the previous evening and gone home.

George and Andreas were having their first experience of the press and they could not believe it. 'They mad,' George announced. 'They come in the big car and they ask me if you drunk, if you argue, if you happy, if you make lots of noise, if you eat the sticky cakes, how much you tip, and they offer me hundreds of pounds to take picture of your birthday cake. I no understand these people!' He had us in hysterics. Hundreds of pounds to take a picture of a half-eaten birthday cake and to their enormous credit George and Andreas turned it down. We were followed by a reporter-photographer from the Sunday paper which had carried Mari's story and the following week Paul Vaughan sent a fax to the hotel to tell us that another big spread about us had appeared in the paper. Linda rang Kerry who had stayed at home because of her job.

'Mum, you'll never guess what Mari's said in the paper,' Kerry told her. 'I have never read such a load of rubbish in my life. She's had a right go at Dad.'

My goodness, she had too, but then as someone close to Mari had told Linda some months before: 'Tell David to keep well away – she only wants to hurt him.' Another Sunday newspaper sent us a fax which included the article. Linda sat reading it, shaking her head and smiling, sometimes laughing out loud, at the fantasy she was reading. It was full of so many amazing untruths and misrepresentations you had to pinch yourself to believe you were reading it. Mari had told so many people so many different stories that they must have been terribly confused by now. She told the paper that I knew about the baby all along and we had kept it from Linda. Yet she had told the healers that Linda had agreed to everything from the start. It was like a verbal version of musical chairs. Whenever the music stopped, the story changed.

The article was one of the most monumental personal attacks by one human being on another that you are ever likely to see. It was aimed at bringing maximum pain and personal damage to me and, in a more subtle way, to Linda because it attempted to patronise her and make her out to be a complete idiot. Most of all it was designed to break us up, but Linda and others had known far more about the situation all along than Mari ever imagined. The article backfired amid a combination of laughter and disbelief from all who knew the truth. My own reaction reminded me of the time when the Irish television programme played in the clip of me being interviewed in the 'turquoise period'. Who is this guy they are talking about? Here I was having a quiet holiday with my family as I had done so many times before and yet I was blasted all over the papers as some kind of womanising religious freak. It was as if they were talking about someone else and not me. It's a very weird experience. When I asked the other levels why all this was happening to me the words that came into my mind were: 'You are going through an emotional crucifixion.' Clearly Linda was too.

So what was this whole episode all about? We asked that question so many times a day for the best part of two years. To be honest I don't think we'll ever know for sure this side of the great beyond. Many psychics have channelled different answers and the truth as usual probably lies in a combination of all of them, plus a few more, no doubt. Nothing happens to us for only one reason, especially something as public and emotionally devastating as the events of 1991 and 1992.

First of all there was clearly a need to bring into incarnation a mind which had the right genetic inheritance and the appropriate life situation to fulfil a life plan which that mind had chosen to serve both its own and the collective evolution. As it happened so publicly, I have no doubt that, as with the Son of the Godhead business, it was designed to affect the collective consciousness in some way. Events that happen very publicly are often designed to make large numbers of people think. Many who have been ridiculed and condemned through history have been minds who have given their lives, mostly unknowingly on the conscious level, to create a situation which encouraged people to think, question, and awaken in some way. You don't have to wear your spiritual purity on your chest or around your neck to serve humanity. Service to humanity is more often than not done in much less obvious ways.

Another reason for what happened was certainly my own development and that of Linda and Mari. I thank Rebecca for coming into incarnation to provide a catalyst for change within me that helped to blow away the conditioning that the system imposes upon us. Her arrival and all the emotional shock waves it created allowed me to let go of the perspective I had been conditioned in this life to hold about conception and the creation of life. It forced me into a situation in which I could see amid the emotional typhoon of extreme experience played out in public that the taboos and prejudice that govern sex, conception and the birth of children are but another self-imposed prison cell, invented by ignorance and perpetuated by tradition.

It is time for humanity to walk free from these misunderstandings which generate such sorrow, guilt, condemnation and fear. All life is equally sacred, a magical expression of Creation, no matter through whom, or in what circumstances, it is born into the physical world. Anyone who says otherwise is allowing themselves to be conditioned by the system, by religion, and self-righteous ignorance, and not by the wonderful truth that we are all one, all part of the same consciousness. I am Rebecca and Rebecca is me. I am Gareth and Gareth is me. I am everyone and everyone is me. The divisions, and therefore the prejudice and judgement of others, are all a figment of the collective imaginations of the human race.

Mari Shawsun was also an enormous catalyst to bring about fundamental change in my perceptions. I thank Mari and all those who have ridiculed me for expanding my potential to love unconditionally. It has not been easy to do that in Mari's case or with those who have chosen to mock and I have really had to work at it. Don't let anyone tell you that loving everyone without condition is easy. If they convince you it is easy, that leads to guilt when you struggle with it. Unconditional love for everyone, no matter what they do to us, is something we have to work for until we get there in the end. Even then there will be moments when we find it impossible. I remember the moment when I let go of the negative feelings I had about Mari. I felt such freedom, joy, peace and contentment. When you find it possible to love without condition or judgement, it is not only others who benefit – the biggest beneficiary is you.

I would like to think that Mari could now accept the learning experience that she, too, was given and move on. From what I hear, however, that is not yet the case at the time of writing. I find it so desperately sad for Mari that she is still thinking in such terms. Those who lash out publicly at others always seem to forget the pain it causes for those close to the intended target, their children, parents and others. But again, maybe it's a pre-arranged experience; I don't know. In some cases it will be, in others it will not.

I wish Mari limitless joy, love and happiness in whatever she chooses to do, but she, and anyone else who is thinking of hurling abuse at me and those around me in the future, should realise that the whole world working together cannot destroy me and the information I am passing on, and neither can it destroy the bond between those close to me.

Psychics have channelled or offered other explanations for what happened in that spring of 1991. Among them was the need for two energy fields to interact physically to generate particularly powerful energies for earth healing and activate energies within both people. As those in the East have long understood, sexual contact is far more powerful and significant than people in other parts of the World have been led to believe. It is not only about the conceiving of children or some physical release or desire. It has also to do with energy interaction and the stimulation and activation of energies within us and our environment. It is the motivation behind the contact that decides the type of energy, positive or negative, that is thus created.

Other psychics have talked of the need for all involved to work out personal karma, collective karma on behalf of the whole, and to blast away all fear of what people say or think in preparation for what is to come. I repeat, it is almost certainly a combination of all or some of these things and many more. The common theme of every channelling, and my own intuition, is that what happened was necessary, meant to be, and, at least in total if not in detail, part of the life plan of all concerned. The circumstances were most certainly part of Rebecca's life plan because, as with all children, her mind was in total control of when and where to incarnate. I hope her life plan includes a time when we will get to know each other. If it does, then circumstances will ensure it happens.

I have been through so much pain and anguish trying to work out why everything happened. Hardly an hour has gone by since then that I have not thought about it, analysed it, questioned it. I have looked up to the sky and demanded answers to put my turmoil to rest. But in the end you just have to accept that many things happen that we don't understand on this level. The time will come when we step out of the space suit, at the moment we call physical 'death', when we will appreciate why situations and experiences were necessary. In fact we will no doubt laugh about them with the very minds which, in physical bodies, we disliked or had problems with. The reality of life is so different from our current perception. All the world really is a stage and we are the cast. The trick is staying with the script!

Another reason why many people go through certain situations and emotions is that they act as a kind of kidney machine for the collective energy sea or collective karma. Personal karma is the imbalances we retain within our own energy fields, and collective karma is the imbalanced energy we generate into the environment. It is vital that the latter is cleansed if the planet is going to survive. Again there are large numbers of people in the world doing this today. Most have no idea of the role they are playing. It involves taking on different emotions and so tuning in to the collective negative energies created by those emotions over the centuries, be it guilt, fear, anger or whatever. These energies are then channelled through your energy field, just like blood passing through a kidney machine to be cleansed, or in this case balanced. This is another explanation for why some people suddenly feel emotions that they cannot explain, and why sometimes our emotions appear almost to overwhelm us, such is their power. Some refer to such people as psychic vacuum cleaners and I have also heard it called 'redemptive karma' – agreeing to take responsibility for some of humanity's collective karma and, through experiencing certain situations, removing it.

This has been done by many people throughout history. It might have been a misunderstanding of this process that led to the idea that Jesus 'died so our sins could be forgiven'. 'Sin' really means karma and perhaps his lifetime was designed to take out some of humanity's collective karma to ease the burden on those who were being swamped by personal karma and could not cope with the collective imbalances too. But what he didn't do was die so that humanity's 'sin' or karma could be forgiven forever more. On the personal level at least, we have to face the consequences of our own actions – 'What you sow, you shall reap.'

Judy Hall's reading talks of the need for 'scapegoats' to attract the negative energy of others and then diffuse it. I feel all the ridicule I attracted was part of this. She said:

The role of the scapegoat is to be a focus for carrying away other people's negative energy. It is possible to be a passive scapegoat, no more than a victim who simply absorbs all this energy and feels helpless to do anything about it, or one can be a positive scapegoat who takes the energy and transforms it. Many people are incarnating with this ability today ... You may well have volunteered for the post of Scapegoat-in-Chief because of your care and concern for humanity ... I think your time of being the total scapegoat is coming, but if you do it in the right way, it's going to be an incredibly positive experience. You won't do it by denial. You will only do it by transmuting what is thrown at you, clearing the energies, and simply reflecting them back to those people. But in reflecting them back the energies are subtly changed because they have shifted up a vibration.

The take-over energies, that hypnotic state, or whatever it was which led to all that happened, are not a cop-out of my responsibility because I would have agreed to that take-over before I incarnated. It was all part of the personal and collective plan. But no doubt many will fire their custom-ised, selective, designer-morality in my direction; indeed they already have. There will be people making judgements about my morality on their way to their offices in the City of London to make decisions that cost the lives of thousands of children through the exploitation of the poorest countries. There will be church officials condemning my immorality while accepting their church's investments in projects that destroy people and the environment and in countries with regimes that are anything but 'Godly'. Evangelists will condemn me while supporting the work of 'missionaries' who seek to impose Christianity on native peoples and destroy their whole way of life in the process. There will be intensive animal farmers, slaughterhouse owners and meat producers condemning me on their way to cause more fear, pain and misery for fellow members of the universal family. Some politicians and businessmen will condemn me while making decisions that leave the poor sleeping in the streets, children hungry and the planet on the brink of ceasing to be.

I invite those people to take a few moments to redefine their understanding of immorality: as I said in Chapter 6, every twenty-four hours an area of tropical forest the size of the Isle of Wight is destroyed or degraded; deserts advance by a similar area; two hundred million tonnes of top soil is lost through erosion; increasing numbers of species become extinct; and a hundred thousand people, nearly half of them children, die through hunger or hunger-related disease. Every day.

Now that, my friends, is immorality.

Some of our most outrageous 'values' are merely the imposition of someone else's misguided idea of morality, often from centuries before. For instance, what arrogance to condemn a child as 'illegitimate' just because it was conceived by two people who had not signed a piece of paper in a church or registry office. There is no such thing as an 'illegitimate' child. All life is equally legitimate. I respect those who wish to go through a church marriage because everyone should have the right to make their own choices and have those choices respected, but I would not have got married if my awakening process had been activated before I met Linda all those years ago. I would most certainly have still spent my life with her because that was meant to be and our energies are so in harmony, but today I do not consider a church service and a piece of paper has any relevance to a relationship whatsoever. It's just a ceremony based on a misunderstanding of Creation, I would suggest. As the church's authority and influence continues to wane and collapse, and its subtle influences on our behaviour disappear, our entire view of conception, birth and children will begin to change. The word 'illegitimate' will be struck from the dictionaries as no longer having any part to play in the language of the new tomorrow.

The strength of my bond with Linda has nothing to do with a piece of paper saying 'married'. The bond is created by the compatibility of the energies passing between us and endless lifetimes together. If we had both been married to others when we met it would have been just the same. In the future the concept of 'family' will move away from two parents and two children to the whole of humanity. Who decided that people should live only within the concept of the family we have today? We merely inherited it from the last generation who, in turn, inherited it from the one before and so on. In this way we end up living our lives in a way someone decided was right centuries ago, and often it can be traced back to someone's interpretation of the Bible.

So much that we see as 'normal' and acceptable only survives because it was here when we were born. We accept things because they have been around for so long when if those same things, the church among them, were being introduced for the first time today, they would never be allowed the power and influence they have enjoyed. There is no 'normal' family situation in reality. It is whatever people feel is right for them. The time for 'norms' is over. We are entering a time when to be different will be something to celebrate not scorn.

It is the same with abortion and all the controversy that surrounds that subject. Once you realise the true nature of life, you see that the incoming mind does not incarnate into the physical form until the mother has made a definite commitment to go ahead with the birth. So, except in the rare circumstances where a mind chooses to experience the rejection of abortion, there is no taking of life, no 'murder', because the life force, the mind, will not be there if the mother has decided not to have the child. There are so many old and misguided values that are about to be challenged by the information now being made available from the higher levels.

The extreme events that I and others have been through in such a remarkably short time have blasted away most of the influences of forty years on this planet and life has become so much easier to understand. I now think the way I think, not the way society wants me to think. My bond with Linda has reached new heights. Only such a bond could survive this ultimate test. There were times when I thought neither of us would ever laugh again. But we did and we do – now more than ever before in the wake of a new mental and emotional freedom. After such fantastic mental and emotional pressure played out in public, the roses and the rosebowl are not only still intact but more united than ever. Linda gave me a greetings card to mark our twenty-one years together and it summed up so wonderfully what we had come through. The words will give comfort, I'm sure, to many others who are going through personal crises and karmic release. They were written by Deanne Laura Kennedy and entitled 'You and I':

Relationships are never easy,
And you and I have had our share of struggling and troubled times.
But together we made it.
Together we cared enough to face our problems;
We loved enough not to let go.
And now what we have is stronger because of all we have been through,
All we have struggled with.
I sometimes worry about the future,
But with you by my side the future seems much brighter,
The present more precious, more meaningful.

We need the tears to appreciate the laughter.
We must share our problems to realise how much we truly need each other.
To give our love the chance to expand, to strengthen, to endure.
We deserve nothing less than a love that will remain through all aspects of our lives.
Together we will face all obstacles with confidence,
Because we already know our relationship can endure even the worst of times,
As long as we love, share and stay together.

The true test of love is not when things are going well.

Indeed the opposite is the case. The events of 1991 and 1992 have built a relationship that can survive anything, including the enormous strains that the future will bring. I have seen Linda blossom so much through the troubled times, which also included the death of her mother soon after our return from Crete as one emotional crisis continued to follow another.

I know the hardest part for me and others is yet to come when the condemnation begins to gather pace as the system sees that this challenge to its suicidal self-destruction is having an effect. If the system in all its forms wants to stop a message it doesn't like, what is the most effective way of doing that? To attack the vehicle of the information, either physically or by undermining the person. This is why it is vital that people judge the information, not the vehicles for it. There is going to be so much disinformation and so many false accusations put around about me and others involved in passing on this information in the years to come. They will make what has happened so far seem mild. I have no doubt there will be many invented stories and other more sinister attempts to discredit the truth by discrediting the messenger. Two channellers have passed on communications warning me to beware of attempts to discredit me in the eyes of those who might otherwise listen, of many likely plans to get me out of the way including, they both said, attempts to plant drugs. Don't be surprised at anything you read and hear about people like me and what we are supposed to have done or said!

Thanks to previous lives and the experiences in this one, I hope I am ready for whatever may come, although I don't promise to enjoy it all. It is time for those who share the same thoughts and beliefs to stand up and say so because it is going to get tougher for those who speak out for the truth and the more who are prepared to do that, the easier it will be.

12

The Acupuncture Needle

Early in 1992 I had a letter from an astrologer and psychic in the English West Midlands predicting that this would be the year when more people would begin to take me more seriously.

His name was Philip Solomon, a lovely man, very balanced, with his feet firmly on the ground. He made predictions for a Midlands Sunday newspaper and also appeared regularly on a local radio station, but while all his other New Year predictions had been published in the paper, they declined to use the one about me, even though Philip said that was the strongest message he had received. Perhaps they thought there was no way I would ever be taken seriously, never mind so soon. When we returned from Crete, Philip wrote again. He had seen all the stuff in the press, but he stood by his prediction. His letter should have been laughable given what had happened, but I knew he was right. I had no doubt that by the end of the year the tide would have begun to turn.

This was confirmed when I was introduced to Jane, a tarot card reader and friend of Judy Hall. Judy led me to many people as I tried to make sense of what had happened and I'll always be grateful for the magnificent and unwavering support she, and Joan in Wales, gave to me and my family through such traumatic times. Tarot cards are symbolic pictures and these, together with psychic vision and feeling, can, in the right hands, help to project forward the likely outcome of a situation, although exact timings can be very difficult to predict. She said the cards indicated there was some kind of deception around me. There would be one more dose of 'poison', as she put it, to come out in relation to this and then it would be over. 'Your time of sacrifice will then be over,' she said. Eventually it would seem that the pain of the previous two years had never happened. Also, she said, the autumn would see the start of a changing public perception of me and what I was saying.

She said that I needed to talk to a newspaper about what had happened before I would find a publisher for this book. We were approached immediately after that by the London newspaper *Today* which published two articles written by a journalist called David Jones. He was someone I had met back in the Green Party days when he had been the paper's environment correspondent. He is a decent man and a journalist with a mind he is prepared to use, but it was a terribly painful experience for both Linda and me, going over with him what had happened. I didn't realise just how much inner pain there was to bring to the surface. But from the moment those articles appeared things began to improve.

Soon afterwards I had a letter from Salford Green Party. Some of their members had heard me speak in Manchester a few months earlier and they wanted to set up a fringe meeting at the upcoming Green Party Conference in Wolverhampton in September so I could outline my view to the wider membership. I jumped at the chance, but it was to cause considerable unease among some prominent members of the national party. Sara Parkin, my one-time fellow national speaker, was appalled that I should be asked to speak and said so publicly. She was supported by Jonathon Porritt, a man who had done so much to bring the danger to the environment to public attention. I had an official letter from the party asking me not to attend because, in effect, they did not want to open the party to ridicule. I had to smile at that because the party had been ridiculed since the day it was formed for saying humanity was destroying the planet, only for public opinion to catch up and agree with them eventually. Being ridiculed is part of the price, initially, of speaking true.

What those who opposed my invitation to speak could not see was that they were acting in precisely the same way towards me as others had once acted towards them in the days when they were saying something radical. This happens all the time. I see the journey to truth and understanding as a long spiralling road climbing ever higher. We all set out on that road, but we all choose a different point to stop, pitch the tent, and rest a while. Some do this after a few steps, and to them the environmentalists who have travelled many miles further to reach their stage of understanding will be seen as extreme, cranky and loony. But if you are prepared to keep walking, keep seeking, after the environmentalists have pitched their tents and said this far and no further, then they, in turn, will see you as extreme, cranky, and loony. This is what happened to Jonathon and Sara, it would seem. They pitched their tent alongside the conventional human scientific analysis of the planet's problems and could see only political and 'scientific' solutions to them. Anyone who went beyond that, and I had gone well beyond it, was not to be taken seriously. For years environmentalists had been told by the system to live in the 'real world' and now here was Jonathon telling those in the party who wished me to speak that they should live in the 'real world'. A full circle.

I hope that those environmentalists who have pitched their tent will look at themselves honestly. If they do they will be horrified at just how much they have been absorbed and made impotent by the very system they were once so keen to bring down. That realisation might crack the concrete that has been solidifying around their feet and allow them to start walking again. This applies to the whole Green movement because unless it has the courage and vision to go beyond human scientific analysis and into the areas outlined in this book and others, they will become an irrelevance before very long. That would be sad given the contribution they have made to human understanding and could still make in the future with their organisation and communication network. But if they refuse to evolve they will fade and die because the agenda will have moved beyond them.

The European election success in 1989 had a down side for the Greens. When they were in the wilderness they said what they believed to be right, and in the end, as public awareness grew, the party began to set agendas for change. But after the European elections, as our opinion poll rating soared, too many put being popular ahead of being true. I can understand this. When you've always been on one per cent in the polls or less, it's nice to be liked, but it is also dangerous to the cause if popularity in itself becomes the goal. That is how traditional politics operates. The radical edge of the party's view lost its sharpness as it became absorbed into the political game, and words were watched more carefully in case they cost a single new-found supporter. There is a lesson here for everyone seeking change. Don't seek popularity; seek truth. If being true makes you popular, great, but if being true makes you unpopular, then so be it if that is what is necessary.

The controversy over my appearance at the Green Party Conference focused the party on where it wished to go and it led to both Sara and Jonathon stepping back from upfront influence. I spoke to a packed fringe meeting and was given a tremendous welcome from the large section of the party who had either supported these ideas since the sixties or were now awakening to them. I left the Civic Hall in Wolverhampton that Saturday afternoon highly elated. Somehow I just knew I had turned the corner. Jane the tarot card reader had said someone would come out of my past to publish my next book; in fact, this happened twice when Jon Carpenter, the man I worked with on *It Doesn't Have To Be*

Like This, offered to publish the basis of my speech to the Greens in book form under the title *Days of Decision,* and Alan Samson, a man I had met in my snooker days, agreed to publish this book. That left only one more in the predicted sequence of five to complete. Maybe if you count *It Doesn't Have To Be Like This,* the sequence was already finished. We shall see.

I went with Linda and Gareth on a short visit to St Malo and Normandy in France. We travelled along the invasion beaches where the Allies had landed on D-Day. It was, not surprisingly, a very negative area. We went also to two big Earth energy sites, the Cathedral at Bayeux and Mont St Michel, a French counterpart to Cornwall's St Michael's Mount. It was so depressing to see how such an important and awesomely beautiful energy site as Mont St Michel had been turned into a place for tourist day trips with all its fast food bars and tacky souvenir shops. If only they realised what they were doing to the energies of a spot that helps to keep this planet alive. Our most memorable moment on the visit came when we arrived at the former home of the remarkable Frenchman, Count St Germain, who in the eighteenth and nineteenth centuries was dubbed the 'Wonderman of Europe' for his feats and abilities. One, so it was claimed, was the ability to disappear. No-one knows how long he lived except that it was a very, very, long time. Voltaire called him 'the man who never dies and who knows everything'. It is widely held that the mind or aspect of Infinite Consciousness I call Rakorski had incarnated as Count St Germain, and the moment we saw his house both Linda and I had the same reaction: wow! We were both very moved just looking at the place and the energies were incredibly powerful. It was lunchtime and we couldn't go inside, but as I stood there a very clear thought came into my mind: 'You will come back here with your family and your new son next year (1993), and you will release energies that will have an enormous effect on the world.' Again, we'll have to see what happens.

Back in England I was preparing to play a serious football match again for the first time in twenty years. Philip Solomon had come along to that Green Party Conference to see me and just as he was leaving he said: 'I am being told you are going to play football again.' I had been coaching goalkeepers at the Ryde Sports Football Club and I assumed that he was relating to that. But the next time I went to the club, one of the managers asked if I would be free to play in October. I agreed because my arthritis was now all but gone, and I was training with no pain at all. Three weeks later I walked out on the pitch at Haylands, a local club in Ryde, to play in the Isle of Wight Cup Competition. Lined up along the touchline were national newspaper photographers and reporters who had come to record the return of the 'Son of God' to football. All the 'Icke has discovered religion' myths and clichés were already prepared and waiting to be put into service even before the whistle had been blown.

The match itself was very strange. There was a peculiar atmosphere from the start. The game was going on around me, but it was as if I was not part of it. I would have taken the whole thing to be my own imagination, but others noticed it too. My good friend, Mark Firmin, the Ryde Sports general manager, who was standing behind my goal, commented on the weird atmosphere that had prevailed in the first half. The pitch was just awful, rock hard and bumpy, but the opening minutes went well for me, considering I was clearly not totally there at the time. It was like being in some kind of dream. Then one of the Haylands players went to cross the ball into my goalmouth and mis-hit his kick. Instead of the ball going high to the far post as he intended, it headed for the near post at about waist height. I remember seeing the ball leave his foot, but everything else was a blank until I found myself lying on the floor with the ball in the net beside me. I was sickened about the goal and confused about how it had happened, but what was worse was that I felt pain in my right hand and I could not move my little finger. It was already badly swollen and past experience from my playing days told me it was either broken or dislocated, maybe both.

I thought about coming off, but as it was my first serious game for so long after once being virtually crippled with arthritis, I wanted to use the event to make some points about illness and how Western medical science has such a limited view of the causes and cures for disease. I decided to carry on. From that moment the strange atmosphere disappeared and it became just like any other football match. I was pleased with my second-half performance despite a bit of pain and we won the game 2–1. That evening the hospital confirmed a broken finger.

Actually football is a big part of my life, particularly through Gareth who has the potential to become a top-class goalkeeper. You will probably have gained the impression from what you have read since the account of my first visit to the medium that my life is one round of psychics, channellings and energy sites. That is because I have had to condense everything into a short space. But the great majority of my life is spent doing all the things that everyone else does. Talking about the home, going out with the family, watching television, going to the football, having a beer with my friends at Ryde Sports. I do not get involved very often these days in contemplating the navel of some communication or other. There are times when my pulse races because I know some particular information is significant and I act upon it, but I am extremely selective. Most channellings should be treated with great caution until common themes across many different channellers emerge. I prefer to follow my own intuition and stand or fall by it. I am waiting for the day when my intuition tells me that Leicester City Football Club will win the English Championship, but so far I wait in vain!

One of the few psychics I worked with after 1991 was the lady in the West of England. She was in her sixties and had been involved in these areas of thought for some time. She had a vision of me as a sort of walking acupuncture needle, constantly putting energy into the system or balancing the flows. She saw me holding 'the blue sword of truth, a sword you have held many times'. She channelled that both Linda and myself had the 'new' energies flowing through us and that the mind who was incarnating as our next child had been around Linda for some time waiting for her vibration in this life to reach the level required to create the necessary physical form. The child would be a boy, she felt.

The prediction that I would be taken more seriously before the end of 1992 was also coming true as more people began to realise that much of what I had said in *The Truth Vibrations* was happening. This increasing realisation was strengthened by a series of major weather events and by the changing attitudes that were beginning to become more evident. A comet called Smith Tuttle appeared in the sky and there was a major fire at Windsor Castle. Channellings in *The Truth Vibrations* had said that what we call a comet would be seen in the night sky and that there would be fires at many energy sites. The hill on which Windsor Castle was built is a big acupuncture point and I had been there for energy work the year before. A long letter published by *The Independent* in which I challenged many fundamental aspects of religion helped enormously to highlight the myth that I had 'discovered' the church. This led to further opportunities to question the power and privileges enjoyed by the church at the expense of other explanations of life and Creation. The perception of me was definitely changing among those who were prepared to open their minds and think for themselves.

I was invited to more lectures at British universities. Sometimes there would be a few hostile people in the audience who had been mind-controlled by the tabloid press, but most people came along to listen. Something was definitely happening in the collective psyche because I could see from event to event how people in the audience were beginning to think differently. I could also feel the power of the energy passing through me to the audience. When I went to speak at the renowned Cambridge Union I gained some idea of what was happening on these other levels.

The West Country psychic came with me and on the way north the feeling was getting stronger that what would happen in Cambridge was particularly important. A significant event was about to happen, my thoughts were telling me. This feeling increased when we were sitting in a tea shop in the city and the most enormous energy descended upon me. There was a loud humming in my ears and my eyelids would barely stay open. Something was going on. To me Cambridge is one of the most beautiful cities in the world and the energies at the Union building where I was to speak were warm and welcoming, as were the people. This was clearly an energy site of some importance. Alongside the building and the debating chamber was the Round Church, an old Knights Templar Church. The Templars knew of the energy system and there is far more to that organisation than history has documented.

The evening went very well and afterwards Paul Vaughan, a former Cambridge student himself, showed us around some of the ancient streets. I slept in a room overlooking the Round Church and the next morning I walked through the city very early with the psychic. She particularly wanted to see the inside of the famous chapel of Kings College. We arrived to find it wasn't open to the public for another hour and we had planned to be on our way before then. But as we stood by the gate barring the way, a man emerged and we told him our predicament. He agreed to let us in for a few minutes just to have a brief look. As I stood inside admiring the superb ceiling another great burst of warm energy swept through me. I said I had a really strong feeling that something very important had been achieved in the twenty-four hours since I left the Isle of Wight. We thanked the man for his help and began to walk back to the car. I was walking in front of the psychic as we passed a spot close to the chapel when I noticed she had stopped. I looked back and she was just standing there with a shocked look on her face.

'I've just seen you on another level,' she said.

She was visibly shaken by what she had seen and became quite ill for a short time later that morning. The incident appeared to happen at a point where two energy lines cross and I had apparently walked through that crossover point when she had seen me. She later described what she saw:

'The lead up to it had a sense of dynamism, like a magnetic energy field working through us and drawing us to a point of immense power, a gateway to another dimension that was so brief, but really potent. The width of it was about a pace and a half, a yard and a half, something like that. As you walked through, it was like your physical body was non-existent. What I saw was the same shape as you. The outer edge was not totally defined, but at the point between your shoulder blades (the heart chakra) were two waving lines of golden light, golden energy, undulating and just drifting. The actual gold was quite sharp, brilliant. And also at the same time there were tiny golden threads of energy going in all directions, straight and hard. It was mostly a kind of gold light, gold radiance. I don't relate this to the aura, I relate it to the level I put myself into to connect to the highest spiritual presence of a being. So for me that was a glimpse of your higher spiritual reality. It was very fleeting, but I caught it and it was very powerful. It affected me very deeply. I felt intensely emotional and then it filtered on to the physical, creating a temporary illness.'

This gave me – and I hope gives you – some insight into how we are all multi-dimensional beings working on many levels at the same time. Our evolution or role in the transformation is not related to how well known we are or what we do for a living. Just as one level of me would appear to be pouring out golden energy into the environment without my physical consciousness knowing anything about it, so an old lady may be living a quiet, mundane existence on the surface while another level of her being generates energy which is helping to heal the Earth. The energy has to pass through a physical form, or at least the etheric level, to be transformed to the appropriate mix and frequency, and often all this physical body has to do is be in the right place at the right time. It doesn't have to know the whys and the wherefores and if it thinks it has gone to a place only for a holiday, a beer, or a day out, that's fine, as long as they go and their other levels can use the body to bring energy through to this frequency.

The energy work I and so many others are involved with relates to the higher levels of the Earth, the mental, emotional and etheric. Most of what happens at energy sites does not affect the physical Earth immediately; it affects the etheric template, the organising energy field, or the emotional and mental levels which, in turn, affect the balance of the etheric. This balance within the etheric energy field of the Earth is crucial. In the same way that our etheric energy field controls the health and well-being of our physical bodies, so with the planet. If the Earth's etheric field is damaged or imbalanced, this will show itself at some point in physical damage and imbalance. The etheric energy field of the Earth is what some call Mother Nature and others have called Gaia. It is the self-balancing intelligence, which weaves the glorious web of birth, rebirth and restoration, that we see all around us. It is this which reacts to changing circumstances and tries to keep everything in balance. It is the scales of nature.

There is, however, a limit to how much it can compensate for the damage and havoc wreaked by the human race. The negative domination of this frequency, the negative thought forms constantly generated by humanity, the physical destruction, and the mental and emotional turmoil this has caused for the Spirit, the Mind, of the Earth, has done terrible damage to the etheric field. This has manifested in part as increasing areas of dead or dying land, the extremes of weather, and the inability of species of all kinds to survive humanity's intrusions. We now have a situation in which mental and emotional trauma and imbalances are not only affecting the etheric, but the damage to the etheric, and its

consequences are passing trauma and imbalance back up the
levels to the mental and emotional fields which then pass
them back, with interest, to the etheric. So it goes on in an
ever greater cycle of perpetuating imbalance. This cycle
must be broken and the etheric field restored if humanity
and the physical Earth are going to survive, as they *are*. The
work of repairing the etheric field goes on all the time
through the etheric bodies of energy workers, even though
they may not be consciously aware of it. The etheric level of
the Earth is on a kind of life support system with immense
numbers of minds, who are not in physical bodies, also
involved in its restoration. Without that round-the-clock
support system, the physical Earth would no longer be with
us even now.

The week after Cambridge when I arrived at the University of Glamorgan in Pontypridd, South Wales, for my
last talk of 1992, I felt a sense of a cycle being completed. As
I drove through the streets near the University in the
darkness and gloom of a winter's evening, it reminded me
very much of driving into Bangor in North Wales ten
months earlier for my first public appearance after the
turquoise period. So much had happened since then, so
much pain had been faced. I felt another stage was over. The
following morning, 12 November, the psychic lady had a
series of visions and channelled messages. Interestingly my
favourite colour has always been green and, since 1990, some
shades of purple, too. The psychic didn't know this. Her
channelling said:

'I am being presented with a picture. It is full of people,
mainly in procession. The significant thing is that purple and
green are the colours for you. All these people are clothed in
purple and green cloaks. So the image presented is of a great
many people connecting themselves to your energy stream
in some way. It is an immense procession. It started off quite
small, now it is a multitude of thousands and thousands of
people, thousands and thousands, streaming. First of all it
was like a slow procession, now they're streaming, endless

lines of them. I can see it keying in to something I saw while we were at Cambridge. What I saw was the stream of energy emanating from your heart chakra ... Purple and green are indicative of two balances. The green is the absolute balance, and the purple is your transmuting energy which raises the vibration of energies within and around you. The purple connects you to a lot of your power source of information which is St Germain. You call him by another name (Rakorski). He's like your overlighting energy field. I can feel him somehow standing behind you.

This day is the beginning of a new cycle, a new empowerment. It is like you will take on a new coat. You will divest yourself of one which is now played through. The tests of the last two years were part of your preparation. You have completed part of the route. You may think you've already fulfilled quite a bit of the pathway. What you have fulfilled is your preparation. Now the true work begins. There's some kind of humour going on because they have felt from you a reaction of 'What!' (exactly what I was thinking!). They're laughing at that. I am looking at you. I know these are symbolic visions, but this time you are clothed in armour up to the neck. It is a radiant golden armour, the true warrior. Talk about electro-magnetic energy fields. You are firmly locked in. I can see your heart chakra. The electro-magnetic energy field (the energy sea) is locking in to your heart chakra and green energy is pouring from you. It's very powerful. That's the energy that people are going to be feeling. It's emanating now.'

This supported a feeling I had that in some way the experiences that I and others had been through had been designed, at least in part, to affect the energy sea, the collective psyche, and so help to change its way of thinking. The channelling said that the energy I had been working with helped to clear people's psychic blockages so they could be opened up consciously to accept new ideas and, thereby, the new frequency. The seeds that had already been sown could be enormous in no time. Once more I say these channellings are symbolic and should not necessarily be taken as a hundred per cent accurate. This applies to all channelled information in this book and elsewhere. We have to follow our intuition on how it feels to us.

Six days later, just after midnight on the morning of 18 November, I was awakened by Linda. The baby was on his way. I say 'his' because we had never doubted it was a boy and those who had channelled or had visions on the subject had all said the baby was a boy. It had been a difficult pregnancy what with all the pain and pressures of that nine months and Linda had been exhausted for most of the time. So we were delighted he was about to arrive two weeks ahead of the scheduled date. I'll never forget trying to wake up Kerry to tell her we were about to leave for the hospital. She's not the easiest person to wake up at the best of times and it was even more difficult that evening. But the moment I uttered the words, 'Kerry, Mum's going to have the baby tonight', whooosh! Not only was she awake, she was past me in a flash. All I heard was 'Aaahhhhhh!!' as a pair of silver-coloured pyjamas disappeared through her bedroom door followed by a pair of feet. 'Don't panic, don't panic' seemed to be her general advice!

As we arrived at the hospital, it was a glorious night with the sky ablaze with stars. The first midwife we saw in those early hours said she had heard on the evening news that a comet could be seen in the sky that night and for the next few days.

'I can't remember what they said it was called,' she said.

'Smith Tuttle?' I asked.

'Yes, that's the one.'

The baby took thirteen hours to arrive and Linda was incredible, refusing all offers of drugs for pain relief in case they harmed the child. The problem was that the baby was in the wrong position to be born and the doctor and midwives had decided to wait until 12.30 that afternoon to see if things would begin to move more quickly. If there was no obvious progress by then they would have to take action.

At around 12.30 there was some considerable movement as the baby turned himself around into the perfect position. Eighteen minutes later at 12.48 pm Jaymie Alexander Icke was born. A friend and healer was with us for the last few hours before the birth to help Linda and just outside the room were Kerry and Gareth.

It was a moment of great emotion for everyone and nothing reminds you of the wonders of life and Creation more than seeing another child, another mind, born onto this troubled, but oh-so-beautiful planet.

Welcome to the world, Jaymie Icke.

13

The Reluctant Rebel

Just before Christmas I was approached by a television programme. Could they fly me to Israel? They wanted to interview me in Bethlehem. My immediate reaction was 'No' because I could see their plan: 'Let's interview this loony Icke who reckons he's the Son of God at the place where Jesus was born.' But the more I thought about it the more I wanted to go. It was nothing to do with the programme; it was a sudden and overwhelming desire to go to Israel and, in particular, Jerusalem. I spent days reading all I could about that city.

Unfortunately a few days before the interview was due to be recorded an Israeli solder was killed by Arab terrorists and the Israeli Government's response was to deport a group of Palestinians. They, in turn, were refused entry to Lebanon and were forced to set up camp in what is called the No Man's Land between the two countries. The television company pulled out of the trip when the trouble flared and I was very disappointed. I was so keen to go I tried to fly out there myself, but I couldn't get on a flight. I decided instead to go in late January just before this book was due to be finished.

I didn't realise at the time, but the trip coincided with a highly significant astrological sequence. On 2 February, the day after I would arrive back in England, there would be the first Uranus–Neptune 'conjunction' (an extremely powerful interaction) for 171 years. More important, it would be the first time this had happened since those planets were 'discovered' by humanity. Once we acknowledge a planet's existence on the conscious level their vibrations affect us much more powerfully. It's something to do with the tuning-in process, I suppose. Furthermore, Uranus and Neptune would conjunct again in 1993 on 20 August and 24 October, making it an immense year astrologically. These conjunctions were certain to increase the speed of change on all levels, mental, emotional, and physical.

After Christmas, in the run-up to my visit to Jerusalem, I became very depressed. It was a major period of questioning – 'What's it all about?' The memories and the anguish of the previous two years returned to hit me like a runaway train. How I wished I could have woken up to find it was February 1990 again before that visit to Betty Shine. In the mood I was in then, I would definitely not have gone if I had known of all that was to follow from that trigger. I felt tired mentally and emotionally, weary of the pounding I and my family had taken. I just wanted out. I wanted to start my life again away from all this. The desire to go to Jerusalem had all but gone, and I almost cancelled the trip.

The day before I left, I received a package through the post from Michael Roll. I had been corresponding with him for almost a year. He is a man of great determination who had been gathering information from various scientists and thinkers who have shown that the mind and the brain are not the same, and that all consciousness survives physical 'death'. Life after death, in other words, is for everyone and not just those persuaded to believe some mumbo jumbo peddled by one religion or another. Those religions have to insist that only their followers have everlasting life or they lose the power to control. The truth is that while 'science' and religion may appear to be on opposing sides of the argument, they are exactly the same in one way. Their empires both survive only through the suppression of information.

I had long been sceptical and deeply suspicious of religion, but the contents of Michael's package sharpened my appreciation of the massive confidence trick it has been through the centuries and continues to be. We should not allow the work of some wonderful people involved with the church to obscure its overall contribution to most of the darkness that has descended on the world. Michael included a paper he had written and published himself in 1983 called 'The Suppression of Knowledge'. It was dedicated to 'the teeming millions who have died in the name of ignorance and religion'. It documents the history of Christianity, but the same themes apply to all religions. So many of the 'truths' and 'facts' taken for granted today are merely the result of what one man or group of men decided was the case centuries after the one we call Jesus had gone from the Earth if, indeed, he had ever been here in the first place.

There is little – many would say no – historical evidence that Jesus even existed. You would think that someone who caused the stir attributed to him in the Bible would have rated a mention by writers of the time. But take away the gospels and he virtually disappears. And bear in mind that the gospels were written by who knows who, who knows when, in who knows what circumstances.

Even in the gospels Jesus does not claim to be the saviour of the world or the only Son of God. If anything, he says the opposite – that God is greater than he. Many of the Jesus myths developed after Saul of Tarsus (St Paul) appeared on the scene. He never claimed to have met Jesus and only turned to the subject after his famous conversion on the road to Damascus. Maybe he saw a ghost or something; maybe he made up the whole story.

The most important moment in the sorry history of Christianity came at the Council of Nicaea in AD 325, getting on for three centuries after Jesus was said to be alive. The Council was called by the Roman Emperor Constantine 'the Great', a man responsible for an enormous amount of death and suffering. His Christian values were flexible enough, it would appear, for him to murder his wife, son and nephew. He became perturbed when the many Christian sects that had emerged in his empire began to argue over the 'truth' of Jesus and his life. Constantine called the sides together at his palace at Nicaea, which is today called Iznik in Turkey. He insisted that a creed was formed that all 'Christians' would then have to follow − or else!

The big question at the core of the argument was this: was Jesus merely a man who was used as a vehicle for God or was he actually God incarnate, the only begotten son? The bishops gathered at Nicaea and, supported by Constantine, decided in favour of the 'Jesus was God' lobby. They also decided that God came in three parts − father, son and holy ghost. It is sobering to think that this decision and others that were to be the heart of Christian belief from that day to this were discussed and made by people who also thought the Earth was flat and that Jerusalem was the centre of the universe! If it wasn't so tragic, it would be comic.

The Council of Nicaea was to have terrible implications for endless millions of people, not least for the Jews who now stood accused not only of killing the vehicle of God, but God himself. Those who refused to believe the nonsense of Nicaea were either banished or killed. At the Council of Constantinople in AD 381, the Emperor Theodosius decreed officially that anyone who would not accept the verdict of Nicaea was a traitor of the state and must be killed. As Michael Roll says in his paper:

> Religious history is a tale of imprisonment, banishment, and slaughter. Priests everywhere were appointed as informers, to become known as inquisitors of the Faith. Heretics, Jews, and witches, all in fact who did not conform to the orthodox teaching of the church were slaughtered, and the roll of victims runs into millions.

At the Council of Ephesus in AD 431 came another layer of man-made myth which survives powerfully intact in the

Roman Catholic Church to this day. Mary, reputed mother of Jesus, was officially pronounced Mother of God. Not that religion has done anything for women. It has been used as a tool for their repression and words are quoted from its pages to justify that repression in the same way that other lines were used to justify wholesale genocide of non-believers. For example, St Paul quotes in Timothy I, 2:12: 'But I suffer not a woman to teach, nor to usurp authority over the man, but to be in silence.' It was only at the Council of Trent in 1545 that the church decided women had souls – and then by a majority of just three votes!!!

After Nicaea, the church set about destroying all alternative knowledge and views that would expose its stupidity and arrogance. The free-thinker Arthur Findlay summarised the consequences in his superb book *The Curse of Ignorance*, published in 1947:

> The Council of Nicaea ... raised the Christian Church to the position of State Church of the Roman Empire. This was the greatest and most tragic event in history. Instead of the world being guided by the thoughts of the great philosophers of Greece and Rome, its most virile inhabitants fell under the domination of the hierarchy of ignorant priests – what became Christendom from that date to the 20th century. The Greek and Roman educational system was replaced by theology, and consequently ignorance took the place of the pursuit of knowledge.

It was the church hierarchy which tried to stop education being available for the masses because they didn't want them exposed to alternative information. The priests and churchmen might have been misguided, but if you are the only ones who can read or write, you are in control. In the land of the blind, the one-eyed man is king. A Member of Parliament, one Davies Giddy, encapsulated their fears when speaking of the proposed Education Bill of 1807:

However specious in theory the project might be of giving education to the labouring classes of the poor, it would be prejudicial to their morals and happiness ... it would make them despise their lot in life instead of making them good servants ... and (here we go!) ... it would enable them to read seditious pamphlets, vicious books, and publications against Christianity.

This still occurs today to a larger or lesser extent in all parts of the Earth. In Britain it is compulsory to teach this rubbish in schools while the BBC continues to allow itself to be a mouthpiece for the church through the guaranteed air-time it gives for Christianity to broadcast its myths and illusions, while helping, by omission, to suppress alternative information that challenges both religion and establishment science. The Queen is both head of state and head of the Church of England, and state and church are linked at all levels. This is quite outrageous. We even put our hands on the Bible to show that we intend to tell the truth in a court of law when the book is a catalogue of untruths and misrepresentations. Any visitor to Planet Earth who was observing all this would immediately report back to base: 'No sign of intelligent life!' It is not a person's right to believe anything they like that I oppose; quite, quite the contrary. What I oppose is the way people are denied their right to have access to all information without bias or suppression so they can make up their minds based on all the knowledge available, not only that which certain groups wish them to believe.

Fortunately, the scales of Creation can only be pushed down on one side for so long. Then they react. The law of cause and effect (karma) now has religion and all the tools of state and mind control in its sights. Their days are numbered and one of the most appalling stories in all human history will soon be over. Good riddance. Religion has been a curse to the world.

How appropriate that the day after reading Michael's work, I was off to Jerusalem, that city of religious control and intolerance. At Heathrow on the way out I spotted a book called *Jesus: The Evidence*, which seemed to support much of the historical documentation in Michael's paper. My plane touched down in the early hours at Tel Aviv's Ben Gurion Airport. I wanted to be anywhere else and preferably at home. The plane was returning to England about four hours later and I so wanted to be on it.

I waited for daylight and took the bus to the 'Holy City'. The weather was cold, wet and foggy. As I looked out from the window the land looked sad, somehow, almost in despair. It was not alone. I felt the same. What the hell did I decide to come here for? I changed buses amid crowds of uniforms and guns at the Jerusalem bus station and headed for the Old City. Within its high walls, encircled as they are by modern Jerusalem, the religions jockey for space and recognition.

This is the city, the guidebooks say, of David, of Jesus, of Mohammed, and countless others who would rate a mention in a religious *Who's Who*. It is divided into 'quarters' for Jews, Moslems, Christians and Armenians. If you want to buy a myth or misunderstanding, this is the place, pal. They've got hundreds of them. On the street corners and at every church or monument there they are, lying in wait, those spiritual used car salesmen, the tourist guides. From what I could see in Jerusalem, many of them wore a black leather jacket and looked like extras from *The Godfather*. These are the silver-tongued repeaters of make-believe who will sell you a myth tour of anywhere.

Even at 7.30 in the morning, as I walked through the Jaffa Gate and into the near-deserted streets of the Old City, I was not safe. I felt someone touch my arm.

'Hello, my friend,' a voice said. 'You from England? I know many people in England. They come from Glasgow. You know Glasgow?'

I knew what was going on. It is the same in every country that attracts the tourists in significant numbers. But I decided to stick with him because I had little time here and

I needed to get sorted out quickly. I also find it fascinating to see these people at work when they think you haven't sussed them. They make out they are helping you because they want to be your friend when you know they are going to ask for a serious fee once they have you dangling on the line. That's okay if it's agreed beforehand, because they have to earn a living, but many people end up paying for something they didn't want and never asked for. This one said he approached me because 'I liked your face'. As he had approached me from behind, I had clearly witnessed the latest recorded miracle in Jerusalem. I have no doubt the spot is being added to the tourist itinerary as I speak.

He showed me the Wailing Wall, that most sacred of places in the Jewish religion. They go there to talk to God. They leave little messages for 'him' which they write on bits of paper and stick in the cracks between the stones. They are now even offering a fax service so that Jews all over the world can fax their message to God and someone then nips it down and puts it in the wall. No, I'm not kidding.

The guide took me to a youth hostel where I left my bag and, within an hour of arriving at Jerusalem bus station, I was off with him to Bethlehem, a short bus journey away. I apologise in advance if this upsets people, but I have to be honest: what a dump. If Bethlehem was once a little town, it isn't now. It is virtually an extension of modern Jerusalem. We walked through 'Manger Square' to the Church of the Nativity on the site where Jesus was supposed to have been born. I don't believe that for a second, but the travel guide to Jerusalem and the Holy Land is in no doubt and states categorically: 'This church is situated above the Grotto of the Nativity, a small subterranean chamber, in which a silver star marks the place of Jesus's birth.' At the height of the tourist season people queue for hours to see this grotto, such is the power of myth and mind control. But this, luckily, was the off-season and I walked right in. What a performance unfolded before me. Watched by a small group of tourists, three men dressed up in various regalia were wailing away at each other. The only word I could make out was the odd 'Hallelujah'. One man in the black hood was leading a ceremonial sing-song, while another put on a crown and drank from a goblet in a manner that suggested he had just returned from the desert. The third man, who looked in urgent need of a good laugh, swished around with some object on a chain which puffed out smoke occasionally. The one with the crown finished his drink and proceeded to read loudly and earnestly from a big red book. In Britain, the most famous big red book belongs to a television show called 'This Is Your Life'. Personalities appear in front of an audience to have their life stories told by a man reading from the said, big red book. The book in the grotto was a sort of 'Jesus Christ, this is your life', and if the television show presented the lives and beliefs of the famous as inaccurately as the Church has with Jesus they would be sued out of existence in a month.

By the time the three guys in the grotto started kissing the book in ceremonial order, I'd had enough and left. The words that came to me were that favourite line of the tennis player John McEnroe: 'You cannot be serious.'

If people only realised that the pomp and ceremony of the church and its myths are largely based on pre-Christian ceremonies and beliefs. They've just been re-hashed, re-painted, and re-named. There's nothing new in Christianity, it's the ultimate in recycling. In Tarsus, the home of St Paul, they worshipped the saviour-God Dionysus; the Jesus depicted by Paul and the Church is one of many saviour-God figures invented throughout history. Humanity has this desire to be 'saved' by someone else and so avoid taking personal responsibility for what needs to be done. Many of these 'gods' incarnate display the same theme – born to virgin mothers, only sons of God, humble birthplace with star above for guiding wise men and shepherds, local king orders the killing of babies, seen by followers after death, and more. James H. Baxter, former professor of ecclesiastical history at St Andrew's University, said this:

If paganism had been destroyed, it was less through annihilation than through absorption. Almost all that was pagan was carried over to survive under a Christian name. Deprived of demi-gods and heroes, men easily and half-unconsciously invested a local martyr with their attributes ... transferring to him the cult and mythology associated with the pagan deity. Before the fourth century was over the martyr cult was universal ... pagan festivals were re-named, and Christmas Day, the ancient festival of the Sun, was transformed into the birthday of Jesus.

Christianity did not destroy the pagan ceremonies, it took them over! Incidentally, the word 'pagan', which, I am told, really means 'country people', has been changed to mean 'uncivilised heathen' and used as an all-encompassing term for pre-Christians. The implication is that all pre-Christians were 'heathen' and that Christianity 'civilised' the world. This is simply untrue. It is the same with the term 'Christian values'. We are supposed to believe that Christianity invented decent values. Nonsense. It is all part of centuries of Christian propaganda.

Outside the grotto in Bethlehem, the guide introduced me to his friend whom he said he had bumped into purely by accident. This friend just happened to own a souvenir shop around the corner, I was soon to learn.

'He likes your face,' the guide informed me.

'Oh, good,' I thought. 'But I bet he likes my pocket a shade more.'

Sure enough.

'He invites you back to his home for a drink with him.'

'Okay, thanks, very nice.'

We arrived at his home after a few seconds' walk. It was a nice home, but strange in a way. It had every appearance of being a big souvenir shop. It was the large front window, the credit card signs, the counters, the cash register, and all the souvenirs, that gave it away, really. As I looked around,

I didn't know whether to laugh or scream. You could buy holy this, holy that, holy anything. I didn't quite see the holy toilet paper, but it must have been there. In fact, given all the crap spoken in the name of religion, I would have thought it essential. Among my favourites were the little crosses made from 'holy earth from the holy land'. In case I thought for one moment that it might be a con, the wrapper assured me: 'Each one inspected by a genuine Catholic family.' But nothing could surpass the plastic baby Jesus, in all sizes to suit all pockets. They were like those cheap dolls you see in the 'nothing over £1' shops in England. If you bought the small version, your Jesus only had a bit of wire for a halo, but really go for it and buy the deluxe model, and you, too, could have a baby Jesus with three genuine, gold-painted, plastic prongs sticking out of his head. The shopowner could see what he took to be my longing looks as I surveyed the rows of baby Jesuses. He thought he would push me over the edge and into my pocket.

'They are genuine,' he said.

'Genuine? A genuine baby Jesus?'

'They are made by local priests.'

'Ah. That kind of genuine.'

My God. This is not only religion we are talking about here. It's a whole bloody industry. Millions are on the payroll. Bishops' palaces, tourist guides, tacky gift shops, entire economies and political systems in some countries. All depend for their survival on the perpetuation of fantasy. From the Vatican to Bethlehem, from Jerusalem to Salt Lake City, the cash registers go on singing to the music of myth. The Vatican and the other bastions of mind control know that information exists that would bring them crashing down. That's why they have worked so hard to suppress it. Unless they do, the party's over. No wonder there is so much opposition to information that will expose this global con-trick when the economic and personal power of church and state depends on deception of monumental proportions.

I returned to the Old City. The man who liked my face, the

first one that is, announced he wanted his money. Anything I gave him would be acceptable, he said. I gave him a fair amount for three hours' work with a meal thrown in and he proceeded to give me earache until I coughed up some more.

We said goodbye and I walked around the outside of the city walls to what is said to be the Garden of Gethsemane where Jesus is reputed to have spent time. When I was close, I asked a passer-by the way. He was most helpful.

'I show you,' he said. 'It's only around the corner.'

'Thanks, very kind.'

Hold on a minute. Isn't that a black leather jacket he's wearing? Oh no, not again. I followed him into the garden and he suddenly switched from his passer-by to tourist guide mode. 'This is the very tree where Jesus was arrested ... these trees have been here for ...'

'Excuse me. Thank you for your help, but I only want to stand here on my own, if it's okay with you.'

'You mean you don't want me to show the church and the tomb of Mary and ...'

'No thanks, all the same.'

'I give you good price.'

'No.'

He left somewhat bemused and mumbled something to another leather jacket nearby.

I have this nightmare. I leave this physical body and return to another frequency. On the threshold, a spirit in a black leather jacket touches my arm.

'Hello, my friend,' it says. 'Are you from Planet Earth? I know many people on Planet Earth. I show you heaven. I like your face.'

As with all the places I visited, the Garden of Gethsemane felt sad. Maybe it was my own mood coming through, but I don't think so. I have often felt places to be happy and joyous when that has not been my own state of mind. I didn't stay long and I decided to walk to the top of the Mount of Olives high above Gethsemane. As I began to walk, a taxi driver leaned out of his car window:

'Where you going?'

'The top of the Mount of Olives. How far to walk?'

'Forty minutes and it's very steep. I take for a good price.'

He was right. It was steep and I was glad I accepted his offer. We stopped near the top and I looked across to the Old City of Jerusalem. It is a stunningly beautiful and moving sight. It must be one of the most impressive views of any city in the world. I could see the famous Golden Gate which is bricked up and, both Moslems and Jews believe, will only open when the Messiah comes. They are in for a long wait. Either that, or they should open it to everyone now because we are all potential messiahs for change and justice. Immediately behind me was the Intercontinental Hotel. What environmental sacrilege to build that or anything else at this spot! I didn't like what I was seeing in Jerusalem and the way it was being exploited. I didn't feel happy here at all and I wanted to go home.

The taxi driver said he was having a bad day for tourists and he would give me a good price to take me to the old city of Jericho and the place where Jesus was tempted by Satan. The thought that Satan might have worn a black leather jacket and the temptation might involve the offer of a guided tour did cross my mind briefly. I was so tired after the flight that I refused the trip. But *this* guy was not letting go. I think if I had stayed my ground for long enough he would have paid *me*. He halved his original price and, before I could say anything, he roared off through Bethany on the way to Jericho. Okay, I thought. Why not? I might as well be depressed there as here.

We talked about the story of Jesus and whether you could take any of it to be true. He came out with a memorable line which summed up all that I had seen since my plane landed. He didn't know about the truth of the story, but, he said: 'Jesus is very good for tourist buses and taxi drivers because he moved around a lot.' If he hadn't, they would have made sure people believed he had, have no doubt.

At least the journey to Jericho was inspiring: the first time I had felt uplifted since I arrived in what was supposed to be the Holy Land. He took me on a minor road through the hills – and the landscape just sang to me. It was a fantastic place and all I could say was 'incredible', 'gorgeous', 'I can't believe it'. Of all the places I have seen, only parts of Peru compare with the way it made me feel. The hills were barren and typically biblical, but they had a beauty and dignity that you would have to experience to appreciate. I could have sat out there for hours.

We stopped at the supposed site of old Jericho where the walls long ago came tumbling down, although I bet it took more than a few trumpets. It is now an archaeological excavation and said to be the place of the world's oldest known city. I sat among the excavations looking across to the rock where, the guides say, Jesus was tempted by Satan, the so-called Mount of Temptation. I don't accept any of that, but I can say for sure that the energies passing through me as I sat on the Jericho site were wonderful. They were calm and peaceful; powerful, but gentle. Whenever you go to places where there has been a settlement for a very long time, they are almost always energy points because that would have attracted the settlers in the first place when they understood the ways of the Earth.

Back in Jersualem, the inspiration of the hills had faded, and I longed to return to the airport. I was feeling so depressed sitting alone in my room that I went for a walk to find the location of the airline office. The next day I meant to get out of here. I couldn't stand it anymore. Night was falling and as I walked all the pain of the previous two years came flooding back. If it weren't for Linda and my family, I could see no point in going on. What was it all about? All this pain and agony, all this frustration, and for what? Where was it leading? The moon and a few bright stars had appeared above the wall of the Old City. I sat on a rock by the road looking up at the heavens.

'Why does all this have to be so bloody painful?' I asked the sky in despair. 'All I want to do is pass on truth. Why does it have to hurt so much?'

The next morning I went to Temple Mount in the Old City. Temple Mount, or Mount Moriah, is where they reckon King Solomon built the first temple. It is a sacred site for Jews, Moslems and Christians and they all claim it for their own. Today it is dominated by the dome of a magnificently decorated mosque. Inside is a large rock which is said to be the place where Abraham offered his son in sacrifice to God, and some say the rock has a footprint of the prophet Mohammed. Somewhere in the building they claim to have some hairs from his beard.

Getting into the mosque entailed more hassle with a leather jacket. 'How will you know the meaning of everything if no-one shows you?' I would struggle by, I said. I walked around the inside a few times and stood at the centre near the rock. I expected it to be a powerful energy point, but instead the atmosphere was very flat. It was almost as if the energies had been switched off.

Outside, as I thumbed through the little guidebook I realised how easy it is for myths to become 'fact'. It tells me that many of the so-called 'fourteen stations of the cross' in Jerusalem were decided by European Christians who had never been there. The 'stations' are places in the Old City where it is said that Jesus fell holding the cross, or had his brow wiped by an onlooker, incidents like that. It turns out that there were once no more than seven 'stations', but European churchmen decided on some more and visitors to Jerusalem from Europe wanted to see the places they had been told about back home. As a result, the monks in Jerusalem included them to keep everyone happy. I also learn that the Church of the Holy Sepulchre at the end of the 'stations' tour is only considered the place where Jesus was crucified because a Queen Helena decided this was so in AD 326 ... a year after you know what. Her son, a Roman Emperor, then had a great basilica built on the site to house the 'tomb' of Jesus. Now who was it again? Ah yes, our old friend Constantine the Great.

As I left the Temple Mount area, I saw a group of little

Moslem children playing football in the street. Every one seemed to be called Mohammed. They would already have been indoctrinated into the ways and laws of the Koran and they would have developed a certain view of Jewish people. It struck me as I watched them that if they had been born only a few minutes' walk away in the Jewish Quarter, they would have already been indoctrinated into a very different view of life and Creation, and they would have developed a certain view of Arab people. Left to themselves with no indoctrination from birth, those little Arab children would have been playing football with little Jewish children and in a few generations there would be only one people, one world, one universal family. In places like Northern Ireland the religious bigotry on both sides claims quite wrongly to be speaking for the people, who even fall out over the interpretation of the same basic religion. After all these years, I can settle the argument for them. They are both wrong, I would suggest.

Jerusalem symbolises all the divisions, violence, suffering, lies and misunderstanding that religion has visited upon the world. How ironic that *shalem* (or *shalom*) means peace and hence it is known as the City of Peace. Poor old Jerusalem. What has it done to deserve all this?

The airline could not change my flight and I had to stay another two days. What's that they say about free will? I couldn't work out why I was so depressed here. Was it the exploitation, the untruths, or just the place? Maybe it was all three. Whatever the reason, Jerusalem and I were not getting on. I went back to my room around mid-day and I stayed there until the following morning. I wrote this whole passage about religion and my visit to Israel up to this point sitting on the bed with a pen and sheets of scrap paper. Somehow it seemed appropriate that such a message should be written within the walls of the 'Holy City'. The way it is written reflects my mood at the time.

There was certainly more energy in that room than I felt at Temple Mount. My feet were burning and there was powerful energy all around me. That night I had a series of vivid dreams, some of the most vivid I can remember. I would wake up after one and go straight into the next. They were very clear, but too complex to detail. My father was involved in one and it was as if he was in the room, so sharp was the figure I saw.

As the Sun rose above the city the next morning I felt very different about the place somehow. I stood at the window looking at the misty outline of the Temple Mount mosque and I knew the anger and depression that had dominated my first two days had lifted. I felt brighter and lighter. I can't tell you what had happened, but it was almost as if Jerusalem and me had made our peace. Perhaps the experience was related to some past life there. Who knows? But something changed that night and when I left I missed the place.

I walked from the Old City below a cloudless sky, an appropriate contrast to the cloud and drizzle that so captured my mood on the day I had arrived. At the bus station the guns and uniforms were there in force again and my eyes caught the headlines at the news-stand: 'Two soldiers killed in Gaza ambush', and 'Thousands march against deportations'.

Another day dawns in the Holy Land.

I arrived at the airport nearly twenty-four hours before my flight because I wanted to hire a car there and see some of the country. The name in my mind was Beersheba to the south, but as I drove from the airport towards Tel Aviv I lost my way on the complicated road system. Eventually I found myself driving inland and I kept seeing signs to the Jordan Valley. That felt good to me and I followed them across the hills and mountains of what the Jews call Samaria. The traffic thinned out the further I travelled and there were long stretches when there were no other people or vehicles to be seen. Most of those I did see were army trucks as I headed into disputed territory. (Actually the whole of Israel is disputed territory, but you know what I mean.) It was a beautiful journey. The plains of the Jordan Valley opened up before me amid the haze of a lovely day. In the distance were the mountains of Jordan and I was now deep into the area known as the West Bank which was taken by the Israelis in the war of 1967.

Driving across Israel you realise what a narrow country it is and I can understand why the Jews feel so threatened. But I can equally understand why the Palestinians felt so aggrieved at having their homeland taken from them so arrogantly after the Second World War. As with so many trouble spots, the only solution is for both sides to respect the rights and feelings of the other and leave behind the religious and political dogma which is at the heart of the division. After all, there are no Israelis or Arabs, Catholics, or Protestants, on the other frequencies. They exist only in the mixed-up mind of humanity and I would love to be there when they all realise that each has had lives as the other! I don't consider myself English or British or European or white or anything, and I never really have. I am just me. We all just are.

I turned right into the Jordan Valley and aimed for the Dead Sea. People had warned me not to go alone to these areas close to the Jordan River, but I never felt in any danger. It is the same wherever I have travelled. I just know everything is going to be all right. On the way I passed the entrance to the excavations at Jericho where I had been with the taxi driver two days before. Then, emerging through the haze and glistening under a brilliant sun, was the Dead Sea. It is something I will never forget. On its far shore were the mountains of Jordan, on the other the mountains of Israel. The Dead Sea is the lowest point on the face of the Earth, 1,280 feet below 'real' sea level. I have rarely seen such a magical place. Mother Earth, you are simply amazing.

Before long I was at Qumran on the northern shore. It was here that the Dead Sea Scrolls were found in a cave by an Arab shepherd in 1947. There were eight clay jars containing parchment scrolls and fragments wrapped in ancient linen. They were bought for a nominal fee by a Bethlehem trader before finding their way to the Hebrew University in Jerusalem where their significance began to unfold. Among the scrolls was the text from the Old Testament Book of Isaiah, but even though they were found nearly fifty years ago most of their contents have yet to be revealed to the public. Why?

The scrolls would appear to be the work of a spiritual group called the Essenes which was based at Qumran at the time Jesus is said to have lived. The ruins at Qumran were almost deserted when I bought my entrance ticket and walked in. I sat for a while in the shade above the cave where the scrolls were found. A gentle energy washed over me. Love, pure love, is the only way I can describe it. From my lips came the words: 'I forgive them everything.' To what that referred or where the words came from, I cannot say. They were followed by: 'Let there be Light, let the power flow again, let the spirit live.'

That was all. The energy lifted and I walked across to an area marked 'cemetery'. Again love surrounded me and my feet began to burn. I looked at my hands and they were covered in red and white blotches, something that always happens when I am channelling energy. There was so much love there. It was like standing in another world, another dimension of understanding.

I continued along the road beside the Dead Sea. If they were making a television series called 'Road Journeys of the World', this would be a certainty. It winds its way between the mountains and the sea, and on the far shore the mountains of Jordan cast a near-perfect reflection on the water. With few tourists, mine was the only car to be seen for long periods and everywhere was so quiet, so calm and peaceful. I stopped at one point and walked down to a beach. Almost a quarter of the volume of the water is made up of minerals and so it is impossible for anything to live in such conditions. It feels more like washing-up liquid than water! The sea is not only dead, it's disappearing. The water is evaporating faster than the Jordan River can replenish it and it is this evaporation which produces a thin haze over the water, giving the landscape a dreamy, mystical quality.

My next stop was Massada, a flat-topped mountain which soars from Earth a short distance back from the water. It is a staggering spectacle and they say that the last group of Jews involved in the rebellion against the Romans held out here for nearly three years. When all was lost, it is believed, they committed suicide rather than surrender. The mountain is 1,450 feet high and yet, because of the low altitude of the area, it is only 135 feet above sea level at its highest point. There is now a cable car to the top. Several coach parties were leaving when I arrived and the mountain-top was relatively free from people. I sat almost in the centre, among some ruins, and looked out across the water to Jordan. Energy flowed through me and I drifted away in the warmth of the sun. Once more words came to me in my semi-sleep: 'Let the key be turned. Let the life force awaken. Let Mother Earth speak to the world in words they cannot ignore. Let there be Light. Let there be peace.'

As I gazed out across the glorious valley, I knew that a new phase of the transformation was beginning. I noticed a couple had sat down nearby and we began to chat about the country and its religious beliefs. They said, without my prompting, how disappointed they had been with Temple Mount. It had felt so negative and lifeless. I think that Jerusalem was once the centre of a powerful pattern of energy lines and it was this that first attracted settlers who understood its significance. It is the same with countless other places. As the understanding is lost, the myths and legends begin to take over from simple truth. Gradually, people are attracted to a place because of the nonsense that is attached to it and it becomes a symbol of political and religious power and dogma. This destroys the energy pattern or causes it to be shut down to avoid polluting the whole system. This, I believe, happened to Jerusalem and also at one point to Massada, but the time has come for them to be re-activated to send their latent power across the planet. What changes this will bring.

The Sun eased closer to the distant mountains and I said goodbye to Massada. I drove away from the Dead Sea and across the hills and mountains of Judaea. I went on past Arad and through Beersheba back to Tel Aviv Airport to complete a vast circuit around Jerusalem and central Israel. It had been a day to lift the heart and inspire the spirit. For that one day alone, I was so glad I had come.

In the hours before my flight, I had time to reflect on many things. I gathered my thoughts in particular on this whole story of Jesus. I have a real problem with the gospels. I think there has been some skulduggery here or – let us be charitable – some serious exaggeration. Much of the New Testament, I believe, is a compilation of a host of legends and myths that existed long before Jesus was claimed to have lived. I think, also, that the words of people like St Paul are not worth the paper they are so widely written on. To be frank, if you were going purely on the historical evidence you would be hard pressed to make a case that Jesus even existed at all. Maybe Jesus is really a thought form, a figment of the collective imagination created and fuelled by the propaganda of the church over so many centuries.

My rational self, that part of me which thinks on the purely factual, provable, level, finds it hard to believe that Jesus ever lived. But I believe he did. Or rather I believe there was a man on the back of whom all the propaganda and nonsense we call Christianity has been built. I can't give you evidence of this because none exists. I can only say what I feel. Around 2,000 years ago I think there was a courageous and gifted man, one of many who incarnated at that time in many areas of the world. But his name was certainly not Jesus. That is a Greek version of a Jewish name, probably Jeshuah or something similar. I believe he was extremely psychic and had a knowledge both of healing and hypnotism. He may well have understood the power of the mind enough to do some things that would have been seen as 'miracles'. I would say he travelled widely and often alone, being guided by his intuition to many people who gave him knowledge and helped to activate his powers. Among those he visited and worked with at certain times, I would say, were the Essenes at Qumran and the one known as John the Baptist. I feel he knew of the energy system and visited many energy points on his travels to many other countries. He was able to channel, I believe, immensely powerful frequencies of the energy that many people call the Christ. I am reluctant to use that term because it has other connotations which go back to ancient times. I would call it the energy of transformation, of pure love.

He would have attracted like thinkers, women as well as men. I feel his explanation of Creation, the laws of cause and effect (karma) and reincarnation made sense to people in the wake of the patent rubbish spoken by the religious hierarchy. I believe he fathered children, but none of this would have been allowed to enter the script we call the Bible. The church sees Jesus as perfect and so they couldn't have him involved in anything as imperfect as sex. The same with Mary; it had to be a virgin birth. From this has come the idea of the celibate priest. Think about it. The church says Jesus was perfect. Being perfect, it seems, means not having sex. The church wants us all to be as perfect as Jesus and so, presumably by implication, not to have sex. In this way we will all be so perfect the human race will cease to exist. If they say it's okay to have sex, then we can never be as perfect as Jesus. Either way, what utter nonsense.

It may well be that the church hierarchy had him killed with the support of the Romans who would not have wanted anyone rocking the boat. It is conceivable that he died on a cross or by the sword. It is just as conceivable that he wasn't killed at all. What I cannot believe, given the almost total lack of historical documentation by writers of the time, is that whatever happened was done in the high-profile way described in the Bible. Lots of people were killed in those days on all sorts of made-up charges. Historians would not have documented just another one. From the foundations of this simple story, you could build on all the exaggerations and inventions and turn it into the gospel version you read in the Bible. This is what I feel happened, but I will be delighted to alter that view should other information emerge.

But in the end, you know, much as we might believe in and pay tribute to one man's courage and love of truth, it really doesn't matter that we don't know the details of his life two thousand years ago. Religion is obsessed with the past. You would think that spirituality and truth stopped twenty centuries ago. We must live in the NOW and look at what *is*, not at what was or wasn't. The character I believe became the thought form called Jesus would have been sickened by what has been done in his name. The man who talked of love and tolerance has been used to justify more war, pain and suffering than any other man in all human history. It is a scar on the face of humanity and it's time it was over.

With these thoughts, I prepared to leave Israel. The security at Ben Gurion Airport is extraordinary. First I was interrogated by a man about my trip. Why had I been there? What had I done? Where had I been? Could I prove it? This continued for a good twenty minutes. I was asked for receipts, names and times to back up my story. When he had finished, a woman arrived to repeat the process, asking the same questions and trying to catch me out. Another fifteen minutes went by and I still hadn't reached the check-in desk. Eventually they swapped notes and decided I was okay. The word in the air was fear. This is a country that fears God, fears everything. But that is what most religion is – fear. That is its power and that is the consequence of its arrogance and dogma, be it Jewish, Moslem, Mormon, whatever. That is its legacy to the world. Goodbye, Israel. Nice country. Shame about the faiths.

Back home I completed this book and looked back over all that had happened in such a short time. It has been an amazing tale by any standards, but after all those experiences, what do I really know for sure? I would merely say that I have a life plan which involves helping to break down the wall of suppression which mind-controls humanity, and that this is to be done by passing on information that will help people awaken to who they really are and what is happening to the Earth. I'm not a 'messiah'. I am merely a bloke who believes people should have access to the information I have set out in this book and particularly in the next chapter. I am a rebel in terms of the established order which is destroying the planet, that's obvious, but I am a reluctant rebel. I wish the state of the world were such that there were nothing to rebel against. Being a rebel is a lot of hassle!

I have long felt that my life has been on some kind of spiritual railway track with another level of myself or Creation constantly switching the points and changing the direction. As this book was going to press, I was struck very forcibly by a channelled passage in a fascinating book called *The Only Planet Of Choice* (Gateway Books). The channelling was said to come from a highly evolved consciousness known as The Nine. The term 'angel' here is just a symbolic name for a certain type of 'job description' and has nothing to do with beings with wings so beloved of religion. In the book, The Nine were questioned about 'angels'.

Q: How can we recognise [angels]?
A: Always look for the golden light. Those angels working for the evolution always radiate a golden light. They are messengers from the Creator, they are messengers from the civilisations [other frequencies], and they do not have free choice.
Q: Why?
A: For they have given their free will to the Creator.
Q: So it's another form of service?
A: Yes.

That had such an impact on me because after all that I have experienced I feel that my own free will on this conscious level is at the very least subject to limitations in the cause of the transformation.

Does anyone seriously believe that this conscious level wanted to stand up in a turquoise shellsuit in front of tabloid journalists to say all that I did? Does anyone believe I wanted to go on 'Wogan' and take all that ridicule? Or to face laughter in the street wherever I went? Or put my family through all that happened? Does anyone really think that I sat down and made those decisions given the obvious consequences I knew would ensue, especially as a member of the media myself? All the dies were cast for the consequences that followed in one tiny period in March 1991 and when I see pictures from that time of what was claimed to be me, I simply do not recognise him. If ever there was a picture of someone in some kind of hypnotic state, then it is that guy in the turquoise.

After Jerusalem there was nothing I wanted to do more than bring information to public attention that will transform this troubled world. I knew that all that had happened had been necessary, horrible as it was at times, and I knew that I had agreed to go through it before this incarnation. It was my choice and it was a choice that had to be made because, let's face it, someone had to stand up and launch this subject into the main public arena. Otherwise it would be denied to the vast majority and mind control would continue to imprison them. Those who mock and ridicule me have as much right to hear the information as those who support what I say. It belongs to everyone without exception. I may not always like what I have to do, but I know it has to be done and I will therefore do it to the best of my ability. After all, there was hardly a queue of people waiting to put their head on the block in the same way.

There's no shortage of those who tell me what I should do; and there are countless numbers who say the truths must be made available to everyone. But put most of those people in a position where their name might become known to the public and suddenly you can't see the horizon for dust. I can understand their reluctance, but with knowledge comes privilege and everyone who has information that can help others has a duty to pass it on in the most effective way possible, even if the consequences are less than pleasant. Whenever I see a news bulletin, when I see those who go hungry in a world of plenty or the latest assault on the dignity of Mother Earth, I know that I am doing what must be done, much as I may wish it was different.

I know also that I will go on doing what I believe to be right in the face of whatever may come. Fortunately I am extremely stubborn when necessary and the more anyone tries to stop me the more determined I become to go on. That doesn't mean that I won't sometimes crave a quiet life with my family away from all this, but if the Tumi reading is anything like accurate, a withdrawal from the firing line would not seem to be on the agenda. It said of the future:

Your progressed Moon is moving into Capricorn which will help to bring the whole vision back down to the Earth because Capricorn is an Earth sign and the last time this happened for you it sparked off with Chiron the rheumatoid arthritis. What Chiron is going to throw up this time I'm not sure, but it feels much more like it's to do with the healing processes of the Earth (my arthritis returned to a limited extent right on the changeover). I feel that probably your gift for the next two or three years is actually to walk the earth, to take your message out, communicate your ideas, and at the same time know that on an energy level, regardless of what you say or the way you choose to deliver your message, you are healing the Earth. The energy of Chiron infiltrated you the first time around when you were fifteen and now you have that healing energy within you for the Earth.

This book is the story of my life and so naturally it has focused on what I have done. But I am only one of many, many thousands who are involved in some way in working for the transformation. Soon it will be millions and tens of millions. Some have already been activated, at least to an extent, and the rest will follow. Although my awakening may seem astonishing because of the speed with which it happened and the extremes of experience that suddenly unfolded, the preparation for that time had begun from the moment I was born. If you are looking at a dam, the first signs of trouble only appear when water begins to seep through the concrete. From that moment, things can move very quickly until the whole structure collapses. But the weakening process and the tiny faults and cracks that lead up to that collapse may have started a long time before without anyone noticing. It is the same with spiritual awakening. Many people have opened up unconsciously over a long period to the point where it is about to become conscious – like the water visibly beginning to leak from that symbolic dam. Many of these people are in significant positions to influence others and we will see them emerge in the months and years ahead.

We will see famous people from all walks of life, music, show business, the arts, politics, television, etc. speaking out in support of the truth. There will be others in the church and the media who are about to realise what they are really here to do and they will start to break ranks and challenge what their organisations believe or promote. These people have been put here unconsciously to infiltrate these organisations, and when their moment of activation comes they will be in position to bring down pillars of untruth from within. Even some of those who speak and act in ways that undermine public confidence in 'the system' will, unknowingly, be following their life plan and playing their part in making people think and question the status quo. I have no doubt that the so-called 'young royals', people like the Princess of Wales and the Duchess of York, who have been criticised for undermining the stature of the British monarchy, are simply following their life plans which were designed to do just that. The same with Prince Charles. The monarchy is a symbol of a wholly unjust, misguided way of life and it will soon be no more. You can see from this how quickly things can change, once enough people in the right places are activated.

Against all that are ranged the extreme negative forces which are seeking to wreck this transformation of Planet Earth and they, too, will show themselves in many ways, even working through some of those who have come to play a significant part in this time of change. There are many who had life plans that involved working for the transformation who are not doing so, or are no longer doing so. This is disappointing because it makes the task that much more difficult and leaves them open to be used as a means of discrediting the very truth they had come to pass on. These disruptive, misguided forces, however, will not win through, for the power of love that will soon be sweeping this planet is the ultimate power in Creation. Love will change everything. Love will heal the world.

As I complete my own story and move on to the wider picture of what is happening and what we can do, I'd like to thank all those people who have helped to increase my understanding whether they acted towards me in a negative or positive way. All are equally important if that is what I needed to experience. And this works in the other direction, too. I have done and will do in the future many things that people will condemn and not understand. I ask only that they appreciate that there are many things that have to be done to awaken humanity from its slumber of so many centuries, and there are many ways in which people can give their lives to the cause of human understanding and the transformation of this planet. Many, indeed most, are not the most obvious ways. I hope that people will at least accept that whatever I have done and will do, my motivation is at all times the preservation of this planet and the freeing from bondage of the human mind. If that means upsetting people sometimes and shaking up the status quo until it crumbles, then so be it. As the communication said: 'True love does not always give the receiver what it would like to receive, but it will always give that which is best for it.' Whatever happens, I refuse to be a victim. No matter what is thrown in my direction it will be used to positive effect and I will not let any scale of opposition break my spirit. One day what I have done and will do will be seen in its true light, but that time is not yet. Standing up for the truth has made me a punchball for the media and many other groups and individuals, and that was always going to be a by-product of the job. But look more closely at a punchball. No matter how hard you hit it, a punchball always bounces back to its original position as if nothing had happened. In the end it is the puncher who always gets tired and has to give up. His muscles are aching, his body is awash with sweat, and his arms are able to punch no more. When he walks away, there stands the punchball exactly where it was before the first punch was thrown.

This punchball is just the same.

14

The Messenger

Since those first communications in the spring of 1990, I have been piecing together all the information I have received about the future of the planet.

Even through some dark, dark times which took me to the point of despair, the processing of this information continued and during the writing of this book I went through an enormous leap in consciousness which opened up so much to me. It allowed me to weave together the key strands of knowledge that people need so urgently at this time to understand what is happening and why. What follows is an outline of that information, the culmination of all that I have learned and experienced up to the moment this book went to the presses. There is a tremendous amount still to know and we are all learning something new every day. By the time you read this I will already know much more, but this is the basis of what humanity needs to know now. This is the Message:

It is worth repeating at this stage that there is only one Infinite Consciousness of which we are all a part, and consciousness is energy. Everything that exists in Creation is the same energy vibrating at different speeds, even those things which appear to be solid. At the fastest vibrations it is pure energy. At slower vibrations it turns into what are called sub-atomic particles. At even slower vibrations these particles come together to form the atoms, etc, which make physical matter – what we see all around us today. So your body, your home, your mind, your emotions, the water, the air, everything that exists in any form, is all made from the same energy, but it is vibrating at different speeds and has different levels of consciousness. If you have the knowledge of how to use thought or sound to change the nature of the sub-atomic particles and energies, you can change the nature of the atoms they form and you can change the nature of matter. You can make it appear, disappear, do anything you want with it. As the Magnu channelling said, such things are not miracles, but a matter of order and knowing what you are doing.

Creation is an infinite stream of consciousness – energy – and this is the Infinite Mind, 'God', working through all of us. Names like Rakorski and Magnu are simply a way of identifying different minds or groups of minds, but in fact they are all part of the Infinite Mind. There are no divisions, only what we perceive to be divisions in our part of Creation. The various areas of the stream of energy and the individual droplets – minds – are, however, at different stages of evolution and the Infinite Mind consists of many different levels of consciousness and understanding. These are the frequencies I talk about but they are all created from the same basic energy. The highest level of consciousness, the guide to all the rest, is that original consciousness I talked about right at the start of the book. You might call this the 'Creator' for simplicity.

There is most certainly a plan to sort out the serious problems facing Planet Earth, but there is no Divine Plan with everything pre-ordained into infinity. With free will as a law of evolution, in our part of Creation at least, there can be no pre-ordained Divine Plan because you cannot predict for certain what collective and individual free will choices will be made. The Infinite Mind as a whole is on a never-ending journey of learning and experience through making choices on all levels and learning from the consequences of them. As the individual droplets learn and evolve, so does the whole.

According to information channelled by an excellent channeller and healer called Geoff Bottwood, there are occasions when a vortex emerges in the infinite stream of energy. Again, think of this vortex as a whirlwind shape within the energy, or like a whirlpool or eddy in a fast-flowing river. These vortices are not created by the Infinite Mind saying: 'Oh, I think I'll create a vortex today.' They apparently emerge as a natural consequence of the constant evolution of the whole. There is no need for us to understand exactly how they appear at this stage, only that they do. During the period they exist, these vortices of energy evolve in their own way, and the unique experiences this creates for all within them is another means through which the Infinite Mind constantly learns and experiences. When the vortex has reached a natural conclusion it is absorbed back into the whole Infinite Mind and all that knowledge and experience is similarly absorbed. We live in one such vortex, it seems, but one with a difference.

Our vortex contains all the physical world and much that is not physical. The difference between our vortex and at least the great majority of others is that we have forgotten that we are in a vortex at all. We think that the vortex is the whole of Creation. Even the non-physical levels within the vortex think that, too. The consciousness of the vortex thinks it is *everything* that is, when it is a mere speck of the Infinite Consciousness. When we look out through a telescope or explore space we may think it is infinite, but it is not. It is limited by the walls of the vortex. It is outside the vortex that we will find infinity. Because it has lost touch with that reality, the vortex forgot where it came from and therefore lost the connection with the Infinite Mind outside. You don't seek to reconnect with something you don't think exists.

The vortex has taken on a life, mind and momentum of its own within the Infinite Mind to such an extent that it has effectively become separated from it. So everything within the vortex is created by that part of the Infinite Mind that is within the vortex. As it is not created by the whole Infinite Mind the amount of knowledge, wisdom and understanding is much more limited. This does not mean the vortex energies are stupid – far, far from it. But they are de-linked from the full wisdom of the Infinite Mind. The mind within the vortex is a mini version of the Infinite Mind, you might say, and separated from it. The law of karma does not exist in the same form outside the vortex. It is a process of evolution that has developed here and once you raise your vibration high enough to escape from the vortex the need for repeated physical lives comes to an end. We evolve outside in a more collective way, what one learns we all learn because minds are linked in a much more powerful manner.

The collective mind of the vortex created everything we see in our dense physical universe and, of course, as part of that mind individual minds go on creating in their own way all the time whether they are inside or outside a physical body. Something as simple as building a hut or a house is still creation.

But the disconnection from 'the father', the infinite wisdom of the Infinite Mind, began to show itself and, particularly at this level of dense matter, problems began to develop. As the matter became denser and denser, it became more difficult for the incarnating minds to manifest their knowledge on the physical level. Increasingly the wisdom of the higher levels of the mind was dominated and blocked by the world of dense matter, what came in through the eyes and ears. The consciousness, the frequency, of this physical level continued to fall and it dragged down with it all the other levels within the vortex.

It is really no wonder that this dense physical world finds itself in such trouble. Not only are incarnating minds already subject to a disconnection from the Infinite Mind and so subject to much more limited understanding, the dense physical form they enter cuts them off even from much of the understanding they do have. Incarnating into this dense physical world is like being born into a box with the lid closed. You think that everything that exists must be in that box because you can't see and are not aware of anything else. Hence all the illusions of our world and why so much ridicule and condemnation is heaped upon those who tell a different story. What people like me and others are trying to do is open the box.

The Infinite Mind cannot simply intervene and say, 'I am going to change all this'. There is no omnipotent force, no spiritual Frank Sinatra, saying, 'I'll do it my way'. What the Infinite Mind can do, and decided to do, however, was to ensure that all of its individual minds and life forms could make their decisions and choices on the basis of all the information available, which is certainly not the case within the vortex, especially at this level of dense matter. So as it became clear what was happening, minds began to enter the vortex from outside to bring the information that would challenge the illusions that had developed. These minds could well have been part of that original consciousness, 'the Creator', and perhaps this is where the idea of 'Sons of God' first entered the human psyche. The idea was to awaken that part of every one which knows where it came from, so they would remember that they are part of the greater whole and that the greater whole is far more than just the vortex in which they currently exist. We are often told that there is a 'divine spark' in all of us, that there is a part of God within all of us. But we are more than that. We *are* God. Our consciousness is part of the One Consciousness, the Infinite Mind, and the energy it has created is everything we are and see.

I would suggest that this idea of a 'divine spark' within us is really a misunderstanding of that part of us – the part deep, deep inside and constantly suppressed by the illusions of the vortex and the physical world – that still remembers where it came from and where it seeks to return. That is the part of every mind that I and others are trying to awaken today. It is the faint memory of the situation I have just outlined that has led to the constant theme through the centuries of lost souls 'returning to God'. These are symbolic of souls – minds – breaking away from the whole, becoming trapped in this misguided vortex and then seeking to reunite with the whole, 'the father' again.

The biggest influx of highly evolved minds to enter the vortex from outside came at the time known as Atlantis. They had the advantage of very recent knowledge of the real situation and a direct link through special energy channels to the Infinite Mind outside. Even that, however, did not protect them totally from being scrambled by the illusions they had come to remove and many were. Their task was to try to raise the level of consciousness and understanding, especially at the dense physical level, so the vibrations could be raised. This would help to lift the frequencies of the whole vortex until, in stages, it could be resynchronised with and re-absorbed into the Infinite Mind. This could only be done by enough minds in incarnation remembering who they were and where they came from, so raising the frequency of the physical level.

These highly developed minds who became Atlanteans did not, at least initially, have the dense physical form of others on Earth at the time. They were so different from the rest and capable of such amazing feats that they became known to those in dense physical bodies as 'gods' and this is where many of the ancient myths about gods originate. Many people believe that Atlantis was a vast island in the Atlantic, destroyed by colossal earthquakes, volcanoes and tidal waves around 10,500 BC, give or take one or two thousand years. Exactly what form Atlantis took is not important. Fascinating, yes, but not important. For me, we only need to appreciate that it was a formidable attempt by the Infinite Mind to make all within this vortex and physical world aware of the true situation and that, to a larger or lesser extent, it was not as successful as had been hoped.

After the demise of Atlantis, many of the minds who had

come in to help the vortex evolve had become caught up in its imbalances and delusions and were no longer doing what they had come to do – quite the opposite in some cases. They now had knowledge without the balance of wisdom and they did some very negative things, indeed they are still doing so. Some of the others began to incarnate into dense physical bodies, albeit more genetically evolved ones, and it was they who started what are known as the great civilisations of human history like the Sumerians, the early Egyptians, the Mayans, Chinese and many others. The Cathars were another expression of this. They had great success in the twelfth and early thirteenth centuries in challenging the Roman Catholic Church's control over human minds. They were particularly successful in Southern France and Northern Italy with their views on reincarnation and suchlike. They were so effective that Pope Innocent III launched a 'crusade' to remove them. This 'crusade' was one of the most gruesome examples of man's inhumanity to man that has ever been documented. The Cathars were finally 'defeated' at a place called Montsegur. Many of those Cathar minds are back in incarnation today.

Through this whole period, despite all these efforts, the situation continued to deteriorate until we reached the situation we have now. It has become increasingly difficult for the higher levels of the Mind, the higher self and true self, to manifest their knowledge through the dense physical form, and the destruction this has caused has reached the point where if it continues there will be a catastrophe for all within the vortex. The Earth Spirit, the mind of this planet, does not wish to go out of incarnation, she wishes to evolve, and that will happen if at all possible, even if this means every human form must go to achieve it.

Not all the physical level will be raised to a higher frequency. There will be many minds and planets who stay at this level of understanding or, rather, misunderstanding. It is a sort of harvesting process, raising up and out of dense matter all that are ready and willing, and it is vital that the

Earth Spirit and this planet be among the current 'wave' who will rise to a higher frequency. Unless this happens, she will be forced out of incarnation by a misguided humanity and the consequences of that will spread far and wide for reasons I will explain shortly. When the present transformation process is complete, the dense physical level will be smaller and therefore its 'drag' on the rest of the vortex will be less. In simple terms the fall into dense matter is, in stages, being reversed. In due course, when the time is right, there will be another 'harvesting' of the dense physical level and so on until everyone is freed from the delusions it creates. As a communication I was given for *The Truth Vibrations* said: 'Not one single being is left alone, uncared for. All are gathered in at the end of the day and not one sheep will be left in the field.'

This raising of consciousness on the level of dense matter is now underway and this affects not only the Earth, but every planet, star and life form. The time has come for the vortex, or universe as it is called, to make a leap in evolution. Crucial to that is the leap in evolution that must happen at the lowest level, that of dense matter, or at least a significant part of it. The Earth's frequency is already rising, but it needs to rise by a phenomenal amount before the massive shift in vibration that is necessary can take place. This is why it is so vital that the information which I and others are passing on is accepted by the widest possible number of people.

Every time one individual makes a jump in consciousness it helps to push up the overall frequency because it is raising the vibration in the energy sea and the collective psyche – as the communication said, 'One man cannot change the world, but one man can communicate the message that will change the world.' It is through the collective mind of a species that you can get the so-called hundredth monkey syndrome: when a certain number of a species learns something new, suddenly the whole species can do it without being shown. It also helps to fill the energy sea with thought forms carrying truth and these will challenge the domination of the 'system' thought forms and those of science and religion which have controlled humanity's thinking.

There are extreme negative forces in many forms which are trying to stop this transformation. This planet has been controlled by these forces for a very long time and their grip has tightened over the last two hundred years. Again you will see these forces depicted symbolically in all the ancient legends. They are not evil, they are seriously imbalanced and themselves controlled by the pressures created by the separation from the Infinite Mind. These forces have as their aim the control of all Creation. It is important when you receive channelled information to learn to distinguish between communications that are coming from outside the vortex and those from inside. Communicators inside the vortex are often misguided and confused themselves, and a significant number are seeking to destroy the planet. It is from these sources that you get the disruptive information, extreme negative energies taking over human beings, and phenomena like 'poltergeists'. As someone once said: 'Death is no cure for ignorance.'

The highly negative forces seek to control us through our emotions and to keep us from any knowledge that will set us free. They want to see us at war with each other and the Earth because that creates yet more negative energy on which they feed and grow. They know that every war creates more negative energy and so sets the climate for more and bigger wars to follow. Instead of seeing war and conflict as one side against another, we would be nearer the truth if we asked about the forces working through both sides at the same time.

These forces have also created conflict elsewhere in the vortex, and some of the science fiction we see like 'Star Wars' is not as far-fetched as it might at first seem. Much science fiction, including 'Star Trek', is merely the manifestation of faint memories the writers have of how things really are. Remember, these extreme negative minds and energies are as much the Infinite Mind as you are. Everything is 'God' if you want to use that term and extreme negative forces are merely abusing the gift of consciousness they have been given. But they are playing their part, also, in helping us to experience and learn, if you think about it.

Another key consequence of all the negative energy engulfing the planet is that the link between the higher self and that part of the mind within the physical body can be seriously affected. It is like a radio signal that becomes weak or subject to interference. The messages from the higher self designed to keep us on our life plan are not able to get through as efficiently as they should and once that happens we lose touch with all that knowledge and wisdom. This is why so much human behaviour is not part of the life plan 'script', but free will running riot. Massive karmic implications often ensue from the way we subsequently behave. It is the same with our birth chart programming. The severe negative imbalance can make it more difficult to tune powerfully in to the planetary energies people need to guide them, and that makes the life plan harder to follow.

There is now a massive transformation going on around us to bring an end to the separation from our higher selves and true selves and all the mental, emotional and physical pain this has caused. The situation is this: Each frequency needs to have at least some form of balance between negative and positive energies if we are to enjoy the best characteristics of both energies and not suffer the extremes. We need the interplay of negative and positive energies and we have negative and positive experiences to achieve this until we reach a state of perfect balance between the two. When this happens we progress, or have the choice to progress, from one frequency to another, and then the whole process of negative-positive interplay starts again to lift us to the top of the next frequency and so on.

It is not negative energy as such that is the problem – it is when negative or even positive energy dominates and swamps the other. Negative energy is not a bad thing in itself, it gives us determination, the ability to organise, keeps out feet on the ground, and much more. In the same way positive energy gives us the ability to love in the true sense, to care, to do all the things we would say are good and desirable, but it, too, has its extremes.

When positive energy dominates to an extreme we get what I call the 'hey man' syndrome when you sort of float away in some spiritual mist and lose touch with the practical side of life on the physical level. But that is not the problem that faces humanity as a whole at this time because we are suffering from an extreme imbalance of negative energies and that shows itself in conflict, anger, materialism, self-ishness, and a desire for power and domination. This has come about over thousands and thousands of years because humanity has been generating through its thoughts and actions far more negative energy than positive. A negative thought creates negative energy, a positive thought creates positive energy. This negativity as it is called has polluted, unbalanced the sea of energy in which we live and it has become a self-perpetuating process. As the sea of energy has become more negative, this has encouraged people to think and act more negatively, which has made the energy sea even more negative and so on. This is how the extreme negative forces have taken control of Planet Earth.

It is no accident that it's in this century, with this process gathering pace all the time, that we have had two World Wars, more wars and conflict than ever before, more pain, suffering, anger and an assault on the environment that is beyond belief. And all the negative energy created on Earth affects everything else within this universe and beyond because it is destabilising the balance point of the universe – Planet Earth.

Chakras come in series of seven and the balance point is, not surprisingly, the one in the middle, the heart chakra, signified by the colour green. If the heart chakra is imbal-anced then so is everything else. It is also the point from which the energy we call love emanates. If the heart chakra is diminished so is the flow of love.

Every level has chakras – a plant, a person, an area of land, a planet, a universe, etc, – under the principle of as above, so below. All this is extremely relevant to our predicament when you consider that Glastonbury Tor is the heart chakra for the British Isles; a triangle of land with points at the Tor and in Warwickshire and Hampshire is the heart chakra of the planet; and the Earth is the heart chakra of the universe. This planet is designed to be the balance point between the spiritual and physical worlds. In short, if the Earth is imbalanced then, as the heart chakra for the universe, it must mean the universe becomes increasingly imbalanced. This is what is happening. A communication for *The Truth Vibrations* said: 'The Universe needs the life that the Earth brings forth. It is not for you alone that we do this work. There has always been an order in the way the planets have been governed. Man has not understood the linkages that bind everything together.'

Many early channellings referred to the Earth spirit as the 'Goddess of Love' and this, I was to learn, was because she is a source of love energy for the universe – the heart chakra. It follows that if her own heart chakra can be rebalanced, that triangle of land in England, then this will have a tremendous effect on rebalancing the universe. This is why England is so vital to the plan for human and planetary transformation. A Magnu channelling in the early days of my awakening had said this, although I didn't realise its relevance at the time:

As in your human body, there are energy lines around your planet, through your planet, which correspond, I suppose, very much to the acupuncture lines and meridians in your body. Where two lines cross you create a vortex, a whirlpool of energy, a tiny vortex if it's two. The more lines that intersect, the bigger the vortex. Therefore when you have a chakra you have a large vortex of intersecting energy. It is the same with your planet.

Where most lines cross, there is the biggest vortex. Now you could say the plexus (network) in and around the islands you call the British Isles is the hub of the wheel of plexuses and energies which surround your planet. It has acted in other times like a fail-safe device. In order to activate these chakric points upon your planet, the energies must pass through the central point. They must pass through the heart of the pattern.'

The energies that go into that massive energy centre in England affect the entire planet and it is so, so urgent that this area, especially, is rebalanced. According to many channellings to people all over the world, we are close to the point where the mind of the planet, the Spirit of the Earth, can take no more punishment, and should that mind depart the effects on the physical planet will be the same as on our physical bodies when we depart. It will be no more. This is not going to be allowed to happen and humanity must understand this. The process is now underway to rebalance the energies that encircle the Earth to ensure that such a catastrophe is avoided, and this decade and those that follow in the next century is the time it *must* happen. The Earth is already on a spiritual life-support machine because she cannot continue to operate independently without constant help from the unseen levels.

We should not be surprised at this. The surprise is that she has stayed this long. This planet is the physical body of a glorious spirit. Think what state we would be in if our physical body was plundered in the way hers has been ... if we were gouged, drilled and poisoned ever more severely with every rise in economic growth. She is only still here because she knows the consequences for everyone of not being here. Every negative thought and act we produce she feels and absorbs because she is part of us and we are part of her. Her energy system has been devastated, her emotions have been devastated, she is in turmoil, and that is why so much of the Earth's surface is dying. If we are going to end this process now – and we *are* – we must remember who we are and the true nature of Creation. We must wake up from our spiritual slumber and reject the programming the system seeks to impose upon us.

The Earth Spirit is preparing to take a gigantic leap forward in her consciousness and frequency. This has long been planned. But this needs to take place at a time when she is being raped and ravaged by the imbalances of this frequency and the misunderstandings of the sleeping minds controlled by the illusions we call the physical world. This means that instead of being a gentle transition from one frequency to another, it is going to be the spiritual equivalent of the Bob Beamon long jump which staggered the 1968 Olympic Games in Mexico. The timing of that Beamon leap was appropriate because it was in the 1960s that Operation-Save-The-Earth really began to happen.

In the 1960s the process began of bringing in positive energies from other levels to balance out the negative domination of this one. It was those positive energies that affected the young and created the Flower Power period among those who were ready to tune in to the appropriate vibration. Unfortunately many chose to use drugs to experience other levels of reality when the only way to do it safely and permanently is by thinking, seeking, removing psychic and karmic blocks, and expanding consciousness. Through the 1970s and 1980s as the energies continued to come in, they affected many others in a way that spawned the Green movement, the animal welfare movement, and vegetarianism. Through the later 1980s and into the 1990s with these positive energies pouring into this frequency in ever greater quantities, we have seen the incredible growth in spiritual awareness among many millions. They are being awakened to who they really are and the true nature of Creation. Soon it will be a flood that no-one, no system, can stop.

The positive energy already channelled to the Earth is having tremendous effects on humanity, effects that will become more obvious and pronounced all the time. As *The*

Truth Vibrations said, this will show itself in enormous geological events, the like of which we have never seen in the modern world; extremes of weather, such as great droughts in some areas, fantastic rains and winds in others; and in the minds and emotions of humankind. The strange weather patterns being monitored all over the world have less to do with the Greenhouse Effect and everything to do with the changing nature of these sub-atomic energies. These changes will lead eventually to a shift of the Earth's magnetic poles and a shift in the physical axis. This axis shift is necessary to synchronise all levels of the Earth with the new energies and the new energy system throughout this universe. How severe the changes need to be depends to a very large extent on humanity, and what I set out here is how events are likely to turn out if we go on as we are. But we are not helpless onlookers in this – we can change the outcome in many ways.

But from now on, as things stand, we will see this process of change gather pace. The economic system of the world will continue to decline, despite a few false dawns, and together with other events such as drought, geological events, extremes of weather and war, this will bring food shortages and prices will rocket. Look at the economic cost of the hurricane in Florida and Louisiana in August 1992, and in Hawaii soon afterwards, and imagine what will happen to the economic system when such natural disasters become more frequent and powerful. We will see insurance companies collapse as the amount they are paying out increases dramatically while opportunities to make money through investments will fall equally spectacularly. The banks will follow, as will the entire economic system. We will need to organise barter economies in local communities with goods and services being exchanged for other goods and services rather than money. In the end, though, we will need to help and care for each other irrespective of what we may get, or not get, in return.

The weather will become more and more unpredictable

and extreme with records for heat, cold, drought, rainfall, snow and wind speeds continually broken. The inundations of land by water will likewise increase through high seas and tidal waves. The geological effects will gradually build up with earthquakes and tremors happening in places that have rarely or never experienced them in modern times. And as the energy changes increase the scale of these events will increase until unprecedented volcanoes and earthquakes strike all over the world. The map of the world could be about to be redrawn and scientists will realise there are many, many fault lines or fracture lines that they never realised were there. Similar upheavals have happened many times before in periods when the Earth has taken an evolutionary leap or when humanity has created the need for the planet to be rebalanced. The difference today is that both are happening at the same time.

Think of this process in terms of that symbolic bowl of water. What happened to me in the spring of 1991 is happening to the planet. We are entering that period when the tap is on full and the water, the energy, is thrashing about in chaos and turmoil before it finds the new balance at a higher level. In the 1960s the positive energy 'tap' was turned on slowly and it has been gathering pace all the time. 1987 was a significant year when a big energy shift took place, and now in the 1990s and the decades of the twenty-first century the tap is being turned on more and more until it reaches maximum. It is no wonder that we and the planet are being affected on all levels, physical, emotional, mental and spiritual.

Those who are able to tune in to these new vibrations will find themselves speeding ahead to greater enlightenment, understanding and wisdom because the new energies carry more of all those things. These people will reject the old ways of living and turn to a simpler, non-violent lifestyle, based on respect for all life. We will see people who have been in opposition through their lives suddenly working together for a common aim as the economic system falls and breaks down the divisions between 'us' and 'them'. We will appreciate that in Creation there is no us and them, only 'we'. People will change in ways we could not imagine. The rising vibrations are stimulating those who can tune in to think for themselves and question their personal and collective way of life. 'Why?' is the most liberating word in any language. Ask it enough times and the system falls apart before your eyes. Thinking and seeking is the key and I believe there is another planet, as yet undiscovered, beyond Pluto that is increasingly triggering this process of questioning and change.

It is much easier in the short term not to think and this is why much of humanity has become like a flock of sheep following the one in front – the system. But increasingly we are seeing the sheep asking where the one in front is leading them and why they are following him in the first place. They are receiving no credible reply because there is no credible reply, and the flock is breaking up and going off in the direction each individual feels right for them. These quicking vibrations are making it easier for the wisdom of the higher self to manifest on the conscious level and this is adding to these changing attitudes.

Female energies will also come to the fore as they begin to balance out male domination. We will see women taking their rightful place as the equal of men and men will increasingly show the characteristics of female energies like gentleness, compassion and service to others, as they move closer to a male-female balance within their energy field. There are so many effects that are already there to be seen in ourselves and people around us as the vibrations rise. The Magnu channelling said:

> I feel you are sensing now the energies coming in, the energies surrounding your planet. This is causing many of you to ask questions. It is causing many of you to re-evaluate completely your way of life, where you wish to go, what you want to do. It is causing tremendous

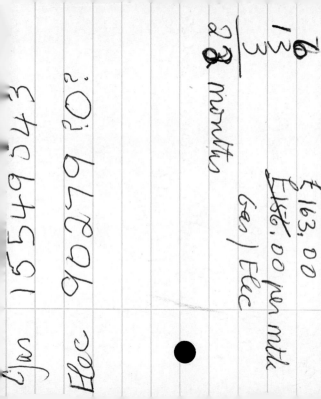

6
13
/3
23 months

£163.00
£156.00 per mth
Gas / Elec

15459543

96279 50?

Gas

Elec

338.95 credit
680.48 Total Bill
341.53 Debit

● New monthly Payment £220.00
on 16/4/2016

£12 Saving on monthly
Payment 15/3/2016

upheavals. Some of these upheavals are very confusing, very distressing, very disturbing. Some people in relationships are finding they can no longer continue in those relationships because their partners cannot tune into what they are tuning in to. It is causing a great deal of disturbance.

Those who choose not to find their own negative-positive balance by thinking, seeking and changing their attitudes, will find themselves increasingly out of sync with the energies as the vibrations continue to rise. This will show itself in more violence, crime, aggression and authoritarianism. We will see the emergence of the extreme Right, including the religious right. Conflict will arise between people fighting over dwindling food and water supplies and between those demanding change and those wishing to hold on to the status quo.

There will also be an increasing belief, among those falling behind the rising vibrations, in ethnic superiority as the insecurity they are feeling at a deep level of their being seeks what it sees as the 'security' of living only with their 'own kind'. The gathering vibrations are feeling increasingly 'alien' to these people at that deep level and this is showing itself on the physical level as a desire to remove all 'aliens' from their lives. We have seen this in the former Yugoslavia very powerfully and we will see this manifest increasingly throughout the world. The United Nations will be so overwhelmed by trouble-spots, it will not be able to respond.

We will see all that has been hidden on a personal and collective level rise to the surface. Everyone will be brought face to face with past decisions and behaviour as karma is worked through, and we will see story after story emerge at all levels of the political, industrial, military and church establishments to expose their nonsenses and encourage us to question and think for ourselves. The old has to crumble before the new can take its place and negative energies locked within all life forms have to be brought to the surface so they can be faced, dealt with, and dispersed. This process will hasten the end of our destructive way of life.

In the midst of this transformation there will be many who will say, understandably, that what is befalling the Earth and humanity cannot be the work of a force of love. It is vital that we appreciate that it is. This is not the way those guiding the Earth through these changes would have chosen to do it. They would have preferred a more gradual approach, but the planet is in such a state of imbalance that their job is so much more difficult and urgent. It is like having an infected wound. Sometimes dabbing on the antiseptic is more painful than the wound. But you know that unless it is treated and healed, the whole body will eventually die.

We can ease this process by starting to organise now, today, the local barter economies that will be needed when the system has collapsed and money is worthless. This is a role the politicians can play, particularly the Green Parties who have long campaigned for local economies and barter economics. But more than anything, we will need to co-operate with each other and share what we have as the economic system comes tumbling down.

In time those minds who cannot stay in sync with the energies will go out of incarnation as the vibrations get even quicker, and they will return to a non-physical level where they will be welcomed with indescribable love and spend some time reassessing and deciding where they wish to go and what they wish to do next. As the inflow of positive energies increases, this decade and beyond will see a collapse of all the economic, political, scientific and religious systems, including institutions like the British monarchy. We should see this as positive, chaotic and traumatic though it will be in the short term, because the danger was not that the system would collapse, but that it would not collapse before it had completed its job of destroying everything.

As the energies around us become more balanced and the

vibrations quicken it will have a phenomenal impact on human thought and behaviour. It is already doing so. It is obvious when you think about it. If everything that exists is a different form of the same energy and the nature of that energy is changing in our part of Creation, it must affect everything whether it be the physical body of the planet, our physical bodies, or our minds and emotions which are themselves energy fields created from the same energy.

We can expect much more apparently inexplicable behaviour that is out of all proportion to a situation as the changes in the energies quicken through this decade. Borders will become meaningless; such will be the numbers of refugees fleeing conflict, geological disasters, drought and environmentally devastated lands. This will help us to see that carving up the planet in some arbitrary way saying this is ours and that is yours, often quoting inaccurate historical events as justification, is quite the wrong way to proceed. Areas of this planet do not belong to this people or that people just because their physical shells share the same ancestral line as those who lived in the area thousands of years ago. This planet belongs to all Creation. We are simply the tenants for a short period.

As the energy changes continue and increase, they are affecting time as we know it. When people say there doesn't seem to be enough time to do everything any more they are right. Time is getting faster and this shows itself not in the hands of the clock moving quicker, but in more and more events happening in a shorter and shorter period. Look what has happened and changed in this century compared with the last, and the last compared with the one before and so on. We need to be aware of this and simplify our lifestyles because this speeding up of time will go on until the transformation is over and the final massive leap in consciousness takes place.

Humanity has become enslaved by its illusion of time governed by the clock. We are moving from our concept of time – one of sixty-second minutes and sixty-minute hours

– to what you might call cosmic time, a state of being that exists on the higher frequencies and has nothing to do with ticking clocks. It is an attunement to the natural ebb and flow of energy and planetary movements. This quickening of time will bring karma back to us at an ever increasing pace. If humanity has come to remove its karma before the transformation, it must also remove the karma created in this life, too. The nearer we get to the final leap to another state of being, the quicker our actions, positive or negative, will return to us so we can stay in balance. This is what we call 'instant' karma.

There will be many effects on health as the energies change because of the pressure this will put on the structure of the human body. We will discover new diseases and some established ones will fade. The more we can get in sync and stay in sync with our higher mind and find inner balance, the less we will be affected by disease old or new, although there are many people who have come into incarnation to take out negative energies and that often shows itself in illness. Just because you are ill doesn't mean you are imbalanced through your own actions. You could be serving the planet or giving those around you a learning experience. I feel Aids is part of this whole process of change, energy cleansing, and the teaching of non-judgemental love and compassion. The rising vibrations will also make it easier for people to consciously leave their physical bodies in what are called Out Of Body Experiences or OOBEs. Many people have experienced this and the numbers will increase dramatically in the years ahead. People simply float out of their physical forms in just the same way that we do when we 'die', except that an energy link remains with the body and so they can return whenever they wish. This was once an accepted part of everyday life on this planet and it is about to return.

Those who stay with the rising vibrations will see their intuition and psychic powers increase in ways they did not think possible, and they will start to sense the emotions of the Earth Spirit to such an extent that they will know when an earthquake is imminent, just as animals have always done. Technical explanations will also emerge that will be able to measure many of the phenomena I have talked about in this book and we will see that hunger, illness and environmental destruction can be ended once we open our minds to the potential of sub-atomic energy.

The basis of the plan is to encourage people to think, seek and question and by doing that raise their own vibratory rate so they can stay with the rising vibrations of the energies surrounding the planet. This is one reason why I put myself on the line because the information I am passing on is helping to awaken people at a deep level so they can raise their own vibration. Only by thinking, searching and seeking truth can our inner knowledge be released and only from within can our vibration rise. To somehow manifest 'happenings' that proved everything to people is not the way this awakening is going to be done and if people wait for absolute proof until they begin to move, they will wait forever. As a channelling in a book called *The R.A. Material* said:

> We offer no concrete proof ... We offer truth. This is an important function of our mission ... to offer truth without proof. In this way, the motivation will, in each and every case, come from within. An offering of proof or an impressing of this truth upon an individual in such a way that they would be forced to accept it, would have no usable effect upon their vibratory state.

It is only by raising our vibratory rate that we can break free of the system's control. The system is a thought form, a mass of thought energy encircling the planet, and the only way out of its control is to raise your vibratory rate higher than that system energy. The very second you do that, your eyes open and you see it for what it is: global suicide. I have had so many letters from people who could not understand why they suddenly saw everything in a new light after a lifetime of system serving. Their sudden revelation was the time their vibratory rate climbed out of the range of the system. This applies also to the massive thought form that we call religion. This escape in vibratory terms from the system's clutches is like that moment a few minutes after an aircraft takes off when you break through the cloud base and look down from the clear blue skies above it. While you are climbing through the clouds you can only see a mist outside and the enclosed cocoon of the aircraft within. Once you get above those clouds, that mist, you look out of the window and you can see into infinity.

When that happens you begin to understand the most important truth of all ... love changes everything. This is not I love you *if* or I love you *when*, it is I love you *whatever*. It is the sort of love, free from conditions, that we have for our children. No matter what they say or do, much as we may not like it sometimes, we still love them and care for them the same. When we think and act on this level of unconditional love we are generating tremendously powerful positive energy which will defuse the negative. We need to see everyone on Earth in the way we see our children. When we love unconditionally the whole of humanity, or at least begin our journey towards that, we are both increasing the rate at which this balancing process can happen and ensuring that we as individuals can get ever closer to our balance and tune in to the new vibrations. It is true, then, that love changes everything, but there are many kinds of love, not just the one we have come to understand on Earth.

The positive energy called love is the creative force behind all that exists. It is love that will get us through this time of change as everything we have known falls apart. We will see amid the mayhem that loving each other and caring for each other is all that really matters. Life, we will appreciate, is not about the latest car, video recorder or hi-fi unit. It is about living together and loving together in its true sense. As we raise our vibrations through love, we will not miss the trinkets of life we worship today. We will see them as the illusions they are, as a whole new understanding and love of life opens up before us. We will see that it is the energy called love which binds the whole of Creation together. It is time to celebrate with joy, love and laughter the realisation of who we really are, eternal beings that never die. The only death is the death of fear and that is within our grasp.

We minds have been around for an incomprehensible amount of time as we measure it here, but never have we faced such a moment of decision. The pressures in this area of the vortex must be removed and harmony restored. We can play our part and help to move everything forward to a level of love, peace and understanding we could hardly imagine. Or the human race on the physical level could cease to be and the effects on even the non-physical levels close to the Earth would be deeply unpleasant. The choice is ours, and when you see the choices in stark contrast you can appreciate why I will do whatever is necessary, no matter what people may think of me at the time.

Some effects on the surface of the earth are now inevitable because of what has gone before and the geological activity will build as the years go by, but how far it and other events have to go depends entirely on us as a human race and how many of us change and start to work for, rather than against, what is necessary for the planet to survive. The future is not pre-ordained – we can change it. In fact the events have already been reduced by the changes that have taken place in the consciousness of many around the world.

You may have heard it said that the past, present and future are all happening at the same time. This is a concept that most people understandably find impossible to comprehend given our conditioning that time must have a beginning, middle and end. But I explain it like this. At some deep level of your mind, you retain all the memories of everything that has happened to you since your creation. Your past is retained as thought energy and is therefore continuing to happen in your memory. You are also experiencing the present and your mind is continually taking the information from those two sources, the past and the present, and projecting forward what it *thinks* the future will be based on that information.

In the same way, the vortex carries the memories of all that has happened within its boundaries in the past, it constantly experiences the present, and on the basis of both, projects forward the likely future. So, on the largest scale, does the Infinite Mind. If we tune in to those vibrations that carry the projected future, we can see and experience what is currently projected to happen. But that is all it is, a projection. Prophecy is about passing on the current projection so that people can change it if they choose to do so. The more positive energy, the more love, we send to the Earth Spirit, each other, and out into the energy sea, the smoother the transition will be. The bottom line is that the Earth needs love and humanity needs love and each of us is capable of generating that love. We are part of the Earth Spirit and she is part of us, we are all part of each other, for we are all expressions of the same infinite energy stream. What each of us thinks and does affects, positively or negatively, everything else. We can use that knowledge to make the transformation easier or harder, but either way it is going to happen because it must happen and it is happening now.

What I have outlined here is the way things look from all the information I have seen and heard so far. Obviously as our minds continue to expand the knowledge and understanding will grow and be refined. But I have no doubt whatsoever that at least the basic themes of what you have just read are correct, and this is the message I and many others are trying to communicate to the world. It will not be easy and some of it will not be popular to those in power, but there is no-one – no group, no government, no system – that will stop what has to be.

The times they are a-changing like never before, of that there can be no doubt.

15

The Awakening

No matter how evolved a mind may or may not be, when we incarnate on Earth we are all subject to the limitations of this planet's physical vibration and energies.

Compared with other levels, incarnating on the Earth has been a little like entering a very thick fog, such has been the domination of negative energies over positive. To a certain extent it is like starting again. Only by learning the hard way, through experience, can we begin to conquer the imbalances and influences on this frequency and the karmic imbalances we bring into each incarnation, and allow the knowledge and wisdom of our eternal self to manifest more powerfully on the physical level. There are no short cuts and life plans are designed to guide this process of relearning and re-awakening.

We are all going through this same basic process in a form most suited to our needs: you, me, everyone. Everything you have read about in this book everyone has the potential to do – and more. No-one is created better or with more gifts than anyone else. On the level of the mind we are equal with equal potential. We simply have to make the choice to use that potential for the good of all.

I have learned so much since those first communications in 1990 and that has only been possible in such a short time because my experiences have been so extreme. If I had not been through them I would not be able to pass on so much to help others. As one communication said: 'How can you help others if you have not been through it yourself?' Before I finish I would like to point out a few of the things that you might find helpful in your own journey and awakening. Above all I have learned not to judge people. That doesn't mean I won't comment on their behaviour and say how it has affected me or what effect it is having on other people and the planet. But we don't know the life plan of every individual and so we have no idea what is making people behave in certain ways and do certain things. Again, as Rakorski said: 'True love does not always give the receiver what it would like to receive but it will always give that which is best for it.'

Love doesn't mean we should lie down and let people walk all over us. It could be that they need someone to challenge and expose their behaviour for their own learning and evolution. Nor should we expect always to have wonderful thoughts about people or feel guilty when we don't. We don't always have wonderful thoughts about our children when they are playing up, but we still love them. When people have laughed at me in the street or shouted pathetic remarks, have I immediately sent them loving thoughts? No, actually, I have often thought something like: 'How can a prat like you have the nerve to laugh at anyone?' That is just the initial reaction which soon passes. I know that really everyone is on a journey of learning and everyone is at a different stage. That doesn't make them any better or worse than anyone else, it makes them different in their outlook on life. By not judging people I mean not holding grudges or seeing them as inferior beings. When we judge others we are inviting others to judge us.

Even judging ourselves should be done with caution. Yes, of course we need to assess our behaviour and attitudes constantly and allow them to evolve as new information comes to light. We need to look at what we have done and ask if we could have acted differently and more positively.

But yell it from the rooftops to everyone you know: DON'T FEEL GUILTY. There is no need. Our chance to right our 'wrongs' will always come. Learn from the experience and remember that tomorrow is the first day of the rest of our eternity. We can only love others when we love ourselves. We can only forgive others when we have learned to forgive ourselves. What we project out to the world is merely a manifestation of what we think of ourselves, and one of humanity's biggest collective problems is that it is awash with guilt and self-hatred. Religion is responsible for much of it. Humanity not only doesn't love itself, it doesn't even like itself. Yet no-one is perfect within the confines of the physical form and the pressures of the energy imbalances affecting this planet. And what does 'perfect' mean anyway? Your idea of perfect might be very different from mine. Don't be frightened of making mistakes, they are part of our evolution. In fact there are no such things as 'mistakes' – only learning from experience.

As you go through your spiritual awakening try to keep one word in your mind and never let it out of your sight. The word is ... balance. We are in a physical body on a physical frequency and we need to balance this with the need to tune into the non-physical levels of the spirit. If we are off-balance we switch off the spiritual part of us and see only the physical world around us. We can see the consequences of that in pain and destruction. But if we go too far in the other direction, we float away in some spiritual daze and forget the practical side of living on a physical planet. We do not incarnate into a physical body to then ignore that we have done so. We are here to experience life on a physical vibration and *balance* this with the spiritual part of us. We need to understand who we really are and listen to our guidance from the unseen levels, but we also need to appreciate that there are practical things to be done on the physical level, without which there would be chaos. It is that balance we are after.

Balance is not passing on our responsibility for what we

should do or say to some guru, cult, movement or 'Living God on Earth' as I heard one guru described. Listen to others by all means, but *we* are the ones responsible for what we do, no-one else. We are not here to let someone else think for us, we are here to think for ourselves. If you don't agree with anything I have said in this book, for instance, then reject it. Reject it all if that's what you feel inside. The same can be said of those with whom people communicate through channelling, pendulums and suchlike. They are not there to do our thinking for us. They are there to guide us. And don't forget, they make misjudgements too, because they are also on a journey of learning. Not all communications are from highly evolved minds and some can be from very imbalanced and negative sources trying to control and disrupt. Be careful. Are the communications coming from outside the vortex from the highest levels, or from within the vortex? The quality of the information between those sources is vastly different.

You will receive information from less evolved sources that can wreck your life if you don't follow your instincts. A woman I had met only briefly with the West Country psychic wrote to inform me that her 'impeccable' sources had told her we were 'cosmic lovers' and I should leave my wife and family and go away with her. When I made it clear that I had no intention of doing anything of the kind, she informed me that her sources now considered me 'a jerk'. She told her husband I was sending her telepathic automatic writing saying all sorts of astonishing things. Some people would judge this woman's behaviour as appalling, but they would be wrong. She was going through a stage of spiritual awakening and she was confused and mixed up as a result. Most people come through this confusion stronger than before and a few get stuck there for a while. Some, sadly, stay there for the rest of their physical life. I tell this story because there will be a great deal of this going on as people open up to the higher energies and become confused. Again, be very, very careful. Don't be fooled. Check everything out with as many people as you can and most of all be honest with yourself and trust your own instincts. The best way is to sit quietly, free your mind from all irrelevances and listen to your higher self speak to you. If what you hear feels right to you in the light of all the information available, then act upon it, but only if it feels right.

Beware, too, of the 'spiritual arrogance' which can be found within a few elements of what is known as the 'New Age' movement. These are people and groups who say, 'We know how things are and we know best.' They might have some useful information for you to act upon, but then again they might not. In the end the only one who knows what's best and right for you is ... YOU. I view with some concern the way parts of the New Age movement are turning themselves into little more than another church. They reach a certain point on the journey to enlightenment and then stop. Like most organisations that begin to gather rules and rigid belief systems around them, they start to see new information that questions some of those beliefs as a threat. That is no different from what the churches have done. Evolution is a continuing process. Remember it matters not what you believe, but what you do.

It is also easy to become obsessed with the extreme negative forces at work around this planet. That obsession can lead you to see everyone as a person 'from the other side' and this brings paranoia and fear. Both states of mind attract to you those very negative energies. The woman I have just mentioned was going around saying all sorts of people, including me, were under the influence of 'negative forces'. But, in reality, the common denominator in all of us was our refusal to do what she thought we should do. It was her ego at work: 'If you don't do what I say, you must have been taken over by the "other side" because I can't possibly be wrong.' I have come across many in her state of misunderstanding and paranoia during the opening-up process and I expect the number to increase. It happened to me for a short period in 1991, which gave me an essential understanding of those who think in this way. They are not 'bad' people. They just need to understand what is happening to them. Everyone, but everyone, gets mixed up during the awakening process as you shift through many levels very quickly. The danger is getting stuck at the mixed-up stage and staying there.

It is right that we should all acknowledge the existence of extreme manifestations of negative energy and be aware of how they work, but the best way to reduce their effect is not to fear them. Fear creates and attracts negative energy very effectively and it is fear that the system uses to control us. In truth, most of what we call power is the ability to make others fear, and not being fearful is the key to self liberation.

It is vital never to lose your sense of humour. There is no greater antidote to extreme negative forces and the extremes of karmic experience than to laugh, especially at yourself. It is so very hard to keep a sense of humour amid the confusion sometimes, but remember that a sense of humour can give you a sense of proportion. Have fun! We make our own reality and if we think of life as joyous and fun it will be. Life is not meant to be full of fear and misery. We are not meant to be serious all the time, forever looking into the deep significance of everything that happens. Let's all have a laugh whenever we can. The more joyous and happy we are, the stronger the channels of guidance become because there is less negativity around us to get in the way.

On our journey of evolution we are all seeking peace, but so often it is the wrong kind of peace. If we see peace as the removal of aggravation around us we will never find it on this dense physical level. Real peace down here is not the absence of hassle and pressure; it is not being affected by that hassle and pressure. This kind of peace comes from within, not without. We also need to appreciate that life within this vortex, particularly at the lower level, is much, much tougher than evolution elsewhere within the Infinite Mind. The suffering we see all over the world is not how life is lived elsewhere in Creation outside the vortex or even on other non-dense physical levels within it. The time is here for all of us to work together to lift the frequency and step out to freedom once again. Exponential economic growth is destroying the planet; exponential spiritual growth is going to heal her.

This is not a time for opting out – it is a time for opting in. It is a time for courage, for action and for non-violent resistance to the system of control. Why should we worry about what people think about us? Why should we allow their misunderstandings and limited view of life to set the limits to what we do and say? They have a right to their beliefs and a right not to be judged as people, but we have that right too. We should, I would suggest, step into the light of freedom that comes from being true to yourself and what you believe, and not allowing others to control your life because you fear what they will think and say. There is nothing to fear. It is time to say what we truly believe and not wait for it to become 'acceptable'.

Truth does not become truth only when it's acceptable. In fact if you look around you, when something becomes acceptable under the present system, it is often because it is anything but the truth. This planet did not become round only at the point when it became acceptable to say it was round. It was always round, even in the days when you were a 'loony' if you said it was anything but flat. Let go of the fear of what others will say and stand up, speak out, and play your part in this transformation of human understanding.

Through these years of change we need to keep focused in our minds the world that can await us when all this is over. It is the kind of world, created by the energy called love, that now we can only dream of, a world in which conflict on the scale of war will not be able to manifest. It is a world in which there is no hunger, no division, no judgement of others who do not share a certain view. Think of all the fantastic people there are on the planet today helping others despite the negative influences all around them. Think of those moments of sheer joy, love, peace and happiness that we can experience even on this imbalanced and troubled planet. Now think what it will be like when the negative domination is no more. I can do no better than to leave you with the words of John Lennon who described this new world so magnificently in his beautiful song, 'Imagine'. It is such an inspired description of what awaits us that I have no doubt it was knowingly or unknowingly channelled through him from a higher level:

> Imagine there's no countries,
> It isn't hard to do,
> Nothing to kill or die for,
> And no religion too.
> Imagine all the people,
> Living life in peace.
>
> Imagine no possessions,
> I wonder if you can,
> No need for greed or hunger,
> A brotherhood of Man.
> Imagine all the people,
> Sharing all the World.
>
> You may say I'm a dreamer,
> But I'm not the only one.
> I hope some day you'll join us.
> And the World will be as one.

The time to build that world has come. We can all be part of that glorious tomorrow if we want it badly enough. The choice is ours and ours alone. But the energies are speaking to us, the crop symbols are speaking to us, our higher minds are speaking to us ... and they are saying very clearly that the time to make that choice – is NOW.

Postscript:

I have received thousands of wonderful letters from all over the world and they are a great source of support and information. I read every one, but unfortunately there is not time to reply to them all. If you feel you do need a reply, I would be grateful if you could send a stamped, addressed envelope and I will do my best to help in any way I can.

Index

In the
Light of
Experience

The Autobiography of

DAVID ICKE

WARNER BOOKS

A *Warner* Book

First published in Great Britain in 1993 by Warner Books

Copyright © David Icke 1993

Acknowledgement is made to the following, in respect of reproduced extracts:

Michael Roll, for permission to quote from his paper 'The Suppression of Knowledge' (1983); *The Curse of Ignorance: A History of Mankind* by Arthur Findlay (2 vols.) (The Psychic Press, 1947); *The Only Planet of Choice* (Gateway Books); *The R.A. Material* by Don Elkins, Carla Rueckert & James Allen McCarty (Unilaw Library); BMG Music Publishing Ltd, for kind permission to reproduce lyrics from 'Imagine': words & music by John Lennon, copyright 1972 Lenono Music, administered in the UK & Eire by BMG Music Publishing Ltd. All rights reserved.

A CIP catalogue record for this book is
available from the British Library.

ISBN 0 7515 0603 6

Typeset in Palladia by Solidus (Bristol) Ltd
Printed and bound in Great Britain by
Clays Ltd, St Ives plc

Warner Books
A Division of
Little, Brown and Company (UK) Limited
165 Great Dover Street
London SE1 4YA